"Finally, a practical, easy-to-read book that teaches us how girls become deeply engaged at school, and why. The authors shatter outdated myths about how girls learn and tell us what the research really says about girls' brains. Most importantly, they listen to the voices of girls and teachers. Now, more than ever, it's crucial to understand what girls' education is meant for and can be. If you're an educator of girls, you need this book."

—**Rachel Simmons**, author of *Odd Girl Out*
and *The Curse of the Good Girl*

"Those of us with daughters and those of us who teach girls need to read this book. This timely, engaging, and highly accessible study is an invaluable resource. The authors have gathered an incredible amount of information from girls themselves as well as their teachers, presenting a wide range of exciting ideas and strategies. I couldn't put it down!"

—**Katherine Schultz**, dean, University of Colorado Boulder

"What I like best about *Teaching Girls* is how commonsensical and accessible it is. There is no pretense that much of what is said wouldn't also be helpful to boys, but rather a continuing emphasis on how much potential girls have, how most schools have under-valued and under-developed that potential, and how those shortcomings can be readily overcome."

—**James H. Lytle**, former superintendent, Trenton
Public Schools, NJ

"This remarkable study reveals how girls think, how girls learn and why gender matters. The challenge and mandate for schools today is to provide an education that is relevant and prepares students for college and most importantly for the lives they will lead as adults. At a time when women and girls continue to experience barriers to success due to the pressures of stereotype threat, role continuity and the impostor syndrome, we need to identify and employ remedies that remove these barriers and optimize the learning and growth of the girls in our care. Educators and parents alike will benefit from the understandings and tools outlined in this beautifully written and easy to understand guide to the life of the girl in the classroom."

—**Dr. Katherine G. Windsor**, head of Miss Porter's
School and board chair of the Oprah Winfrey Leaders

"Putting the voices of girls at the center, this superb book offers unparalleled insight into the learning lives of adolescent girls. Rooted in rigorous methodology, Kuriloff, Andrus and Jacobs illuminate the vital ways in which relationship, personal relevance, passion and content-rich studies are intertwined and central to deep learning for girls. By highlighting the place of gender in students' lives, this book provides both a practical and inspiring text that can help teachers and administrators work against pernicious stereotyping and open up worlds of possibility."

—**Miriam Miriam Raider-Roth**, EdD, professor,
University of Cincinnati

Teaching Girls:
How Teachers and Parents Can
Reach Their Brains and Hearts

Teaching Girls

How Teachers and Parents Can Reach Their Brains and Hearts

Peter Kuriloff, Shannon Andrus, and
Charlotte Jacobs

ROWMAN & LITTLEFIELD
Lanham • Boulder • New York • London

Published by Rowman & Littlefield
A wholly owned subsidiary of The Rowman & Littlefield Publishing Group, Inc.
4501 Forbes Boulevard, Suite 200, Lanham, Maryland 20706
www.rowman.com
Unit A, Whitacre Mews, 26–34 Stannary Street, London SE11 4AB

British Library Cataloguing in Publication Information Available

Library of Congress Cataloging-in-Publication Data Available

Names: Kuriloff, Peter J., author. | Andrus, Shannon, author. |
  Jacobs, Charlotte E., author.
Title: Teaching girls: how teachers and parents can reach their brains
  and hearts / Peter Kuriloff, Shannon Andrus, and Charlotte Jacobs.
Description: Lanham, Maryland: Rowman & Littlefield, [2017] |
  Includes bibliographical references and index.
Identifiers: LCCN 2017039931 (print) | LCCN 2017048860 (ebook) |
  ISBN 9781475820409 (Electronic) | ISBN 9781475820386 (cloth:
  alk. paper) | ISBN 9781475820393 (pbk. : alk. paper)
Subjects: LCSH: Girls—Education. | Motivation in education. |
  Sex differences in education.
Classification: LCC LC1481 (ebook) | LCC LC1481 .K87 2017
  (print) | DDC 371.822—dc23
LC record available at https://lccn.loc.gov/2017039931

ISBN: 978-1-4758-2038-6 (cloth : alk. paper)
ISBN: 978-1-4758-2039-3 (pbk. : alk. paper)
ISBN: 978-1-4758-2040-9 (electronic)

♾️™ The paper used in this publication meets the minimum requirements of American National Standard for Information Sciences—Permanence of Paper for Printed Library Materials, ANSI/NISO Z39.48–1992.

Printed in the United States of America

This book is dedicated to Flannery Andrus-Lundy (age 9),
and to the other wonderful girls in our families:
Scotia Imogene Brown Kuriloff (9),
Ruth Eleanor Klein Kuriloff (9),
Avery Andrus-Lundy (5),
Lucy Elaine Klein Kuriloff (3),
Greta Riva Kuriloff Sicks (2),
and
Norah Faye Snyder (2),
as well as to the 1,328 girls and their 550 teachers who took the time to
share their stories about memorable lessons.

We hope this book will help teachers of girls everywhere find ways to
improve their teaching by making it more lively, engaging, and exciting. We
hope too, that it will provide parents with a framework for assessing the kind
of educations their daughters are receiving in their current schools or what to
look for when they seek a new school for them.

Flannery's Story

One day, when Shannon Andrus was toiling away drafting a chapter for the final report on our study of girls' schools, her daughter Flannery came into her office. Noticing a copy of Reichert and Hawley's book next to her desk, she read the cover and said to her mom: "*Reaching Boys, Teaching Boys.* Where is the book about reaching girls, teaching girls?" Shannon told her daughter that there wasn't one yet, and Flannery replied: "Well, Mom, you have to write it." To which she replied, "That is just what we plan to do, Flann." Three years later, we finally have the book completed for Flannery and for all girls.

Contents

Foreword

In 1963, a survey of college-educated women revealed a surprising and disheartening finding: many were unhappy and feeling unfulfilled. That survey of unhappiness was described by Betty Freidan in *The Feminine Mystique.* When that book was published, a great "aha" descended across the land. For the first time, millions of women realized that they were not suffering in isolation, that they were part of a national epidemic of female heartache. Friedan called this desolation "the problem that has no name." A few years after *The Feminine Mystique* was published, the word "sexism" entered the lexicon.

Teaching Girls: How Teachers and Parents Can Reach Their Brains and Hearts reminds me of this history. Back in the 1960s, in order to move forward, women needed to name the problem they faced. Today, if girls are to move forward, we need more than a name, we need concrete tools and strategies for the classroom. We are well beyond the days when "awareness training" about the perils of gender bias in school will suffice. What Peter Kuriloff, Shannon Andrus, and Charlotte Jacobs provide in this book are specific, authentic resources to stir girls' academic achievement. These pages are filled with insights and information to help girls gain the skills, confidence, and resilience they need for future success.

Teaching Girls focuses on how we can promote curiosity, happiness, risk-taking, and friendships in school settings. The authors surveyed over five hundred teachers and more than a thousand students to mine the lessons that work, and work well. More than that, they analyzed why these approaches were working, what were the underlying connections that they shared. They teased out the lessons' commonalities and characteristics that worked for girls. Visiting schools, observing classroom interaction, and talking with teachers and students led to deeper insights still that they readily share in this well-researched yet easily accessible book. So direct and fruitful was their approach in uncovering how best to teach girls that one is left to wonder: why hasn't this been done before? (I am among the wonderers!) The authors have harvested wonderful lessons and uncovered underlying characteristics that inspire girls. Their efforts demonstrate the power of the academy and practitioners working together.

Here is a book that answers the critical question: How can schools come alive for girls?

Teaching Girls offers "best practices" for parents and educators seeking lessons and strategies that work well with girls. (And don't be surprised if many of them are useful for boys as well.)

I would be remiss if I did not point out how well the book integrates instruction and curriculum. The power of good teaching is evident in every chapter. Teaching a curriculum that includes previously forgotten women demands that there be no forgotten students in the teaching act itself. Unfortunately, the hectic pace of student–teacher interaction too often creates such "forgotten students." It is not uncommon that the teacher's attention goes to the "fastest hand" in the class. Research indicates that a student's race, social class, and gender play a role in this dynamic, and those groups least valued in the culture too often receive the least attention in the classroom. The authors attend to effective instruction, to the central and critical role of teachers, and to the best ways to organize and plan for equitable classroom interaction.

Teaching Girls offers a number of entry points to those looking for real-world resources. Interested in humanities, science, social studies, or physical education? Lessons in most content areas are provided on the authors' website: www.TeachingGirlsWell.com. Interested in age level, you will find information for a variety of age groups. How about lessons to promote creativity, relevance, collaboration, or hands-on learning? Yes, those modalities and more are offered, so happy hunting!

I must mention that *Teaching Girls* is a much-needed antidote to the current crop of "male brain, female brain" books, the ones that advocate sex-segregated schools and classrooms. Such books advise that boys should be spoken to in louder voices and be disciplined harshly, while girls learn best when embraced by soothing, quieter voices that allow them to flourish in a nurturing school climate. Unfortunately, hundreds of schools (and who knows how many parents and teachers) have bought into this notion that boys and girls have different brains requiring separate and different educations. Current neuroscience teaches that this is indeed a myth, and a potentially damaging one at that.

Fortunately, *Teaching Girls* propels us into a more constructive and promising arena. Boys and girls share much in common and learn in similar ways. But the world treats them differently and constructs different social barriers for each gender. This book will help teachers and parents prepare girls to better navigate our world and to overcome its gender roadblocks. How gratifying that we now have a practical path we can travel to become catalysts for girls' academic success.

David Sadker, PhD
Coauthor with Myra Sadker,
Failing at Fairness: How Schools Cheat Our Girls
Tucson, Arizona

Preface

It is a warm, sunny day. My colleague and I are visiting a girls' school as a part of our study exploring what kinds of lessons work best for girls. We sit in a small classroom at lunch time, waiting for the next period to begin. There is a window facing a courtyard. Through it, we notice a wiry girl, probably a seventh grader, walk across the yard. In the middle, she stops and notices a large trashcan, maybe 3 feet in length, lying on its side. The girl, who can be no more than 5'2", begins rolling it across the flagstones with deep concentration. She chooses a spot, places the can upright and then walks several feet away. She turns, and with a sudden burst of energy and speed, she sprints toward the trashcan and at the last minute leaps over it and lands triumphantly on the other side. The grin on her face is exuberant as she runs back to her starting place and repeats the jump. She accomplishes this several times. Soon, other girls start to take notice and wander over to see what is happening. A small crowd forms, and then a self-organized line, as each girl takes her turn at running and jumping over the can. There are cheers and excited talk as each girl successfully clears the hurdle. Joyous smiles abound.

The girls' joyfulness reflects our impressions of the school. It is a place of public happiness, where girls' curiosity and risk-taking are prized, where their friendships are fostered, and where their voices are cherished. As our observation of the school continued, we found that the culture of the school is not an accident; it has been carefully crafted by the teachers and administrators who have worked to create a place where challenges are embraced and risks are taken in classrooms and corridors, on sports fields, and in school-wide activities. It is a place where girls singly and together learn to master all kinds of academic, intellectual, and social hurdles in the service of their development into competent young women.

If you are a school leader or teacher who wants to help girls experience school the way these girls do, this book is for you. If you are a teacher interested in learning how to teach girls better or a parent trying to figure out what type of teaching is best for your daughter or what school would be really good for her, this book is for you.

Currently, there is nothing else like this work available. If you search Amazon.com for books about raising girls, your efforts will reveal hundreds of works—even thousands depending on the scope of your search. There are many titles about helping girls through the emotional and psychological issues involved with growing up female. You would find scores of books describing ways to help girls cope with their anger, develop friendships, and relate to boys. Similarly, it would be no problem to get advice about helping girls become comfortable with their bodies and their looks. You would find dozens of authors offering suggestions about how girls can cope with bullying. You would discover books designed to help parents manage their daughters; even some written specifically for single moms or dads. And of course, you would locate parallel books designed to help girls handle their parents. There are works offering guidance about getting girls to join sports teams, improve their self-esteem, and talk about sex. You would even discover guides suggesting how teenage girls can manage love, both requited and unrequited.

If you teach girls or you are interested in your daughter's education, however, you would discover very, very few books about lessons that interest, engage, inspire, and motivate them. Until now, in the mountain of writing on raising, helping, understanding, and teaching girls, there is nothing that *gives voice to what girls and their teachers believe to be great lessons*—lessons that encourage their involvement and excite their curiosity. No major study has ever asked girls and their teachers about their actual experiences in the classroom and what works for them. Until now.

In a seminal work, *Reaching Boys, Teaching Boys*, our colleagues, Michael Reichert and Richard Hawley, did just that with boys and their teachers. We were inspired to follow up their research by applying the same methods to study what kinds of lessons effectively engage girls. We asked a sample of 1,328 girls, in grades seven through twelve, from fourteen secular independent, religiously affiliated independent, and public girls' schools across the country to describe lessons that were especially memorable, interesting, and motivating to them. We also asked 560 of their teachers to tell us about lessons that they believed to be especially effective in advancing their students' learning. The responses were overwhelming, providing us with hundreds of richly detailed narratives about great teaching.

These stories enabled us to see the variations in the ways girls experienced powerful lessons as well as to discover the central tendencies among them. Within the great variety, we were able to find key themes that characterized what girls view as outstanding lessons. The stories provided to us by teachers largely agree with what the girls told us, suggesting that when it comes to what constitutes great teaching, the picture that emerges from our work is consistent and reliable.

Together, the narratives and what we learned from them should be useful to teachers and parents. If you are a teacher, the book will provide you with a very wide range of lessons that girls and teachers find effective. It will help you figure out how to engage girls optimally in either single-sex or coeducational settings. It will explain what you need to modify when teaching girls and boys together. Perhaps as important, because the findings can be explained by the ways in which great lessons implicitly meet the developmental needs of girls, they will enable you who are parents to know what to look for when you search for a good school for your daughter. Careful reading will give you a useful grasp on what developmentally appropriate education looks like. And finally, for the same reasons, the findings will suggest to those of you who are educational leaders and school designers what the contours of a great school for girls should be.

These lessons are vital if we want our students and daughters to be competitive in the twenty-first century. It stands to reason that actively engaged, intellectually curious girls are more likely to pursue higher education. Engagement and motivation are key in bringing girls into high-paying, highly rewarding disciplines in which they have been systematically underrepresented. They can encourage girls into studying science, math, technology, and engineering and in reaching higher levels of success in any field they choose to enter.

Women have been underrepresented in leadership positions in most segments of society from industry to politics to education. Our findings point to how great teaching fully engages girls in all areas of study, as well as in questions that stir their imaginations around issues that are of concern to them, including matters of social justice and, ultimately, changing the world. Powerful teaching can change the way girls imagine themselves and their futures.

Up until now parents and teachers who desired such outcomes have had to rely on anecdotes to guide their thinking about connecting with and inspiring girls. Teachers have had to base their work on their own experiences and on literature that too often makes claims based on little evidence about how to teach girls' "pink brains," or about how to overcome girls' perceived resistance to taking intellectual risks and getting their hands dirty—literally or figuratively. There was little knowledge—and none that was grounded in the deep, collective wisdom of girls and their teachers—about what really works.

Such knowledge, presented here in a systematic, usable fashion, can lead to transformational teaching—and to excited and engaged girls who love going to school and who have the necessary education and experience to become leaders in both their chosen fields and in civil society. What we present in this book also may serve as a guide to designing more effective schools for girls in the twenty-first century.

Acknowledgments

We are grateful to many people for helping to make this book possible. Foremost among them, our colleague and friend, University of Pennsylvania, PhD student Amanda Cox, who was involved in every stage of our original research. She did everything with us including helping to code our almost 2,000 narratives and bringing her keen observational skills to our school visits.

Most important, perhaps, Amanda mastered the use of the qualitative coding program, ATLAS.ti, and figured out how to turn the data we entered into it into a relational database. Without that help, we could never have analyzed the narratives with the degree of sophistication that became possible. Nor would we be able to continue to interrogate the data going forward in response to new questions that arise.

Though we take full responsibility for our manuscript and the claims it makes, the book is vastly better than it would have been because of the generous feedback we received from several people who put astonishing time and energy into reading an earlier draft.

Besides helping us clarify our organization and presentation, professors Yasmin Kafai of the University of Pennsylvania and Lyn Mikel Brown of Colby College reminded us of the need to emphasize that girls' have multiple identities. Depending on context, their sense of gender, though ever-present, always becomes more or less salient as it interacts with their experience of their race, ethnicity, socioeconomic status, and other identities. We have taken pains to remind readers of the importance of making space for girls to attend to those other identities while thinking about how our findings relate to teaching them well.

Dr. Maggie McQueen, a psychologist in private practice in Wellesley, Massachusetts, and author of a book contrasting women making their way through elite graduate schools in both humanities and hard sciences, did a beyond-the-call and wonderfully meticulous job editing the manuscript. More important, she provided us with a vital, big-picture critique.

Drawing on her experience trying to both support and improve her boys' public schools, Maggie helped us appreciate the importance of qualifying the lessons we were learning from girls and teachers in mostly highly resourced, independent schools. Dr. Brown and Dr. Kafai also stressed the importance of this point. In response, we have tried hard to show how and in what ways our results are relevant to less well-resourced and even under-resourced schools.

Many thanks to Bethany Calhoun, who provided invaluable feedback on an early draft of the book and helped us clarify and focus our message. Her perspective was much needed, and there were many times during this process that we asked ourselves, "What would Bethany think?"

Dr. John D'Auria, a man with a long, distinguished career as a public school teacher, principal, and superintendent, and now president of Teachers21 in Newton, Massachusetts, added to our understanding of how to frame our lessons for public schools and insisted we do a better job finding strong STEM (science, technology, engineering, and mathematics) examples.

Dr. D'Auria, together with Dr. James "Torch" Lytle, a former principal and superintendent in urban schools and a retired practice professor of education at Penn, helped us gain a better understanding of the power of school culture to shape the experience of teachers and students. They both drove home the vital role of what D'Auria calls "fractal leadership"—leadership that educates and relates to teachers in the ways that students should be treated and educated, so the entire school becomes what Lytle calls a "leaderful" community.

Last, but in no way least, we must appreciate Dr. Katherine Windsor, head of Miss Porter's School in Connecticut, and her academic dean, Ms. Jessica Watkin, for their close and critical examination of the book based on their perspectives as leaders of a distinguished independent girls' school. More than anyone else from whom we got advice, they know girls in girls' schools. Dr. Windsor's big picture response was as valuable as her continued, deep, and enthusiastic support for our project. The research literally would not have happened without her.

Ms. Watkin's careful, thorough, and thoughtful review was invaluable in so many ways. She provided us with a close edit that picked up many errors the rest of us missed. She insisted we get rid of jargon and be clearer about our terms. Ms. Watkin's deep knowledge of girls' schools in general, and of the demands and foibles of teaching math and science to girls in particular, as well as her broad understanding of educational "innovations"—effective and not—was an invaluable anchor for us. We could not be more appreciative.

Finally, we cannot close without acknowledging our most significant others. Peter's wife, Peshe, made it possible for him to have the space to work on this, sometimes seemingly endless, project. He will always be grateful for the generosity and good spirits she expressed while coping with his health issues; issues that interrupted his efforts and sometimes inspired fluctuating moods. As a professor of education herself, Peshe's knowledge of urban schools helped to keep Peter grounded and alert the central importance of positive relationships in schools.

Shannon is ever grateful to and appreciative of her spouse and three children. They let her retreat to the office for writing time even (and, at times, especially) on the weekends. David is an amazing partner who was there to bring in a cup of coffee, help edit a tough paragraph, and, especially, think through complex issues and how to write about them thoughtfully and clearly.

Charlotte is deeply thankful for the ongoing support of her family and friends. They have always stood by her side, cheering her on even though working on this book sometimes meant cancelled friend-dates and hiding away for a couple of hours to work during family vacations. The check-in phone calls that often turned into deep, thoughtful conversations always helped Charlotte to remember the importance of giving girls the space they need to tell their stories.

Chapter 1

Introduction

This book is about teaching girls. It is about the lessons that pull them in, motivate them, and keep them engaged. It is about wonderful relationships they form with teachers and peers that enhance and deepen their learning. It is about the classroom experiences that stay with girls days, weeks, or even years later. It is about the assignments, field trips, lectures, and projects that drive a concept home; make a girl feel connected to what she is learning; and, in some cases; entirely change the way she thinks about herself and her future.

We will discuss the activities, practices, and experiences in school that motivate, inspire, and resonate with girls. To accomplish this, we analyzed nearly 2,000 descriptions of lessons from teachers and students in girls' schools located across the country to uncover those that are most motivating and effective. Our approach, actually *asking* teachers and girls what works, is, in truth, revolutionary. Most books about how girls (or boys) learn are rooted in decontextualized assertions plucked from quantitative studies and broadly applied with no basis in real classroom practice. Instead, we went to the source.

We asked more than a thousand girls and over five hundred of their teachers to tell us about captivating lessons—and what made them so compelling. The responses from the teachers and students were a joy to read. We were immersed in descriptions of girls feeling empowered, inspired, valued, and enriched, and of teachers taking pride in having discovered ways to reach them. Our goal in writing this book is to share with teachers, administrators, and parents our discoveries about lessons, classrooms, and schools that genuinely work for girls.

Some people may wonder if this book is necessary. It's true that, on average, girls in this country have higher GPAs, are more likely than boys to graduate from high school, and enter college in greater numbers. While in

1

school, girls are suspended and expelled less often than boys, and fewer girls are referred to special education classes.

From these perspectives, it may seem that girls are doing just fine when it comes to school. Indeed, over the past two decades there has been much more written about boys' struggles in schools. It is important to remember, however, that not all girls are doing well.

Low-income students of both sexes are still far less likely to attend and graduate from a four-year college than their more well-off peers. African American and Latina girls, like their male counterparts, still receive harsher discipline compared to girls of other races and ethnicities. These policies too often lead to increased rates of suspension and expulsion.

Further, in American society, one's socioeconomic status often dictates the quality of education to which one has access. As a result, there are many girls who attend schools that are under-resourced, lack quality teachers, and have a limited curriculum that does not seek to engage students in meaningful ways.

What's more, the idea that "girls are doing fine" falls apart when we examine trends in the U.S. labor market. Women still earn 80 cents to the dollar compared to men[1] holding similar positions, despite constituting 57 percent of the workforce.[2] Only 4 percent of the Fortune 500 CEOs are women,[3] and women only make up about 20 percent of the U.S. Congress.[4]

Gender bias is still very real and prevalent in our society—influencing both the opportunities women are afforded and the career choices they make. Beyond these statistics are the stories of girls and women who were not given the educational opportunities or avenues to careers they would have had were they male.

We chose to write this book because of the personal and professional experiences that have shaped our commitment to girls' education. Peter has been studying various ways gender, race, ethnicity, and sexuality affect the possibilities of girls in schools since the 1980s. His interests were sharpened as he began to observe how his own daughter and her girlfriends experienced their schooling in comparison to his two sons and their male friends.

Peter's paternal curiosity was heightened when he began helping teams of high school girls do participatory action research on issues of concern to them. Their studies have ranged from why highly capable, academically successful girls lack academic self-confidence, to the effects of social class on girls' experiences in school, to the reasons Black girls in schools with majority White student bodies often do not get asked to the prom—by either Black or White boys.

Now that Peter has four granddaughters and observes how they navigate school in comparison to their three brothers, such issues have become even more compelling to him. Given this background, discovering how little research had been done to find out directly from girls about what kinds of teaching is especially engaging for them motivated him to work with Shannon and Charlotte to conduct this study.

While teaching English at an alternative high school, Shannon thought often about her own time as a student and wondered why, by third grade, she had decided that math wasn't for her. She was surprised, then, when she began teaching SAT and GRE preparation classes after college, including math, and discovered that she actually wasn't at all bad at it.

Always interested in matters of gender in education, Shannon was fascinated when she began mentoring new teachers in an urban, public, single-sex school as part of her doctoral work. While the school staff was completely committed to helping the girls succeed, Shannon found the lack of clarity about the purpose and implications of single-sex education at that school troubling. She continued to work for several years with teachers in the school, ultimately forming a teacher inquiry group committed to exploring with the teachers the ways that gender affected their teaching and the students' learning experiences.

As a Black woman who attended suburban public schools for her K–12 education, Charlotte found that her experiences of being one of the few Black students in her honors and AP classes mirrored the experiences of the Black girls in independent schools who were her students when she taught in Chicago, and with whom she worked while conducting different research projects in graduate school in Philadelphia.

Across different geographic regions and in different kinds of schools, Charlotte experienced how Black girls in predominantly White schools have to learn how to navigate encounters of race, gender, and class. In her work with high school girls, as part of a gender justice nonprofit, Charlotte also saw that public school policies and practices often marginalize Black girls.

For Black girls in all schools (public, religiously affiliated, and independent), issues connected to race, gender, class, and status permeate their academic, social, and emotional lives. These issues shape what perspectives and beliefs are valued in the curriculum; what characteristics help someone fit in (or not) in their schools' social environment; and how, on a daily basis, Black girls' emotions are read (and misread) by peers, teachers, and administrators.

Charlotte's work as a teacher and researcher has led her to seek ways that schools can be more supportive and inclusive of the needs of Black girls. She is dedicated to finding ways to promote their optimal academic, social, and emotional development.

Finally, all three of us have worked together at the Center for the Study of Boys' and Girls' Lives (CSBGL; www.csbgl.org). CSBGL is a collaboration of nine independent schools with faculty and graduate students at the University of Pennsylvania's Graduate School of Education. CSBGL supports teams of students at each school doing participatory action research about questions that concern them that lie at the intersection of gender, race, ethnicity, and social class.

The goal of CSBGL is to create student-generated, evidenced-based interventions that help the schools systematically improve school culture, policies, and practice. Our long and varied experiences at CSBGL continue to energize us to try to understand how gender and other social identities affect students' well-being in schools.

Together, our experiences have shown us how gender colors students' experiences in education and every aspect of our society. We believe we must strive to ensure that every student has access to quality education and as many opportunities as possible. For girls, this not only means helping to provide them with excellent teachers and well-resourced schools, but it also means finding ways to instruct them that make them feel connected to what they are learning and make them both confident in and capable of pursuing any future they choose.

The findings we report in this book can further those efforts. They do not, however, support arguments that girls and boys having fundamentally different learning styles. As we show in chapter 6, despite adamant, widely spread claims, there are *few known innate differences* in how the brains of girls and boys work. Differences in how individuals are raised and the influences of society upon them certainly have large effects, but there is *no* compelling research that shows that boys categorically learn in different ways than girls when it comes to taking in and processing information.

Our study began with the premise that there is profound, untapped value in asking the teachers and students in girls' schools what works specifically for them. No one had gone to the source before so we weren't sure what we would find. After analyzing the data we discovered that girls are compelled by hands-on activities, deep classroom discussions, and collaborating with peers on large multimodal projects. They love to have choice in their studies, appreciate lessons that demand they take intellectual risks, and relish projects that challenge them. *So do boys.*

Our data also show that girls greatly value relationships with their teachers. And that they thrive when they can bond with their peers. *So do boys.* As we will make clear, the reality is that while boys and girls are different in many ways, there is little evidence that their *brains* and *learning styles* are meaningfully different.

This leads us to an important question: If boys and girls find the same types of lessons effective and motivating, and also value relationships with their teachers and peers, what does this book add beyond establishing those facts? We answer that question by first stressing the importance of identifying the specifics of what works in girls' education according to their teachers and the girls themselves—and why. Beyond those findings, there are two additional contributions this work makes to the world of girls' education.

First, we address the fact that there are many in education who contend that boys and girls have different kinds of brains. People who share this belief assume that because girls have "pink" brains and boys have "blue" brains, they don't respond to the same forms of pedagogy. The writers of those books would have you believe that girls and boys need almost completely different types of instruction. Some even argue that how loudly a teacher talks to a student should be based on the student's sex, or that the colors school rooms are painted should vary by gender. We will explain how research on adults has been misapplied to children and how good research on minor differences between boys and girls is often overblown and leads to these kinds of extravagant claims, often to the detriment of students.

The second important reason to write this book is to focus on the ways that gender *does* matter. There hasn't been enough attention paid to what works for girls in school and why. In this book we talk about girls' developmental needs and the cultures of classrooms that can support them. While we reject the notion that there is a girl brain that learns in one particular way, we know that being a girl carries intense meanings in school and in society at large.

We look at the qualities of lessons that girls and their teachers told us made lessons most memorable, motivating, and engaging; the activities in lessons that are most effective; and the ways that girls' relationships with each other and with their teachers matter. While our findings indicate that girls and boys are both engaged by hands-on activities, class discussions, and many other types of instruction, we will delve into how to make them particularly effective for girls and show how they can be designed to be powerful tools for enhancing girls' confidence and learning.

Girls are inundated daily by messages telling them what it means to be a girl. These messages influence what they do, how adults and peers interact with them, and what paths their lives take. Schools play a particularly large role in shaping students' gender identities, their beliefs about themselves, and the possibilities they picture for their lives. This book fills a void in the literature by describing the most effective ways to help girls be successful in school and to be prepared for what comes after.

OUR STUDY

Our study was qualitative in nature, meaning that we asked participants directly about their personal experiences. Both quantitative and qualitative studies are important in learning about educational practices. Quantitative studies are good at taking a snapshot of a phenomenon and providing concrete data—usually expressed in numbers.

A quantitative study of boys' and girls' GPAs could tell us on average about how girls and boys are doing in high school as well as how they vary on average by race and ethnicity. It could tell us which of two methods of instruction improved students' math grades more. A qualitative study of GPAs could help us understand *why* certain students' GPAs are different from their peers; *why*, for example, White boys' and Latina girls' grades are higher or lower on average. It could help explain why one method of teaching math worked better than another. It could also help us understand why students in two different schools serving the same kinds of students with the same kinds of demographics score differently.

The goal of qualitative research is to get rich data—complex, detailed information from members of a group that can be studied for patterns. One way to think of it is that while quantitative research may just take a single picture, qualitative research can tell a story about what is happening in the picture.

The following true story illustrates the power of qualitative research. Peter had a professor at Harvard, William Perry, who, as a graduate student, worked for the famous behavioral psychologist B. F. Skinner, in Skinner's, rat lab. After a few months, Perry started to record his predictions of the rats' behavior in the mazes. Skinner became more and more frustrated when Perry's predictions proved more accurate than his own.

Finally, in exasperation, Skinner confronted Perry. "Bill, how are you doing so much better than I am at predicting the damn rats' behavior?" he asked. To which Perry replied, "Professor Skinner, you know your theory but I know your rats." Good qualitative research is designed to learn about the lived experience of the people being studied.

The responses from the students and teachers who participated in our study were both staggering and thrilling, providing us with hundreds of richly detailed narratives about great teaching based on the participants' lived experiences. These stories enabled us to see the variations in the ways girls experienced powerful lessons as well as to discover the central tendencies among them. Within the great variety, we discerned key themes that characterized what girls view as outstanding lessons as well as what their teachers understand as their most effective ones.

We analyzed our data in multiple ways, looking for any differences among schools, age of the students, and the subject matter taught. We also gathered and analyzed demographic data about the students to see if variations emerged based on race or socioeconomic status. We did the same kind of analysis based on teachers' gender, race, and years of teaching.

We did find minor differences in the types of lessons middle school students described compared to high school students and some variation based on subject matter (more hands-on lessons in science, more discussion in English, and the like). We did not, however, find any important demographic differences among student responses. Neither did we find important demographic differences among the stories the teachers told us.[5]

Strikingly, the stories provided to us by teachers agree in very large measure—remarkably in fact—with what the girls told us, suggesting that when it comes to what constitutes great teaching, the picture that emerges from our work is consistent and reliable. The one major difference was that girls told us much about how influential their teachers were. Not surprisingly, teachers made no such claims about their value (though based on what their students said, they legitimately could have).

We situated our study in public, religiously affiliated, and independent girls' schools. That meant the participants in this study were reporting solely on experiences designed for girls. Studying girls in all-girls schools allowed us to uniquely focus on the nuanced complexity of what it means to be a girl in school and in society. As we will argue in chapter 6, while the great preponderance of current scientific research makes it clear there are few, if any, significant and broadly applicable differences in how boys and girls learn, they do have qualitatively different experiences navigating the classroom and the larger world due to their gender.

Being a girl matters. It matters in how people see them and how they see themselves. It shapes their opinions and experiences, often dramatically. For these reasons, we wanted to be able to explore girls' experiences in the classroom without the need to compare them with boys.

The schools in our study are in the south, west, and northeastern parts of the country. A few have relatively small student bodies, others have 1,000 students or more. They include K–12 schools, secondary schools serving middle and high school students, and stand-alone high schools. Most of the schools in our study were private or independent, but two were public schools located in urban areas.

This means most schools in our study are highly resourced and may not face some of the challenges that many public schools experience. However, our participants do represent a wide range of family, racial, and socioeconomic backgrounds.[6] What's more, we found remarkable overlap and consistency in our findings across all our schools.

One of the main findings of our study is the importance of personal relevance to girls' learning. When teachers invite girls to bring their personal histories, family lives, and opinions into their assignments, there are myriad benefits. Girls feel connected and involved in what they are learning, and they make real-world connections that help the material sink in and stay with them.

Teachers learn more about their students, how to connect with them, and how to provide learning opportunities that resonate with them when their students are studying topics that matter deeply to them. Teaching that is personally relevant can be adapted to any classroom in any school but will look different depending on the age level, subject matter, and individuals in the class.

Many of our other findings are likewise dependent on the situations in which they exist. While some of the great lessons we describe can be lifted by a teacher directly from the examples we include, most will work better as starting off points to create a lesson for the subject and, more importantly, for the specific students a teacher is teaching.

We are cognizant of the fact that many (though not all) of the schools in our study were quite privileged. Some of the examples may be difficult to accomplish with a class of thirty students instead of fifteen, and some labs or trips may be out of reach for many schools. However, while some examples in this book include class trips from afar to places like Washington, D.C., or the use of specialized computer equipment, many are adaptable to most classrooms regardless of the school's budget or where it is located. We explore the question of how adaptable our findings are in chapter 9.

This book is about what's right in education. We want school to be a place of engagement, not boredom; of possibility, not frustration. Our hope is the findings we present here will help teachers and administrators find more and better ways to connect girls to their schools, to each other, and to the curriculum. We also hope to help schools center gender in a meaningful way: not by using it to cull boys and girls into different groups based on incorrect assumptions of how their brains work, but by recognizing the place of gender in students' lives. Too often assumptions about gender are used to stereotype and limit girls. To undo this, we must understand the reality of the influence of stereotypes, actively work against limiting assumptions, and leverage gender to foster girls' learning and development.

NOTES

1. Hill, Catherine. "The simple truth about the gender pay gap." *American Association of University Women* 4 *(Fall 2015)*, http://www.aauw.org/resource/the-simple-truth-about-the-gender-pay-gap/.

2. https://www.dol.gov/wb/stats/stats_data.htm.

3. http://fortune.com/2016/06/06/women-ceos-fortune-500-2016/.

4. http://www.cawp.rutgers.edu/women-us-congress-2017.

5. Readers who wish to read more about this may write the senior author, Peter Kuriloff, for a copy of the full report of the national study.

6. Again, readers interested in the full demographic breakdowns may obtain a copy of the final report from the senior author.

Chapter 2

The Qualities of the Effective Lessons

It was inspiring to read through almost 2,000 stories from girls and their teachers about excellent lessons. It's a rare opportunity in the world of research to be able to go to a group of people and ask them to tell you about what's right and good—about what is working. The students' and teachers' stories showed great variety. Some were succinct and to the point, others rich and detailed. Some focused on a single brief encounter during a lesson, others described an entire year in a particular class. The responses included lessons from just about every field of study, as well as nonacademic school events.

We poured through these wonderful data looking for patterns. Why did that 11th grader describe that particular biology lab? What was it about that team debate that so captivated the ninth grader? We then sorted all of the student and teacher responses to capture the major dimensions of lessons that they found especially engaging, interesting, motivating, and effective.

Almost every vignette included a description of a pedagogical activity or technique: a lecture, game, experiment, discussion, and the like. But almost every one also included a description of those qualities of the lesson that made it engaging and motivating. It was clear from what the students and teachers told us that these qualities are every bit as important as the activities—in some cases perhaps more so.

Three main qualities were most consistently referenced as strongly connected to effective teaching by the participants in the study: *relevance* to the students' lives, *clarity* of presentation, and *collaboration* in learning.

RELEVANCE

This I Believe

I am a sixth-grade literature teacher, and each February I ask my students to write a personal essay modeled after National Public Radio's "This I Believe" segment. Students are asked to think of and write about a memorable experience that demonstrates something that they have come to believe about life. This assignment pushes students to not only recall a moment or experience but also asks them to make meaning from that experience. This is very challenging for them, and I often get responses similar to, "I don't know what I believe" or "I haven't had anything interesting happen to me." The leap that they must make is that often what we come to believe about life comes not only from the life-changing experiences that we have but also from the day-to-day interactions and routines in which we engage. . . . Their initial sentiment is that they are too young to have had enough life experience to shape their beliefs, but they soon discover that this is not the case. I have found that girls are eager to share their essays not only with their peers but also with their families and some even want to submit their work for possible publication on NPR's "This I Believe" website. This assignment pushes sixth graders to think beyond the present and the concrete and make abstract meaning out of their past experience. They exceed my expectations every time! —*Ms. Anderson,*[1] *Middle School Teacher*

When the material that girls learn daily is relevant to their lives, goals, and ongoing questions, they find it particularly meaningful and memorable. As Ms. Anderson's lesson illustrates, creating learning opportunities in which girls can see themselves and their experiences reflected in the curriculum is an important key to motivating them. Lessons that ask students to examine their own thoughts, beliefs, goals, and selves are powerful learning tools.

In a society where the experiences of young people in general, and girls in particular, often are overlooked or devalued, a curriculum that emphasizes the importance of *girls* as experts about their lives and the world in which they live—and prioritizes the real-life application of the material—is vital. The "This I Believe" lesson leads girls to discover that they each have a story worth sharing and beliefs that they can be proud of, and it pushes them to think about themselves and their life experiences through a different lens. It empowers them.

When we read through the student and teacher responses, we see that relevance takes many forms, both on practical and personal levels. In a practical sense, girls appreciate lessons and activities in which they can directly apply what they are learning in the classroom to real-life tasks and challenges. For example, Brittany, a ninth-grade student, describes how she found particular joy in her physics class because the lesson provided hands-on, real-life application.

Real-Life Physics

An example of one school assignment that particularly motivated me was a lab we completed in physics. During this lab, we recorded data about a car rolling down and off a simple plastic ramp. We discussed various properties including velocity, acceleration, and inertia. The challenge: calculate the precise landing location of the car, place a metal can on it, and watch and see if your car lands in it. So why did I enjoy this one average lab so much? It combined a subject that I really enjoy with a challenge and allowed me to apply what I have been learning in the classroom to a real-life situation. It allowed me to look forward to more of these challenges in the future as well as to get excited about plenty of real-world situations that I will encounter after I graduate from high school.

Teachers are as enthusiastic about taking lessons out of the purely theoretical realm as their students are. They describe the importance of giving their students chances to apply what they are learning in a real-world setting. In one example, a high school chemistry teacher describes a lesson in which students learn how electrolytes function in everyday household products. The teacher goes on to state that the girls had an "aha" moment about the connection between how everyday products are labeled and what their actual chemical properties are. This newfound knowledge inspired students to bring in groceries from home and to ask a myriad of questions connected not only to chemistry but also to their own lives.

In another example, students in a statistics class gathered data from real-life sources as a way to better understand how statistical functions work. Ms. Sherman, the teacher, describes the following lesson:

Discovering Statistics in Everyday Life

This is a project I do with my 11th-grade students. They study a unit on statistics that deals with mean, median, mode, standard deviation, graphing data, least squares regression lines, correlation, and independence/dependence of two variables. They first study the theory, and this takes the first semester. This is a grueling process for girls where they cannot see the end result of this theory. At the end of the first semester the girls write down a topic of interest. Usually this is sports, or medicine, or business, or engineering. Based on their interest the girls either collect their own data or find data on the Web that relate two variables. . . . Students gather data and then write a mathematics paper on the relationship between the two variables. . . . The excitement of proving something or using their math skills to prove something is both energizing and brings new life to the theory they have learned all year. Using their skills in an application allows girls to connect the theory with their interest. The paper is like a history paper which has about six sections including an introduction, research, a hypothesis, data collection, an analysis, and thoughts on the process. As they write each section, students work with each other and with me to get feedback on their ideas. They present their ideas to the class and are very engaged when presenting to their peers. This process helps them sort through their ideas collectively.

We find that for most of the lessons that contain real-life applications, what draws girls in is the fact that the lessons not only have a hands-on component (something that we discuss in more detail in chapter 3) but also that the theory comes alive through its reflection in real-life situations. Our findings in this instance reflect what many researchers have found about the power in making curriculum relevant to girls, particularly when working to promote their engagement and excitement in the STEM fields.[2]

When students are able to see and apply scientific and mathematical knowledge to the world around them – to not just learn about science, math, and engineering but also to do it in a real-life setting – they are more able to picture themselves going into these fields professionally.

As we reviewed student and teacher responses, we also discovered descriptions that straddle the practical and personal spheres in other important ways: they are relevant to current events, social justice, and topics particularly germane to girls and women. In these responses, girls appreciate the lessons not only because the material connects to their personal experiences or beliefs but also because they create opportunities for enacting change in the world. Girls find them empowering.

Some students write about how moved they were to learn about wars and conflicts occurring in far corners of the world (e.g., the Arab Spring and its aftermath), while others describe getting involved with local politics (e.g., a local bill that would address overcrowding in their school district). Still others passionately describe learning about environmentalism and taking care of the Earth. Many of the narratives are connected to social justice issues, including those directly affecting girls and women. In this example, Isabella, an eleventh-grade student, describes a class discussion in which students talked about female-focused issues from a social justice perspective:

Discussing Women's Issues from around the World

A class experience that I especially remember is when I was in the sophomore year which was last year, we had an open discussion about rape, abortion, and female-related issues that were occurring in the world. Even though I am not a victim of rape and neither have I faced the abortion decision, as a female, I felt obligated to stand up and have a voice. Some things happening out there CAN be prevented. Society sometimes portrays females as a sexual thing, which then leads to people accusing females that they "asked for rape" because of the amount of clothes they are wearing. Females are humans too and shouldn't be judged whether she "asked for" rape or not according to the amount of cloth she has on the body. This is a touchy topic, and this was one of the most memorable times of being in a single-gender school.

Not only does this teacher create a space where social justice issues relevant to girls can be discussed in detail but also the student believes that the all-girls environment is particularly conducive to discussing sensitive and controversial issues that affect women.

In another example, a student describes how a classroom debate in her seventh-grade history class, inspired by the controversy in France over whether girls should be allowed to wear hijabs in public schools, was particularly meaningful because the topic focuses on issues and events that are happening in their lifetime and allows them to see how history connects to current events. Other responses from girls echo the sentiment that a girls' school provides a unique and safe space in which to discuss and debate controversial topics that they care about.

Long-term projects also serve as vehicles for girls to dive deeper into world events and social issues. Students describe how extended, hands-on units encourage them to have a more detailed understanding of what they are learning. Kathryn, a middle school student, talks about her experience participating in a model senate project. The girls each took on the role of a senator from a different state and drafted legislation, including doing research, crafting the document, and debating the merits of the bill in committee. The project concluded with a class trip to Washington, D.C. to watch the real U.S. Senate in action. She writes, "This unit and this class in general prepared us to go out into the world as informed citizens, aware of how our government operates and able to make more informed decisions and votes as a result."

Kathryn's response and others like it showcase the importance of girls being able to see themselves as active and informed citizens in an increasingly complex world. They appreciate relevant lessons that teach them about the inner workings of society and encourage them to consider how they can begin to change the world.

In the next example, Sydney, a twelfth-grade student, also emphasizes the importance of learning about matters that directly affect her life:

Applying Anthropology Class to Real-World Situations

I would have to say that my favorite topic in anthropology would have to be religion. . . . Honestly, this course has helped me in many real-life situations. All of the different cultures and views that I have learned about have made me more accepting of others. I will not look at someone odd because they are wearing clothes that cover every part of their body, I will not question a girl who has an arranged marriage, and I will not argue with a person who has different beliefs than I. Furthermore, what I have learned in Anthropology has enhanced my everyday experience and my personal characteristics. . . . Every time I step foot in my anthropology class I always get enthusiastic about the next study of humans I am going to learn about. I believe that that is why I excel in the class: a class that is exciting and challenges one's view of the world. I am so glad that I selected anthropology as my elective senior year.

As Kathryn's and Sydney's examples demonstrate, material that connects to girls' personal everyday experiences fosters their engagement in the classroom. The girls' responses illustrate how the power of these lessons lies in their ability to place personal experiences at the center of what they are learning.

Many teachers are understandably reluctant to introduce controversial topics in the classroom. They may avoid discussions of politics and stay far away from matters of religious freedom and sexual assault. And, undoubtedly, these topics must be approached carefully and within a properly prepared classroom environment. But when done well, such discussions can be amongst the most powerful lessons a student may ever have.

The girls in our study are glad to be learning about these important topics, but what is even more important to them is their ability to form and voice informed opinions about them. It resonated strongly with them when they were given opportunities to debate and make up their own minds about topics that even many adults avoid thinking about, and certainly often avoid discussing.

This brings to mind a quote often attributed to William Butler Yeats that "education is not the filling of a pail, but the lighting of a fire."[3] The girls in our study convey the excitement and empowerment they get from their most motivating lessons. These feelings move students forward in their learning and propel them to further inquiries.

Another effective teaching tool connected to relevance involves using lessons and activities that are autobiographical in nature. Melissa, a seventh grader, describes a project that brought her closer to understanding her family while enabling her to be quite creative:

Project 12

In English, we had to do a project called Project 12. We chose three different family members who were 12 in three different decades. We researched those decades and interviewed our family members. Once we had done that, we used *Photostory* to create a slide show. We were able to add narration and music to our slide show. It was really interesting to learn about my family and the past. I now know things I hadn't known about my great-grandpa, grandpa, and grandma. I was in 6th grade when I did this project and I loved it, and I think future students would too.

Mrs. Franklin, a high school biology teacher, used a similar strategy to help her girls understand the personal relevance of genetics:

Family Genetics

I find that projects/labs/activities that allow the students to integrate personal experience or knowledge into the project make for a memorable and useful experience. In my ninth-grade biology classes I have the students create family pedigrees in which they choose a particular trait and follow that trait through the generations. The girls do research on their family, and I encourage them to include pictures of family members in their pedigree. Girls like this project because it has a personal aspect and gives them a fair amount of freedom to be creative. They have to meet certain criteria but have latitude in meeting those criteria. The girls also learn about genetics and how traits are passed down from one generation to the next.

In both of these lessons, the access point to girls' learning is through the connection between the curricular material and the study of their family histories. They reinforce the fact that girls have stories to tell and that their experiences are important.

Influential teachers find ways to link the personal and the academic. We find that the defining element of such lessons is that they strategically promote skills associated with what we term "constructive introspection." By this we mean a process of considering one's own emotions in a lesson purposefully devoted to personal growth.

In an example of this process, Ms. Grady, a high school counselor, describes how she helps her students consider what a healthy romantic relationship means to them. As part of the class lesson, the counselor leads her students through brainstorming sessions that focus on what they look for in an ideal romantic partner, and based on that activity, the students engage in a discussion about which characteristics are "essential" and which are "extras" to developing a healthy relationship. In this discussion the academic and the personal intersect as students are given the freedom to challenge, question, and affirm the ideas that are thrown out about what having a healthy romantic relationship means.

Putting Girls in the Center: Why Relevance Works for Girls

While Ms. Grady's lesson is obviously connected to the personal, we find that girls value the various kinds of relevance found in all of the lessons we describe. Whether it's arguing for a legislative bill that matters to a student personally because of where she lives, researching family genetics, learning about the treatment of girls and women around the world, or applying a statistical analysis to real-life experiences, relevance is a key component in making learning engaging and motivating.

To understand why the relevance of lessons to students' lives, experiences, and beliefs is particularly important for girls, we draw on theories of education that argue that the experiences of girls and women should be placed at the center, rather than the margins, of education.[4] Too much research in education either explicitly or accidentally looks only for key strategies and practices that work for boys in the classroom, or, if it includes girls, strives for a comparison between boys and girls (and often draws erroneous or oversimplified conclusions). The learning needs of girls need to be categorically explored and better understood.

It is not only that the needs of girls and women have been overlooked in what is studied typically in schools but also that the daily curriculum of the classroom plays to valuing the needs and accomplishments of boys and men more than those of girls and women.[5] If you thumb through an average history textbook, chances are most of the accomplishments and events described will feature men fulfilling a particularly heroic or villainous role.

When women are mentioned in history, typically they are described as assistants to men, fulfilling stereotypical feminine roles (nurses instead of doctors, teachers instead of professors, administrative assistants instead of CEOs), or there is a special section devoted to their accomplishments (e.g., women in the Civil War) that confine their contributions to a few pages. In cases in which women were notably absent from an historical event, that needs to be acknowledged and discussed. For the most part, however, women's lives were extremely relevant to world events, even if they were not the general on the battlefield or the governor of the colony. Ignoring their presence and relevance communicates that women are inconsequential.

Similar biases can be found in science and math textbooks where only male mathematicians and scientists are mentioned, or in literature where female characters align with stereotypical feminine traits. Again, teachers need to actively reflect about the content of the material they are teaching and whether it indicates a de facto male bias.

What we find in the responses of the girls and their teachers is that the most engaging and memorable lessons tap into the needs, beliefs, and experiences of girls. Girls need to be able to see themselves reflected in the curriculum. This is important not only in a study of history or of famous mathematicians, as described earlier, but also in hands-on activities.

Asking girls to analyze the level of electrolytes in household products and using an actual ramp to explore different properties in physics speak to girls' interests in knowing that what they learn has some sort of practical and real-life application. This connection is particularly important for girls because these kinds of lessons give them the opportunity to be scientists and mathematicians, roles still dominated by men.

The lessons pertaining to girls that revolve around rape, abortion, and wearing hijabs—and more broadly about women's role in the world—provide a space for girls to talk openly and honestly about complex topics that are often not brought up in schools. Teachers encourage girls to become more aware and involved citizens in their communities by bringing these issues into the curriculum. By giving girls opportunities to learn about them in safe spaces, teachers enable the students to reflect on their own statuses and identities in deeply meaningful ways.

Activities that ask girls to share their beliefs and personal experiences place them directly into the center of the curriculum. The "This I Believe" essay, family-based projects, and focused class discussions all communicate to girls that their voices, beliefs, and values are important and worth listening to.

Though women and girls are making gains in our society, the reality is that a wage gap still exists between men and women; the U.S. Congress is still 80 percent male, and girls are still less likely than boys to pursue high-paying careers in STEM fields. In lessons like the ones that the girls and teachers in our study describe, girls become experts, gaining the confidence and perspective to move forward successfully in society.

A CLASSROOM ENVIRONMENT WHERE THE EXPECTATIONS ARE CLEAR

A classroom environment that many girls find constructive and conducive to learning is one in which teachers make their expectations and procedures clear and present them in a detailed manner that is easy to follow.

The Importance of Structure

What I liked about my teacher was that we had the same routine every day. I liked how first we wrote down the lesson plans for the day in our notebooks and we had one question to answer as a review from the previous class. I liked having a quick review before we plunged into the next topic. Then we would have lecture and take notes. . . . After note-taking and lecture we would do some type of art project to show what we had learned in that lesson. I found being able to show my knowledge in that form was fun, because I am a very artistic person, but also those projects made it stick more in my head having time to practice. I also liked how she gave us homework every night. I liked how the homework wasn't "busy work," but it was more like drawing and labeling a cell, or drawing the digestive system that really made the topic stay in my head so I would be ready for the next class. *Tanya, Eighth-Grade Student*

As Tanya's vignette details, well-defined and established classroom routines helped her feel confident about what was expected and to know what she would be facing every day. Further, the varied modes of reviewing a concept fostered her learning about the topic under study in a deep way.

Tanya's vignette also speaks of how clarity in the classroom exists on multiple levels. In both student and teacher responses, we see descriptions of clarity that range from detailed rubrics on projects and assignments to the establishment of predictable and logical classroom routines, to carefully thought-out and executed lesson plans. It will be helpful to many students for teachers to consider clarity on all of these levels when planning lessons.

On the most immediate level, clarity takes the form of detailed explanations and procedures that accompany lessons and activities. Teachers employ examples, images, videos, or demonstrations to unambiguously explain the material. In most cases, the clear lessons students describe involve the presentation of material in multiple ways to further reinforce understanding. This is illustrated in the example provided by Sasha, a sixth-grade math student.

Metric System Video

We came into class and we watched this video about the metric system. It was a video on YouTube because we were learning about the metric system and converting measurements. Then we watched a *BrainPop* video. After that we took notes on the order of the metric system: kilo, hecto, deka, unit, deci, centi, and milli. Our teacher also taught us an easy way to remember it: King Henry Doesn't Usually Drink Chocolate Milk. Then we went over about converting them, for example, converting 1 kilogram equals 1,000 grams. We did some practice problems and then went over them. We also got a chart that said "kilo, hecto, deka, unit, deci, centi, and milli," and we wrote things underneath it like "1 meter = 100 centimeters" and "1 dekameter = 10,000 millimeters." Then we got homework about converting the measurements and we went over it together the next day.

On the face of it, this lesson does not at first appear to be particularly striking. We have to step back and ask why a young student, when given complete freedom to describe any lesson out of hundreds she has experienced, chooses this one. What seems most important to her is the clear, logical, and multimodal nature of the approach. The example shows how the clarity of concept is established in a variety of ways: students watch videos, take notes, learn a mnemonic device, and then complete practice work all centered around the same concept.

It is important for teachers to keep lessons like this in mind when considering what effective and motivating teaching looks like. Our data set is filled with numerous accounts of exciting field trips, amazing hands-on activities, and other out-of-the-ordinary adventures in learning, all of which appear in various sections of this book. But we also have a great number of responses such as this one describing a clear and organized lesson that melds multiple teaching approaches to instill a concept in a student. Not exciting perhaps but very effective for some girls just the same.

Beyond the clear procedures or practices that are tied to the learning of a particular concept or topic, many of the girls' responses highlight the fact that they enjoy the consistency and predictability of well-established classroom routines. In this example, Donna, a tenth-grade history student, describes in detail the routines that accompany each unit in her history class, revealing how systematically and thoroughly the teacher organizes his teaching:

Tying Everything Together

I really like the way my history teacher teaches because I really understand and am able to grasp the material. He will assign us a reading assignment and have us fill out the related parts in a study guide. Then in class he will usually give us a reading quiz testing us on the reading. Then he teaches off of a PowerPoint that has key points on them, but then he really goes in depth about the material and gives us activities about the material after he teaches it to us. He also makes sure that we are very organized using *OneNote Notebook*. *OneNote* enables us to have an extra copy of every document, homework, or PowerPoint on our computer so that when it comes to exams we have everything to study with. After a few more reading assignments our teacher sets the due date for our study guide, and we finish filling out many pages of the study guide that includes chronology, vocabulary, questions, and identifications about the topic we are learning about. The teacher will also give us a test or an essay to write about the topic that really ties everything together.

Girls appreciate clear procedures and policies in the classroom. In our study they not only describe enjoying the recurring sequence of particular events but also appreciate the explicit expectations that cover even the most routine classroom behaviors such as listening to a class lecture and taking notes. In all the examples, the predictability of the formatting and expectations reflected in the notes and study guides helps the girls feel confident in identifying key information.

On a broader level, clarity in the classroom takes the shape of an explicit scope and sequence of a unit or larger curriculum. In classes that demonstrate such transparency, girls are able to see how the different pieces connect to one another and that there is a clear direction in which all of the work is going. Maya, a twelfth grader, describes this experience in her geography class:

Opportunities to Delve into Material

My favorite area of study at school is geography, and I therefore took AP human geography in my Junior Year. Although I found the entire course engaging, the unit of study I found most interesting and that I felt particularly motivated in was the international politics and relations unit. The combination of class activities, readings, and discussions created an environment in which I could understand and delve into the material more thoroughly than I may have in other units. All the units were structured in a similar manner, but this module happened to be the one that worked best for me. I really enjoyed the articles we read since they helped me to understand and relate material we covered in class to real-world situations. The group projects allowed me to apply my knowledge to current events I find interesting, and the group discussions helped me to view the material from many different perspectives.

When describing the connection between past material and present learning, the girls not only trace the chronology of units in a school year but also provide examples of specific questions or themes that serve as touchstones they return to throughout the year. This, of course, provides connections among the different topics that they study.

In the following example, Emma, an eighth-grade student, explains how as part of a history class she was asked to revisit the same central question several times over the course of the school year. As Emma explains, the activity allowed her to see how her learning and thinking had progressed over time:

This Made Me Realize How Much I Have Learned

One of many projects that I have enjoyed this year is a project where we explained what it means to be an American citizen. The first day of school my teacher gave us a blank card. Knowing nothing about American history, we wrote what it means to be a U.S. citizen for us. After our first unit, again we wrote what it means to us to be an American citizen again, on a bigger card. Our answers had grown so much since the first day of school, which made me realize how much I had grown in just one unit. Just a week ago we finished our second unit. So again, we wrote another card that was even bigger than the second one, showing how much we have grown over time.

Emma goes on to describe her excitement about her own learning:

This made me realize how much I have learned over the course of the semester. I am so excited to learn more and see how much I know by the end of the year.

This project was great for me because I could see the progress I have made. It is great to see the steps of the learning I have gone through.

At the broadest level, clarity in the classroom exists because of the careful and intentional planning of teachers. The fact that students are able to pinpoint specific procedures and policies and, in some cases, trace a particular scope and sequence speaks to the thoughtful design teachers bring to their work.

When reading through teachers' responses, we find that, like their students' descriptions, the lessons and activities that they believe are most engaging for girls are often those that include detailed explanations, classroom routines, and assignments. In the following example, Ms. Higgins, a middle school science teacher, describes what she finds to be a good practice for involving her students:

Actively Involve Students

The most effective practice is to actively engage the students in the learning experience. This is a task that I take seriously in my seventh-grade classes. I find it to be quite effective in the learning of both the subject content and skill sets necessary for success in a science class. I always start off my lessons with a few memory jogger questions, and this typically starts the class on a positive note with students recalling previously learned information typically incorporating some kind of analogy. I then continue with a PowerPoint presentation and tie in the previous lesson to the current one. Prior to this I prepare "fill-in-notes" for the girls and e-mail [those to] them. They use this as a shell to complete as we go through the lesson. This way they are engaged in the lesson, typing in important bits and not bogged down by the notes and worrying that they will not "get everything copied." Students seem to like this system as it allows them the processing time necessary to follow along. Following this we have a question period and reflection. Sometimes we incorporate hands-on laboratory work which highlights the task at hand. Students seem to be very comfortable with the unfolding of the lesson. To me, that is the most important element. When the students are comfortable they are open to learn and to be involved in their learning experiences and this, to me, is the whole point.

Ms. Higgins' response, like many other teacher narratives, describes a lesson plan that includes elements of clarity that girls find reassuring and beneficial: having a consistent classroom routine, connecting the material between different units, having a clear procedure by which the students take notes, and using multiple modes to communicate the concepts.

The Importance of Scaffolding and Knowing What's Next

Girls' descriptions of lessons that involve "big picture" as well as "on the ground" examples of clarity speak to how different methods of review and the careful sequencing of curriculum may deepen their understanding of the material. Both the student and teacher responses echo the pedagogical strategies emphasized by developmental theorist Lev Vygotsky[6] and his work on the interaction of learning and development.

Central to Vygotsky's research was his description of the "zone of proximal development" and the notion of "scaffolding." From a learning standpoint, the zone of proximal development is the level of learning difficulty that is situated between the skills that an individual has already learned and is comfortable with and the skills that are too difficult to learn on her own.

In the examples we have given, girls describe situations where the material that they are learning is particularly challenging, and point to the clarity of the lessons and expectations and the systematic review of concepts as being instrumental in their gaining mastery of what was presented in class. These elements that work to promote student learning all function as "scaffolds" that bridge the gap between what students already know and ideas and concepts that are just out of their reach.

Such scaffolds are particularly important for girls, as the research shows that in classrooms (particularly those that are coed) many girls avoid participating in class discussions or providing answers unless they are confident that they have the right answer.[7] Using scaffolding and making overt connections to skills and knowledge already gained give girls the opportunity to learn the material in manageable pieces. This structure has been shown to develop students' confidence in the classroom and to prevent them from feeling overwhelmed by the task set in front of them.

When teachers present a clear scope and sequence for activities, lessons, units, and curriculum, it helps girls to scaffold their current and future learning by providing a map of where they have been, where they are, and where they will be going. We see once again how much students appreciate gaining a broader understanding of their own learning.

Indeed, often what students describe is a meta-cognitive view; that is, to learn how they learn and understand their own thinking. This enables them to see themselves within the scope of their learning over time and to gain a sense of power over their accumulating knowledge.

In the next section, we look at the third main quality of effective lessons that emerged from the teachers' and students' descriptions. As with the qualities of relevance and clarity, collaboration in learning can not only be employed within a single activity but ideally will also function as an intrinsic attribute of the class.

A CLASSROOM ENVIRONMENT THAT PROMOTES COLLABORATION

Collaboration in the classroom—including pair work, group activities and projects, and grade-wide events—is a major category that emerged as we looked through the student and teacher responses. The girls and their teachers describe a variety of experiences, both inside and outside of the classroom, where working together with their classmates is central to their learning and motivation.

The Decades Project

At the end of last year, during seventh grade, each history class completed a project known as "The Decades Project." This project took place during history class, where each class was divided into two groups. Each group was then assigned a decade during the 1900s. To begin the project, each group did research about what the life was like during the certain decade they were assigned. After the research was completed, our teacher allowed us to start the fun part. . . which would be observed by the parents and teachers of the seventh grade. This part included each group designing a set of the daily life of their decade. The set included places such as clothing stores, markets, or even people just talking on the street about important events that were occurring in their time period. It all depended on the decade you were assigned. Parts were chosen for each member of the groups, such as salespeople, or even just a family in a park. This project helped us learn more about each decade, helped us learn to work in a group, and even helped us become closer to people in our class. —*Suzanne, Eighth-Grade Student*

While there are multiple components that made The Decades Project a success, Suzanne emphasizes the importance of collaboration in both helping her learn and connecting her with her peers.

A reflection from Ms. Harper, a calculus teacher, about the challenges of engaging her students around the "substitution of variables" method of integration provides another excellent example of the power of collaboration.

Engaging Girls in Calculus Class

I had difficulty motivating and engaging my class recently as we studied a method of integration that is called substitution of variables. I began the lecture in my typically rigorous, analytical manner and the students were clearly not with me. They took notes and appeared to be attentive, but when I asked them if they understood the new technique, there was a resounding "no." So, I placed them in pairs at the board. I suggested that the student on the left of each pair be the first scribe and record what the other student proposed in solving their problem. First, I asked them to summarize what they had learned during my brief, theoretical lecture. Then I posted on the projector various problems to be solved. I moved around the room continually and was able to clearly see their work as they attempted to solve each problem. After the entire class of paired students had completed each problem successfully, then and only then did the girls move as a group to the next problem. The girls switched being the scribe for each new problem. If one pair finished first and another pair was really struggling, I suggested that that pair assist the pair that could not solve the problem. . . . The time flew by and all of the girls expressed how much fun they were having and how much they had accomplished during that brief 25 minutes at the board. The class was definitely a success and the girls clearly mastered the material.

Collaborative activities foster engagement and learning in at least three major ways. First, girls enjoy collaborating with one another because it makes learning fun and both emotionally and intellectually involving. Second, working together also provides a way for girls to learn the material by gaining insights from different peers' perspectives. Third, it promotes bonding and the ability to get to know one another in more complex ways.

Suzanne's vignette, presented earlier, describes these themes—working in a group on "The Decades Project" was a way students could have fun learning about historical periods, discover more about each other as they worked together, and dive deeply into learning about the history of their chosen decade. The story also illustrates how learning about history through multiple modes serves to maintain girls' interest in the material.

Similarly, Ms. Harper's description of how her students worked together to tackle challenging material reflects both the enjoyment that girls found in working with one another and the collective confidence that they experienced by being able to figure things out. Ms. Harper's narrative is also an example of responsive and reflective teaching. In noticing that her students were not engaged and seemed to be struggling individually, Ms. Harper used the moment to build on the power of trying something new and of collective thinking to help her students better access the material.

The students and teachers whose responses focus on collaboration often write about how enjoying each other is a key reason that they like group work. Girls describe fun in both the sense of enjoying spending time together with their friends when completing an assignment and in the sense of the satisfaction gained from working together with their peers to accomplish a task and helping each other grow.

In one example, a high school student describes how much enjoyment she and her classmates had doing collaborative activities in their Spanish class. In the class, the teacher made a game out of the students writing sentences to practice present and past participles. The students read each other's sentences out loud and tried to guess who wrote each sentence, and then correct them if wrong. The girl describes how she had fun *while* "absorbing the information."

She derived enjoyment from working collectively with her peers throughout the activity, which made the learning itself fun.

In addition to appreciating the enjoyment of collaboration, and certainly as important, girls value opportunities for collaboration because working together with their classmates on a focused task enriches their learning of the material. The examples that students and teachers gave describe learning experiences in which students were asked to teach their classmates about a topic and also lessons where the key points could be magnified and processed in detail through a small group activity.

Another benefit of working in groups is the opportunity it affords for stronger and weaker students to collaborate. By placing girls of different skill levels in one group, teachers consciously scaffold the learning of diverse students. Ms. Costas, a high school physics teacher, describes collaborative learning in this way:

Process-Oriented Guided Inquiry Learning

I employ a strategy called POGIL. POGIL is an acronym for "process-oriented guided inquiry learning." I break the class into groups. Each group has a manager, a spokesperson, a recorder, and an evaluator. The manager keeps the group on task. The recorder writes down all aspects of the exercise. The evaluator grades the group at the end of the exercise. Finally, when I come around to question the group, only the spokesperson is allowed to talk to me. So, the group must articulate questions to the spokesperson, and then the spokesperson talks to me. Once the groups are formed, I give each group a ramp and a marble. I instruct them to devise a method to successfully hit a bull's eye on the floor if the marble starts from rest at the top of the ramp on a desktop and rolls to the floor. I do not give them any other instructions. As the girls scan their lecture notes, they begin to see that kinematic equations for gravity are separate from constant speed in the horizontal direction. Soon, they figure out to use the vertical height of the desk to find time and then use the time to calculate the horizontal range.

Through the designation of different roles, each girl can capitalize on her own strengths and those of the other students in the group to explore the material from their different perspectives, while working together to solve the task at hand.

Collaborative activities also serve a vital social function within classrooms. They are meaningful to girls because they give them the opportunity to get to know their classmates in a more nuanced and deeper fashion. As we saw in the previous examples, working in groups in well-structured ways allows girls to discover what skills and strengths each member brings to the table and also gave them a chance to explore both the challenges and delights of learning how to work together. In the following example, Theresa, a ninth grader, comments on how the challenges of working in a small group project was a learning experience in itself:

We Had to Figure Out Everyone's Strength

One day in history class we were discussing the four different Atlantic revolutions. We were split into four different groups of about five people. Each group was assigned to create a diagram of a specific revolution. Our group had the American Revolution. We had to fill in boxes with the appropriate answers such as the date, the fighting sides, and specific people that were involved. This forced us to look at the revolution as a timeline and organize it into our brains. . . . The groups were a little big, but we all could collaborate on ideas and come up with a lot of ideas. We had to divide the work evenly amongst ourselves without the teacher's involvement. Of course we came across the problem that every group has; there are slackers, over-achievers, leaders, and followers. We had to figure out what everyone's strength was and divide the task up according to that.

Assessing the relative strengths of different members of a team and learning to effectively manage group projects will, of course, serve these students well long after they have finished school.

Opportunities for collaboration abound within school environments. Girls not only value collaborative experiences that occur within the classroom but also describe outdoor retreats and class trips, which can become places where they get to know each other beyond their academic selves. School teams, too, offer opportunities not only for developing physical skill and character growth but also for forging close bonds with classmates. One tenth grader wrote eloquently about how important her being on the school basketball team is to her. She describes the challenge and personal growth she experiences through sports and the important elements of fun and stress relief she gets from it. She concludes, "Meeting new people while doing something you love makes everything all the better."

Girls' Relationships in the Classroom

Being on the basketball team is not, on its face, connected to academic learning. The student described her love of being on the team with no mention of a classroom. However, she beautifully describes many life lessons she takes from being on the team, as well as the much-needed variety and stress relief it provides. Finally, there is a critical component of interpersonal connection in her participation in that activity.

As we will discuss in detail in chapter 4, girls' relationships with their teachers are central to positive and effective experiences in school. They love it when teachers get to know them on a personal level as well as on academic level by taking the time to meet with them one-on-one, by encouraging their voices, and by taking notice of them when different events (both positive and negative) happen in their lives. Girls' reasons for enjoying collaborative work with their peers are no different. They love the opportunity to get to know their classmates as companions and to bond over the trials and tribulations of being teenagers.

Researchers who focus on adolescent girls' relationships (Lyn Mikel Brown and Carol Gilligan[8] being trailblazers in this area) have found that girls often feel that they must choose between having a voice in terms of expressing their feelings, ideas, and questions, and maintaining close relationships with those around them.

When girls "go underground"[9] as Gilligan describes it, they silence themselves in order not to rock the boat and so they will be loved and accepted by their family members, peers, and teachers. Girls' self-silencing takes the form of not openly saying what they are thinking and feeling. Instead, they go along with what they believe will keep them in good standing with their peers and important adults.

Brown and Gilligan describe the psychological dissonance that is at play here: to feel connected with others, girls actually work to disconnect from their authentic selves. Ironically, this means the relationships that they are maintaining cannot be based on authentic connection.

For girls, adolescence can be viewed as a crisis of a push/pull of sorts—as they mature into adolescence, girls (like their male counterparts) they become more autonomous in directing their own lives and develop a growing awareness of the different dimensions of relationships; yet they also feel pressured to forgo that autonomy in order to be involved in relationships. Gaining voice and developing the courage to speak on matters that are important to them is essential to girls' developing authentic adult selves.

What the girls' and teachers' responses show is how spaces for collaborative work in school provide a counterbalance to their tendency to "go underground." Much educational research indicates that while some young women remain outspoken in class, a great many silence themselves as time goes by. This can become especially true in higher level STEM courses in high school and college where many young women, outnumbered and sidelined, eventually leave a class, a college major, or a job.

In our study, we read story after story filled with examples of classes in which the opposite was happening. Girls were taking responsibility for their learning, exhibiting authority, and enthusiastically jumping into their work. In those vignettes, we see girls willingly taking on leadership roles within their group work and describing how thrilled they are to have opportunities to work with each other. We see how collaborative lessons, activities, projects, teams, and field trips foster conditions in which girls are able to confidently express their ideas without worrying about endangering their relationships.

Something that stands out about girls' relationships in the classroom is their multifaceted nature. Their narratives illustrate how collaborative activities allow them to develop connections based on their academic skills and their intellectual journeys as they learn new material together.

Collaborative activities also give girls the chance to be creative, have fun, and connect around their mutual experiences of being adolescents. In the face of silence and uncertainty, an effective collaborative learning environment in the classroom supports a healthier development of girls' learning by helping them become skillful at working together, relying on and trusting each other, and empowering each other's voices. It fosters learning about how to manage disagreements, arguments, and team dynamics that are part of social life.

But to be effective, such collaborative activities must be well-structured. Pair and group work can just as easily lead to further stifling of a girl's voice and sidelining of her full participation. To avoid this, teachers must help their students create positive norms of group behavior, underline the importance of each student's participation, and monitor the students to ensure that some girls are not forcing others into silence.[10]

A NOTE ABOUT COMPETITION

Though some of the examples of collaboration we presented in this section had elements of competition in them or instances where students described the thrill of competing with teams of their peers, when looking through all of the student and teacher responses, we find that competition was a tiny component of our data. It was not central to what girls wrote about when describing what was most engaging, motivating, and inspiring in their educational experiences.

While a very small number of students did choose to write enthusiastically about games as part of learning, they tended to focus on their social dimensions on the fun they had and about working together with their teammates, rather than on winning or on other competitive aspects of the games.

Overall, only a tiny percentage of students and teachers positively mention competition at all or as a part of the educational experiences they narrated. In contrast, many more students and teachers wrote about group and collaborative work. In all of those cases, the participant specifically emphasizes the benefits of students working together.

Of course, this does not mean girls do not enjoy and even thrive on competition when and where it is appropriate. The tremendous growth of interest and participation in women's athletics at all levels since Title IX demonstrates that. It only means that in the narratives teachers and girls wrote for this study, competition does not appear as a key part of the lessons they most prize.

In this chapter, we focused on the qualities of lessons and classrooms that teachers and students brought up again and again as being conducive to learning. In Chapter 3 we go through the kinds of learning activities that came up most often and most powerfully in the data. While we're isolating these findings for clarity in this book, the participants in our study rarely wrote about just one aspect of a classroom or a lesson. It was not uncommon for a girl to describe, for example, a beloved teacher and how she made the subject matter relevant to the students by a collaborative, multimodal project. While we are unpacking each of those components individually (strong connection to teacher, relevance to the girl's life, collaboration, multimodal project), we never want to lose sight of the fact that it was those pieces together that made the experience so powerful.

KEY IDEAS

What Teachers Can Do to Promote Relevance,
Clarity, and Collaboration in Their Teaching:

- Look for opportunities to infuse relevance, clarity, and collaboration into day-to-day lesson plans as well as the curricular structure of the entire school year and the character of the classroom.
- Ensure relevance by regularly incorporating real-world applications to subject matter:

  - Offer your students opportunities to reflect on their personal and family lives and bring them into assignments.
  - When appropriate, connect subject matter to the lives of girls and women locally and globally.

- Promote clarity by using thoughtful routines in the classroom.
- Be explicit with students about daily lesson plans and the arc of learning over the course of a unit or a year.
- Encourage students to meta-cognitively evaluate the way they learn and the effectiveness of their learning.
- Incorporate different modes of learning into lessons.
- Offer opportunities for collaborative learning at the pair, group, and whole-class level.
- Monitor and structure pair and group work to help ensure that all students have opportunities to participate.

- Help the class create norms to help the girls self-govern their teamwork. Such norms might include: every person in the group needs to be heard, respect and learn from other girls' views, and use "I" statements to own what you feel rather than telling other girls what they feel.

What Parents Can Do to Promote Relevance, Clarity, and Collaboration:

- Help your daughter find real-world connections to what she is learning in school.
- Offer examples from your own life about the skills and knowledge you use in your job or daily activities.
- Talk with your daughter about world events.
- Find out what concerns she has about the world and where her passions lie.
- Encourage her to pursue her passions.
- Help her find voice so she can participate in civic and social life in ways that feel meaningful for her.
- Have discussions with your daughter about her learning. This could include questions such as:

  - Do you know why a teacher has given particular homework assignments?
  - Do you understand how to assess your learning progress as the year goes by?
  - If she doesn't, help her develop realistic ways of doing it.
  - If she is not performing as she would like in a class, discuss with her what changes in her routines or approach to studying may be more effective for her.

- Talk to your daughter about how her collaborations with classmates fare.
- While some students have a natural ability to read other's emotions and participate in pair or group work effectively and seemingly effortlessly, most students benefit from coaching about working on teams:

  - If your daughter complains that her classmates do not listen to her when they work together, help her strategize to change this dynamic; one effective technique can be to role-play possible approaches with her.

- Above all, be alert to the possibility that your daughter may feel invisible or silenced at school.
- If she does, work with her as well as with teachers and administrators to help her be authentically present at school. Getting involved in team sports, clubs, or extracurricular activities can often help.

NOTES

1. All names of teachers and students are pseudonyms. In some cases, to ensure clarity, we edited their narratives for spelling and punctuation. Otherwise, we have let the participants speak for themselves in their own words. References to schools' names have also been removed.

2. Halpern, Diane F., Joshua Aronson, Nona Reimer, Sandra Simpkins, Jon R. Star, and Kathryn Wentzel. *Encouraging girls in math and science: IES practice guide.* National Center for Education Research, Institute of Education Sciences, U.S. Department of Education. 2007.

3. https://www.irishtimes.com/news/education/education-is-not-the-filling-of-a-pail-but-the-lighting-of-a-fire-it-s-an-inspiring-quote-but-did-wb-yeats-say-it-1.1560192.

4. Miller, Janet L. Constructions of curriculum and gender. *Gender and education.* Chicago, IL: University of Chicago Press, 1993: 43–63.

5. Kuzmic, Jeffrey J. "Textbooks, knowledge, and masculinity: Examining patriarchy from within." *Research on Men and Masculinities Series* 11, (2000): 105–126.

6. Vygotsky, Lev. "Interaction between learning and development." *Mind and society.* Cambridge, MA: Harvard University Press, 1978: 79–91.

7. Streitmatter, Janice. "An exploratory study of risk-taking and attitudes in a girls-only middle school math class." *The Elementary School Journal* 98, no. 1 (1997): 15–26.

8. Brown, Lyn Mikel, and Carol Gilligan. *Meeting at the crossroads: Women's psychology and girls' development.* Cambridge, MA: Harvard University Press, 1992; Gilligan, Carol. *Joining the resistance.* Malden, MA: Polity Press, 2011; Gilligan, Carol. *In a different voice: Psychological theory and women's development.* Cambridge, MA: Harvard University Press, 1982.

9. Gilligan, Carol. *Joining the Resistance.* Malden, MA: Polity Press, 2011.

10. Research by Field-Marvin (2016) clearly demonstrates the importance of taking such measures to insure collaborations work to promote girls' growth rather than shutting them down. Field-Marvin, K. *The making of "me": Exploring how an engaging, student-directed learning environment influences the creation of agency in early adolescent girls.* Unpublished dissertation. University of Pennsylvania. 2016.

Chapter 3

Engaging Classroom Activities

In this chapter, we focus on the major themes that emerged from the most prevalent learning activities that we discovered in the teacher and student narratives. Girls and their teachers chose to describe, often in vivid detail, a large variety of projects and exercises that stimulated their curiosity, motivation, and engagement in learning. The five central themes that united these were class discussions, multimodal projects, hands-on activities, use of creativity in learning, and out-of-classroom experiences.

These are all familiar classroom activities, of course. We imagine that most people who have been to school have participated in many of them through the years. But we also know that not every class discussion goes smoothly and not all hands-on lessons result in deep understanding of new material. Our goal was to closely examine the descriptions of these activities to better understand what it is about them that made them so engaging and effective.

The responses from students and teachers provided a wealth of insider information about what transforms a familiar pedagogical technique into a lesson that students remember for years to come. In discussions we found that students especially valued classroom environments that provided a "safe space" in which they could air their personal opinions without fear of reprisal and where they felt free from the pressures of having a single right answer.

Multimodal activities, lessons, and projects included classroom experiences in which students learned about one concept or topic through several channels. Importantly, students found that multimodal projects provided useful breaks from more "traditional" classroom activities and assessments. They also made ample room to appeal to different girls' learning styles.

In hands-on lessons, students sometimes describe a single activity, but often the hands-on nature of the activity was part of a larger project or experience in which teachers employed multiple modalities of learning. Students appreciated how hands-on activities could incorporate real-life applications of what they were learning and, again, how the lessons appealed to a variety of learning styles.

Lessons and assignments that were a part of the creativity and creative arts category were often nestled within the larger multimodal and hands-on categories, illustrating the interwoven nature of our findings.

Finally, a group of the participants in this study described out-of-classroom experiences including trips, field days, and guest speakers. These out-of-the-ordinary opportunities for learning are, for some girls, among the most important they have had in school.

Overall, readers will learn how girls enjoy learning experiences in which they feel comfortable with the classroom structure while being able to challenge themselves and their classmates, and in which they are offered a variety of ways to take in new knowledge.

INSPIRING CLASS DISCUSSIONS

Discovering Things on Our Own

I feel as though I am engaged, motivated, and interested in Mr. Potter's discussion-based classes because he gives us a chance to first discover information on our own. . . . The objective is to attempt to first muddle through a difficult reading on our own and come to class prepared to dig deeper with the help of our peers to discover the meaning or purpose of the text by the end of a class period. . . . He feels as though we should discuss amongst our peers and figure it out for ourselves what the readings are trying to reveal to us, rather than simply sitting down and taking notes on what he tells us the texts are about. —*Gia, Twelfth-Grade Student*

Many students' and teachers' stories focus on class discussions. As we read across the responses, we saw that discussions varied in format, from Socratic seminars to "Harkness" discussions to debates. Girls' reasons for finding discussions engaging speak to different aspects of the experience. One central theme that runs throughout is how such conversations can serve as spaces in which girls may find their voices and take ownership of their ideas.

The opening vignette presents a detailed picture of how class discussions can be especially motivating for girls. Gia's response captures how girls appreciate opportunities to talk about and think through material with their peers. They benefit from sharing their ideas and not having to worry about getting the "right" answer. Class discussions also help girls gain a deeper understanding of the material by hearing their peers' interpretations of the same topic and being able to compare them with their own.

In the next example, Brianna, an eleventh-grade student, writes about the experience of studying *The Adventures of Huckleberry Finn* as a young woman of color. Her narrative is less about the content of the book than the debate over whether they should study it at all given the use of the "N word." Her teacher carefully structured the class so that the students could have an informed and meaningful discussion about this sensitive subject.

Debating Huckleberry Finn

One day in my English 11 class, my class was discussing *The Adventures of Huckleberry Finn* by Mark Twain. The subtopic of the discussion was about the use of the word "n___" in the book and to further stimulate the discussion, my teacher brought in some outside sources such as videos from the Internet. The main video that we watched featured high school students from different backgrounds, teachers, and college professors. In the video, some people argued that the use of the word "n___" was essential in telling a true story that offered historical value in American culture. Others argued that the word could be taken out if it offended people and made them uncomfortable. I agreed with the first perspective because as a student of color, I believe in telling American slave history like it is. I agreed that it was offensive for me to read the story, but I overcame that obstacle and read the book to the best of my understanding and ability. I was lucky enough to have a diverse class to discuss the argument with and a class filled with bright students such as myself.

Brianna's story illustrates several important points that are worth underscoring. While our book is about girls generally, girls always have multiple identities. To engage them effectively, teachers will hopefully be aware of those multiple identities and adjust their teaching accordingly. That means understanding that students' identities shape how they view and experience many topics. It means that to have fruitful discussions, teachers must create ground rules that enable their diverse classes to safely engage without feeling threatened or as if they must represent their entire race, social class, ethnic background, or religion. This is a demanding and important work.

Brianna is a Black girl from a certain socioeconomic status and a certain family background. In this case, her teacher understands both the literary importance of *Huckleberry Finn* and its offensive use of the "N word." By carefully preparing her girls, the teacher creates a safe space in which both the book and its controversial language can be discussed openly by the students in a way that makes Brianna come away feeling she learns much and is glad to have participated.

Being in Charge: Having Ownership of Their Learning

What stands out about the girls' responses about class discussions is that even though their teachers often take the lead in providing a topic or prompt, after that initial contribution, they then step back and students have the floor to discuss, interrogate, and challenge the text and each other's ideas.

Many of the discussions that they describe take place in humanities classes, where discourse stems from a single set of guiding questions supplied by the teacher. These often happen in a Harkness format. Both girls and teachers frequently appreciate the Harkness method[1] in which students sit around a table or in a circle of desks, and the teacher provides minimal intervention. In the following example, Caroline, an eleventh grader, describes how the method is used in her American literature class:

The Power of Harkness Discussions

We sit in a circle in the classroom to analyze, form arguments, and discuss literary works that are relevant to American literature. This exercise is called the Harkness discussion. This method of teaching and learning is effective for many reasons. We are graded on how well we work together as a class. A big issue in our class is that the foreign students do not speak up. The Harkness discussion allows other students to ask them questions, and they are "forced," for lack of a better word, to answer. In our circle, we consider each and every idea that is contributed to our discussion. . . . This exercise allowed us, the students, to teach ourselves and learn from each other, rather than learning from a lecture or PowerPoint.

Caroline's story highlights the sense of power and control over their learning that girls can acquire through these conversations. Discussions give girls the freedom to "analyze," "form," and "discuss" rather than sitting as passive receivers of information. In particular, Harkness discussions provide opportunities for girls to step into the role of being in charge of their learning. Students appreciate how teachers become facilitators or "shepherds" of the flow of conversation rather than dominating it.

The girls then are the ones who prepare the questions and lead the direction of the conversation. This student-led and student-centered structure allows them to explore issues without the "bias" of a teacher (and without her or his authoritative knowledge interrupting the natural development of students' thinking) and to come to their own conclusions and understandings, both individually and as a class. Of course, successful Harkness discussions require a great amount of front-loaded work on the part of the teacher to prepare students to take on these roles.

Discussions also promote students' sense of ownership of their own learning. The girls talked about how conversations provide a collaborative space where peers work together to understand the material. For example, Joyce, an

11th grader, describes one of the first days of her government class in which the entire class sat at "one long, round discussion table":

Engaging Discussions

After reading the Declaration of Independence for homework, we had the whole class period to discuss whether we thought the document was liberal or conservative, or both, and why. My class had people of many different backgrounds, politically, economically, and socially, so everyone had different opinions. This lesson was especially memorable to me because the discussion style made everyone speak their opinion and forced others to pay attention. Due to the fact that we were at one table, nobody had their computers out, was texting, or in general, was otherwise occupied instead of paying attention to the discussion. It was very engaging, and while my teacher would step in if he wanted to make a point, he let us lead the discussion by ourselves and find out knowledge on our own, which was more satisfying than him relaying information to us. Overall, this discussion not only engaged everyone but also gave people the confidence to voice their thoughts and defend them against others' opinions, a sometimes difficult thing to do if one attends a coed school.

Joyce enjoys the fact that the discussion intentionally involves the whole class so that all students can "speak their opinion" and are "forced" to "pay attention" because of the intimate setup around the table. She also comments on how this type of format enables students to express a variety of perspectives. Joyce reflects on how the differing political, socioeconomic, and social identities of her classmates bring different opinions and ideas into the conversations in a way that promotes everyone's learning. As in Brianna's example, the teacher manages to create a safe space in which students learn from each other's diverse backgrounds and views instead of becoming defensive about them.

Being Free from Having the "Right" Answer

Many girls attribute their engagement in discussions to the fact that they know that the goal is not to have the right answer but rather to consider the topic from a variety of perspectives. Jenelle, a 12th grader, talks about how this phenomenon plays out in her government class:

We Were Not Afraid to Be Wrong

Usually, political issues make for cold and strictly partial arguments between two sides, but this discussion was an open opportunity to fully discuss and dissect the prompt and the many sides and factors that contribute to it. We were not afraid to be wrong because we knew there was no right answer. It helped me realize that we need to have this mindset about conversations in politics in general— to understand why each side could reason for their position and respect it.

Like many of the participants who wrote about discussions, Jenelle talks about how she finds class discussions particularly enlightening because the students are able to share their thoughts and opinions in a space that is respectful of opposing viewpoints, especially around controversial topics. Other students describe deliberations focused on racism and Eurocentrism where, again, the emphasis is not on getting to a right answer, but rather on openly trying to integrate a variety of perspectives.

These examples highlight how instrumental teachers are in creating an environment that promotes the notion that there are multiple answers to complex questions. Anna, a tenth grader, talked about how her teacher skillfully moves the class to consider alternative views by asking specific questions rather than lecturing or giving a long explanation about why he might not agree with what students are saying. By modeling a nonjudgmental stance throughout the discourse, the teacher demonstrates how students can do the same.

Girls talk about how this kind of judgment-free atmosphere helps them to find their own voice. They describe how they learn to give their opinions confidently and share their ideas in a group setting. Echoing other responses that we read, 11th grader Tara describes how discussions enable girls to practice how "to assert ourselves in a conversation" and "learn how to argue a point"—skills that encourage girls to productively and confidently share their thoughts and opinions with others beyond the context of their classroom; that help them develop strong, assertive, and well-modulated personal voices.

Girls love well-managed discussions because they provide spaces where they are in charge and where their opinions and ideas are valued and respected not only by their peers but also by their teachers. Girls want to feel that they have been seen and heard; in this format, they are able to develop a strong sense of direction over their learning.

According to the students, a critical aspect of feeling free and confident to share their opinions is that they take place in an environment that is free from judgment and where the expectations are not about getting the right answer. Instead, they appreciate a focus on the process of developing and expressing their opinions while learning to listen carefully to those of their peers.

Education researchers[2] consistently point out that when it comes to classroom participation, girls are unlikely to share their thoughts unless they are confident that they have the right answer. Often, when they do contribute, they preface their comments with disclaimers such as "I'm not sure if this is right, but . . ." or "I don't know, but . . .", indicating a sense of uncertainty about their ideas.

Contributing to this uncertainty is awareness on girls' parts of the stereotypes that abound about how they are supposed to be "perfect" students; they are supposed to be particularly strong in subjects such as humanities and not so great in other areas, such as science, technology, engineering, and math. We explore this idea of the often-negative power of such stereotypes in more detail in chapters 6, 7, and 8.

In the meaningful discussions and debates they describe, girls are eager to jump in and confidently share their thoughts and opinions. From what they and their teachers say, a central aspect of controlling the negative impact of stereotypes is the intentional creation of a classroom environment in which girls feel that their ideas are respected, where they are encouraged to learn from one another, and where multiple perspectives are embraced. Girls thrive amid this kind of discourse, when they are the ones in the driver's seat and their teachers are the encouraging passengers along for the ride.

MULTIMODAL LEARNING EXPERIENCES

The Scavenger Hunt

My most effective lesson was one in which my students applied their knowledge of matrices and used it for a scavenger hunt. This hunt was graded and they worked in teams. It took them around the school, where they used matrix multiplication, solving systems of equations, and cryptology to get from one clue to the next. I enlisted the help of several adults in the community who relayed to me how engaged each member of the group was. The class consisted of sophomores in Algebra 2. The scavenger hunt was in place of a written assessment, however, the groups needed to present the work that they performed for each clue so it was in fact clear that they used their knowledge of matrices to get from one adult to the next. The girls loved working in teams and loved the competitive nature of the hunt (while there was no prize for the group that finished first, they all attempted to finish first). This activity required knowledge of the content, collaborative group work, and a positive outlook to complete this alternative assessment. *Ms. Jones, High School Math Teacher*

This teacher's story exemplifies a form of engaging lessons that both students and teachers find especially effective. Such "multimodal" lessons, activities, and projects require students to learn through several distinctive channels. They naturally overlap with several of the other dimensions of memorable lessons we describe throughout the book. Since multimodal lessons incorporate several lines of instruction, they often are comprised of elements of the classroom environment (relevance, clarity, and collaboration) and classroom activities (i.e., discussions, hands-on lessons, creativity, and experiential learning) that our study found to be particularly effective for girls.

The opening vignette illustrates not only how the teacher uses multiple modalities in her scavenger hunt—solving equations in groups and presenting their work to others as different opportunities for learning—but also again the power of collaborative work and the importance of clear lessons to motivate girls.

In our data set, teachers' and students' narratives about multimodal lessons seem to mirror one another; sometimes they even describe the same lesson. The students' and teachers' responses both tend to describe two different aspects of classroom life. One set highlights elements that focus on the pedagogy or specific teaching strategies involved in multimodal lessons such as their interdisciplinary character and the fact that multi-modal projects offer a break from the norm of daily classroom activities and routines. Another set of responses describe particular activities, such as the use of technology and experiences presenting to others.

Learning across Subjects and Making Connections

The responses from students and teachers illustrate how the nature of multimodal lessons easily lends itself to interdisciplinary teaching and learning. There is much students can gain from working across different subjects and topic areas. The interdisciplinary character of these lessons provides a multimodal experience on a large scale. In these situations, students and teachers embrace the ways in which girls are able to learn about a topic from a variety of perspectives and disciplines. This encourages stronger mastery of the subject under study.

In one example, Ms. Kirby, a middle school teacher, describes how an interdisciplinary unit she created focused on measurement in the core subject areas of math, ancient history, and science. As part of the unit, students use their knowledge of measurement concepts to design and sew pillowcases, and, in another project, incorporate their learnings into bridges they design. They then program their LEGO NXT robots to drive over the bridges. In ancient history, the students participated in a weekly guessing game in which a pair of girls develops clues to different locations around the world based on latitude, longitude, and distance from their school. Their peers then use that information to guess where the locations are. In science, students created their own independent study projects, in which measurement was a key element.

In another example, Stella, a seventh grader, discusses a grade-wide project that focused on hunger around the world. She describes how she has the opportunity to learn about different perspectives connected to the sources of world hunger and ways to end it through her math, science, history, fitness, and English classes. Stella said the interdisciplinary experience "made me aware of the world around us and how much of an impact it [has] on me."

As these two stories illustrate, the several modes through which the students learn take the form of different projects united under one larger topic, while their different disciplinary perspectives serve as vehicles of learning in their own right. The interdisciplinary aspect of some multimodal lessons gives students the opportunity to make connections across different topics and disciplines, and sometimes, as in the world hunger example, also works to situate their learning within a larger global context.

Switching Up the Classroom Routine

Students and teachers both appreciate multimodal activities because they experience them as a break from the norm. Girls like the fact that the lessons require them to do things that are beyond what they typically do in class. Generally, students and teachers point to reading from a textbook or listening to or presenting a lecture as the "typical" way that material is taught in school. The lessons that get away from these ordinary practices involve projects that require students to do things such as conduct interviews of their relatives who lived during the Great Depression, construct a real-life museum as part of their ninth-grade history class, or create timelines of their entire lives.

Narratives containing multimodal lessons often describe how they include some sort of creative element that distinguishes the task from the more mundane, everyday activities usually required of students. As Stephanie, a twelfth-grade student explains, having the opportunity to do a project instead of a "long, boring essay" gave her a lasting memory of what she learned in this class.

Making Memorable Projects

In AP English 12 this year, instead of doing a long, boring essay on one of the main themes of *Othello*, our teacher decided to do a project instead. The best part of the project was that we could literally do any type of art we wanted to present a theme or motif included in *Othello*. Because I am not artistically gifted, I decided to make a Twitter page for each of the main characters. The day it was due, everyone presented their projects. People did monologues, paintings, dances; anything you could imagine. This project made a lasting impact on me, whereas I would've forgotten about the essay the second I submitted it. Including these sorts of activities in a course is very important and leaves the students having fond memories as opposed to just another class.

Similarly, eleventh-grader Jessica comments on how the freedom to break away from even the typical structure of projects when reading *Romeo and Juliet* made her feel more engaged in the class. Instead of having a simple presentation about a scene from the play, she describes how their teacher assigned them the task of rewriting a scene however they wanted, and then required them to construct a "play book" where they took on the roles of being the director, costume designer, or set designer. The student recalls how "truly fun" this take on an English assignment was for her.

Multimodal projects also function as a "break from the norm" because they employ alternative assessments, which allow students to demonstrate their understanding of topics in nontraditional ways. For example, Nicole, an eleventh-grade student, was assigned a research task instead of an end-of-unit exam. Her story again highlights the potential of multimodal projects to serve as exciting alternatives to typical evaluative essays and tests:

The Soil Ecology Project

In my ninth-grade biology class, our final exam grade was the Soil Ecology Project. We were put into groups and had to form our own experiment. The Soil Ecology project interested me because my group could come up with our own concern and test the soil to find if our initial prediction was correct or incorrect. I was motivated to complete the experiments so we could then begin the creative part of the project. For the creative part, each group could make a song, a movie, or another interactive idea to discuss their project. Although each person in the group had to write part of the overall report, the creative part of the project kept everyone in my group engaged. The Soil Ecology project was the most interesting class project, which allowed me to take charge on a topic I was curious about.

Nicole's story illustrates how the novelty of a multimodal project heightened her curiosity and maintained her interest and involvement. It also typifies how the opportunity to be creative is an important reason why many girls enjoy multimodal projects. Finally, it highlights the power of self-chosen experiments, self-directed learning, and group work for girls—all elements that we see emerge in other dimensions of our data as well.

Learning through Presenting to Others

Students' and teachers' descriptions of multimodal activities highlight how student-led presentations are a central element of the positive experiences for them. The presentations vary from developing and showing websites to demonstrating how a product that they constructed worked, to having an open-house event for parents and students, to giving research talks in front of a panel of teachers. Students tell us both how much they enjoy and learn from presenting to others, as well as how much they learn from other girls' presentations.

Indeed, the presentation component serves as another important mode of acquiring knowledge for the students—teachers and girls report that students must think carefully about how they will organize and deliver their information so their classmates will understand it.

In one of the examples we read, Tessa, an eleventh-grade girl, vividly describes her experience from four years earlier in which all 7th graders were given the freedom to develop a research project on a topic of their choosing. She appreciates the fact that students were allowed to pursue a topic that "truly interests them" and that they could choose the modes through which to teach their peers about what they learned. The entire project culminated in a school-wide research fair during which students, teachers, and parents traveled from project to project and learned about each student's topic.

Ms. Sawyer, a high school English teacher, also describes how giving students the opportunity to work in groups to create lessons for their classmates around *The Great Gatsby* not only gives them ownership over their learning but also teaches them more from that experience than if she had directly taught them the book:

The Great Gatsby

In my AP English language and composition class (11th grade), the students are motivated by activities that are hands-on and allow them a chance to be in charge of their own learning. A particularly successful lesson this year was a reciprocal teaching project with *The Great Gatsby*. Students chose their own groups (key for girls: choice), and then constructed a lesson following the principles of reciprocal teaching, as outlined by Palincsar (1985, 1986).[3] The students appeared energized and engaged, and they reported to me that they "loved" *The Great Gatsby*, as well as the way in which they learned about it. The collaboration was a huge part of the lesson's success. The girls very much enjoy working together. They provided a summary of assigned chapters, key questions that they asked the class, and then an activity. The activities they chose ranged from traditional crossword puzzles to complicated games of Jeopardy. In nearly every instance, they chose to divide the class into small groups (as modeled frequently by me) and then require each group to share out. The students read the book, enjoyed taking charge of their learning, and seemed to get far more out of the lesson than if I had just lectured them and pointed out important passages.

MultiModal Lessons in the Twenty-First Century: The Evolving Importance of Technology

When analyzing the different "modes" at play in multimodal learning, that is, the multiple, distinctive channels through which students can take up their learning, we find technology often playing an integral part. Students are growing up in a digital world and hopefully are learning in a twenty-first-century classroom. Many of the girls in our sample clearly are. They talk about using the *Inspiration* computer program to compare and contrast different Atlantic revolutions, the *Photo Story* program to create presentations about the lives of various family members when they were the age of twelve, and the *Voice Thread* program to develop voice-overs for their PowerPoint presentations on a figure that they studied in ancient history.

Girls appreciate using technology because it provides both innovative ways for them to learn about a topic and another way to break from ordinary teaching norms. Shayna, an eighth-grade student, finds it "a lot more fun" to look at websites created by her classmates "than to just read a textbook or have the teacher lecture."

The 13 Colonies Project

One project I found especially interesting and engaging was . . . on the 13 colonies. We worked in groups of two and each group would research a colony. . . . Once we had collected all of our research we made a Google site about our colony. Once all the groups had finished making their sites the class got to look at everyone's site. I thought this project was especially interesting because we got to do fun, interactive things (like making a site) while we learned a lot about the 13 colonies. I learned a lot about my colony, Rhode Island, because I researched it, but I also learned a lot about the other 12 colonies because I found the sites my classmates made very interesting. I think it is a lot more fun to look at sites made by my classmates . . . than to just read a textbook or have the teacher lecture. I thought this project was very engaging and I would love to do another like this.

Ms. Williams, a high school English teacher, also points out how the use of various forms of technology challenges students to think about how they will present their information in an effective and accessible way, thereby "honing a student's analytical, rhetoric, and twenty-first-century skills":

Using Glogster 2.0

In English II, Literature of the World, we assign "outside reading" each quarter. For two of the four quarters, the choices must be one from a list of world literature texts. The other two quarters, the choice is free (with gentle nudging toward increased challenge). Along with reading the text, students are required to complete one of a number of projects that are designed to increase the depth of interaction with the text while honing a student's analytical rhetoric and 21st-century skills. One project was to create a digital advertisement using Glogster, a web 2.0 tool. The students had to combine visual, audio, text, and A/V elements into an interactive hypertext. Multiple students indicated that this was a particularly challenging project because they had to use words economically and were forced to find other methods of communication with which they were less familiar. That combined with the intellectual challenge of designing and executing a hypertext with its many layers and interconnections was certainly demanding. However, that the assignment was to design a digital space allowed students to leverage their rich understanding of media, social media, and advertising to draw out pertinent strains of thought and images from the text.

Taken together, the varying pedagogical and experiential components of multimodal lessons can be an integral part of girls' memorable and engaging experiences at school. Whether the engagement is due to the interdisciplinary nature of the multimodal activities, or the fact that multimodal projects provide something that is fresh and a break from their daily experiences, or that it aligns with students' different learning styles, or some combination of the three, they enthusiastically lose themselves in their projects and activities.

By incorporating multiple ways of teaching and learning, multimodal lessons bring to light the ways in which the experiences of engaging in a variety of different learning activities contribute to students' understanding, mastery, and enjoyment of a range of subjects.

HANDS-ON LEARNING EXPERIENCES

Learning Physics through Building Wind Chimes

Last year in my physics class I had one experience that was very memorable. We spent many weeks building a large wind chime for the school auction. We spent these weeks measuring the pipes, figuring out where the pipes needed to be struck and how long they had to be in order for the sound to resonate well. This activity was not only fun but also very educational. We used the pipes and computer programs to see what different sound waves looked like and the differences between them. This activity was very effective in teaching us about sound waves, showing, and hearing. It also showed us how physics relates to the real world, which I love to see in a class. —*Lizet, Tenth-Grade Student*

"Hands-on learning" is another major category of responses that fosters effective, memorable, and motivating classroom environments. While the majority of the hands-on activities fall within the context of science classes, students and teachers report experiencing and teaching hands-on lessons in a variety of other subject areas including math, English, history, world languages, and health and wellness.

The range of activities is extensive—students engage in hands-on learning in experiences as diverse as dissecting animals, crocheting hats, designing and making Chinese terra cotta soldiers, creating musical instruments, taking field trips to local wetland environments, baking, and making videos.

Both student and teacher narratives indicate that hands-on activities deepen girls' learning by asking them to apply concepts to real-life situations. When they can create, design, and build as part of the lesson, it makes what they are learning more vivid and real to them. In particular, teachers report that hands-on lessons help their students grasp more fully the complexity of the material they are teaching. Girls learn more when they enthusiastically take ownership of their own learning experiences.

Deeper Learning through Real-Life Applications

By doing hands-on activities, students find that they can grasp and remember the concepts they are learning better than when they simply read about the topic in a textbook or hear about it during a lecture. In one example, Ms. Chase, a calculus teacher, describes how she teaches her students about the concept of volume by giving them Play-Doh to create a hands-on experience:

Using Play-Doh to Learn Calculus

In calculus, one of the problems students must solve is to find the volume of solids generated by rotating a curve around a given line or finding the volume of a solid with a known cross-section. The mathematics of the topic is quite simple, but often students emerge with a correct answer, which is completely unconnected to the actual solid whose volume they have found. One of the practices I find most effective is to arm students with jars of Play-Doh. I ask them to picture the rotation of one element of the rotation, a rectangle, then to build the actual physical shape it would generate when rotated around a line. I give no further instruction than that. It takes very little time before they begin to look around, notice that other students have disks (or washers, or shells) of different sizes than theirs and to have someone gleefully walk around the room and assemble the entire solid out of parts made by the different students. If they are not motivated to then build for themselves the actual solid, I encourage them to do so—but that's rarely necessary. We follow up with some great SMART Board demonstrations available on this topic, but I think they learn more from the Play-Doh than from the Internet on this one. Volume is often one of their favorite topics; they are fearless in the face of complex problems on the topic.

In another example, Chelsea, an eighth-grade student, recalls how completing labs in her seventh-grade life science class made it "the most interesting and engaging course I have ever taken." Chelsea goes on to describe how a frog dissection helped her to better understand the creature's anatomy and how it compared to other organisms' anatomies.

The fact that Chelsea could hold the frog in her own hands and study it up close instead of "just reading about experiments that another scientist performed and struggling to understand the information" made this learning experience significant for her. It is striking to note in this quotation that she reveals that she includes herself in the category of scientist.

When lessons afford girls opportunities to make the connection between what they are learning in school to their everyday lives, it becomes more meaningful for them than dry textbook learning. Heather, an eighth-grade student, captures this vividly:

The Submarine Project

In eighth-grade science class we had a challenging project called "The Submarine Project." . . . The student was to research about submarines and build one of her own. The sizes could range from as big as a fish tank to as small as a penny. When the class was first assigned this, I thought that it would be very easy to make and I would easily get a good grade on it. As the project progressed, it became very clear that if I would like to receive a good grade on it, I would have to work as hard as I could.

On the weekends I would spend several hours at a time trying many different methods to get the submarine to work. I began to give up on it, thinking that this one time I would have to accept getting a bad grade. When I went to class the next day, I saw that a small amount of people could get theirs to work, and a large amount of people couldn't. It was then that I decided I wanted to be in the small group. . . . I went in for extra help, stayed after school, and worked endless hours on it at my house, until one day when I found something that worked. The design was a tack with an Alka-Seltzer taped on top of it. I was so proud of my discovery and went to school the next day knowing that my design would succeed. During class, my submarine was tested, and succeeded. I not only felt good for working so hard, but I also felt excited about my grade. In this project my interest in learning and determination was very evident.

Other hands-on activities with real-world connections include analyzing organisms and sediment in a nearby river, learning about physics concepts by studying the dynamics of bicycling while actually riding a bike down a hill, discovering the science of maple sugaring through tapping trees and visiting the local sugar house, designing a dream house to learn about area and perimeter in math class, and completing the daily chores that women engaged in during the Colonial period as part of a history class on U.S. women.

Creating, Designing, and Building

Girls also appreciate how hands-on activities afford them opportunities to be creative through constructing, building, and designing. The students typically then perform or showcase their products as a way of demonstrating what they have learned. A high school science teacher, Mr. Dunham, describes how he uses this approach:

Test Tube Instruments

The girls use previously acquired knowledge of the acoustics of open and closed pipes to construct an instrument from test tubes. They must mathematically determine the appropriate tube length to produce the frequencies in a diatonic major scale. After performing the calculations, they use water to adjust the pipes to the proper lengths. When the instrument is finished each group learns a song to perform. I accompany them on guitar. Often the groups will perform for other classes. The girls really enjoy the activity, and I feel this helps them learn the physics principles involved.

While creations such as this appear in the typical art-related classes such as ceramics, figure drawing, and theater, girls find other subjects incorporating elements of art into lessons highly engaging too (as we will discuss in more detail later in the chapter). Mr. Dunham's example shows how physics and music connect, and he has designed a lesson in which the girls experience them together. In the following example, Mr. Snyder, another high school science teacher, combines the art techniques of Jackson Pollock with his physics class to teach girls about the concepts of distance, time, and velocity:

Art in a Non–Art Class Setting

An effective practice that I have employed is the use of art in a non-art class setting. We discussed the work of Jackson Pollock and then proceeded to drop paint of many colors onto canvases. We did this from different heights and made some remarkable images. However, along the way we learned about gravity. The nature of this force is not easy. We also used our paintings to discuss velocity, speed, distance, and time. When the masterpieces were dry we hung them in our room. This is kind of crazy, but it got the students interested in some concepts that were not very interesting in the abstract text in the book. The other thing is that each student got to throw her colors on to the canvas, and there was some class pride and unity in the final product.

In another example, Ms. Shields, a high school health and guidance teacher-counselor, uses art to tackle the challenging topic of the psychology of depression. In her lesson, Ms. Shields asks her ninth-grade students to bring to class an example of depression in some sort of creative form. The students then take turns presenting their creation and how it expresses depression to them. This enables the class to engage in a discussion about how the different representations of depression speak to their personal experiences in a way that enabled them to share their feelings safely.

Being in Charge of Their Own Learning

Hands-on activities seem particularly memorable for girls because they give them the opportunity to take charge of their learning in the same way class discussions can. Many of the teachers in our study commented on how hands-on projects allow girls to assume responsibility for making meaning through their own self-directed learning – a skill that is a central part of development for adolescents. Ms. Campbell, a middle school science teacher, captures this well.

Fun with Convection Currents

The most effective lessons are those in which the students find the answers for themselves and have some fun in getting them. We recently decided to find out whether there were convection currents in the eighth-grade lab. The girls figured they needed to take the temperature of the room at different heights and locations in the room. This involved the floor, the countertops, and the ceiling. They had to climb counters and be patient while the thermometers or temperature probes read the correct temperature.

The students loved the physical nature of the lab and did not mind taking the time for the instruments to work properly. At the end, they needed to complete a whole lab report (usually a tedious task), but no one complained about the graphing or the determination of independent variables because they felt competent to answer those questions. Everyone understood what convection is about and the grades were higher than normal for a comparable exercise. . . . Fun and ownership of data did the trick.

In another example, a math teacher, Ms. Green, describes how she incorporates hands-on activities for her students to learn the different elements of trigonometry, and how, through these activities, her students assume a sense of ownership over their learning:

Creating Paper Circles in Trigonometry

A particularly effective lesson, which is quite simple really, is one that I do in the beginning of the study of trigonometry. I hand out three pieces of paper all with an identical, perfect circle drawn on it. I ask the girls to take the circles and to section each into 4, 8, and 12 segments, respectively. I then tell them to consider the radius to be one unit and then label the segment of the circumference used in each circle. This begins with them creating their own unit circle. They can then see the complete unit circle when they hold the pieces of paper together and toward the light. The creation of the unit circle on their own gives them an ownership and a self-serving knowledge of the angles we need to have memorized in Trigonometry. Once there, we can then get the values of the sine and cosine by putting triangles in the pie wedges built and seeing that they are special right triangles. Again, once done, there is an understanding and ownership.

Teachers often speak about how giving students the freedom to make choices about different aspects of their work, as well as ensuring that the focus of the task can be applied to real life, helps girls feel ownership over their learning. Ms. Jackson, a high school science teacher explains:

Creating Sunscreen

I am teaching AP chemistry for the first time this year. Instead of just focusing on the course material every day, I wanted to take the time for our girls to explore a research project. My goal was for them to conduct an experiment as a class, of their choosing, and then be assessed on their knowledge by a presentation. . . . So, the students decided to create sunscreen. They each are making a batch, modifying the main chemical quantities, and then going to compare their sample with actual marketed sunscreens. They will evaluate their sunscreen production by looking at the absorption of the UV rays and seeing it in action by UV-absorbing beads. Why I think this practice is effective is because I am asking the students to direct their own learning. They picked the topic and are taking it upon themselves to do the work. They are excited about the presentation side of it and have really had an authentic experience as a scientist. I also hear from them that they have talked about it at home. While some of the processes of data collection might be tedious, I think that the fact that they are coming in after school to work on this also illustrates to me that they want to do the project. What I have seen now is showing me that when I do a project like this, students not only love the hands-on approach but also, as AP kids, get to fully challenge themselves in a whole new way. They might understand the material, but when practicing it in real life, can see how much easier/harder it is to do it. In essence, they discover that while they can do the mathematical problems, they are not guaranteed to succeed in a laboratory/hand-on approach.

The responses in this section illustrate the varying ways in which students and teachers alike find hands-on lessons to be captivating. They agree that such lessons provide opportunities for deeper learning, especially when a topic is particularly complex or abstract. Hands-on learning can be even more powerful when girls are able to make a connection to their real-life experiences.

Students and teachers also view hands-on activities as an effective way to explore difficult subjects imaginatively through building, creating, and designing. In addition, teachers report that hands-on activities provide opportunities for girls to experience a sense of ownership over their meaning-making by giving them the freedom to make their own decisions when crafting their work. In these ways, hands-on learning is a theme that captures the multiple, meaningful experiences of learning, discovery, and inspiration for girls.

OPPORTUNITIES FOR CREATIVITY

Adapting the Canterbury Tales

In Mrs. Holmes' 11th-grade English class, we are currently working on *The Canterbury Tales*. You might assume that we're simply reading the tales, discussing them, and then taking quizzes and/or a test on our reading. At many schools, that might have been the case. In this English class, we do read each tale individually. We do take the quizzes. But we also do more. . . . And perhaps most significantly, Mrs. Holmes is currently working with Mrs. Green, our school's theater director, who decided to adapt *The Canterbury Tales* for the school's next theater production. In class this week and next week, we are working in groups to use the satire and themes of the tales we read for class as inspiration for the adaptation Mrs. Green will use with her cast. Each of us is required to participate in a creative project to write a script, monologue, or story based on one or more tales, and we have so many options and ideas floating around that there will be no shortage of material for Mrs. Green to use for her adaptation of the school play. Not only are we understanding the relevance and symbolism of Geoffrey Chaucer's writing as it pertains to us today, we are also becoming part of a large school project. In Mrs. Holmes' class, we are taught, yes. However, we are also inspired and given opportunities to use this inspiration in a way that will affect not only us as individuals but also our school as a whole. —*Katie, Eleventh-Grade Student*

As this vignette illustrates, and as you will discover reading further in this section, girls often find that their most memorable lessons are ones involving the creative arts. We define "creative arts" as a lesson whose central focus is either art, music, drama, or one that involves making some sort of novel final product in any class. These are frequently components that students appreciated as a part of multimodal lessons.

In the vignette, Katie describes how her reading and understanding of *The Canterbury Tales* were enhanced through the interdisciplinary work that involved adapting the readings into a theater production. She acknowledges the traditional learning and assessment practices that are part of the class routine such as taking quizzes, but what really captures her imagination is the opportunity to play with the material in ways that contribute to a larger and more meaningful end product than simply a test or essay.

Working in multiple modalities that involve the creative arts inspires girls to engage with the material with excitement and energy. The activities themselves often serve as a source of pride and ownership for students because they have the freedom to express themselves creatively. Student and teacher narratives also demonstrate how incorporating the use of the creative arts through technology is quickly becoming a staple in well-resourced twenty-first-century classrooms.

Helping Girls to Think Creatively

The student and teacher responses that describe creative endeavors across the curriculum emphasize that those types of lessons foster fun and engaging learning even in situations that require rote memorization. For example, Whitney, an eighth-grade student, talks about how the use of music as a tool for memorization was a staple at the end of each of the units in her history class. This sequence of learning not only helped her remember information but also increased the enjoyment she got from the class.

Memorizing Material through Music

In my sixth-grade history class, at the end of each unit we had to write a song or a skit. The song had to have about five or six terms from the unit that it briefly explained. Each song was about a different subject matter and was to the tune of a popular song. For example, some subject matters might be war, people, religion, or art. Our groups were then filmed and shown to the rest of the grade. We had to have some movement and costumes/props. This experience stuck out to me because as we would write the songs and listen to other groups, the songs would become stuck in my head. When we would have a test after this I would use the songs to help me answer the questions.

In addition to highlighting how music contributes to learning history, we also see how multilayered the description is. While Whitney points to the importance of having to write a song, she mentions too that she worked in groups that had to develop props and costumes to perform for the entire grade—a rich multimodal experience.

Acting and drama also provide ample opportunities for girls to engage more fully in a variety of subjects. For example, Norah, a seventh-grade student, talks about how acting out scenes from *A Raisin in the Sun* helped her gain a better understanding of the story. When describing the acting that they did in class, she says, "This exercise was particularly helpful for me because rather than annotating the text and simply reading the characters' words, I 'lived' the text by actually feeling each character's emotion as I or another classmate read their words out loud." Adding the element of drama to an English class not only makes the class more interesting but also, perhaps more important, makes the material more accessible for Norah.

Creative writing also emerges as an important way to encourage girls to enrich their meaning-making within multimodal and interdisciplinary work. Here, eleventh-grader Deborah describes a writing assignment through which she demonstrated all that she had learned during her class on forensics:

Rewriting Fairytales

In my forensics class, we had a project to rewrite a fairytale to incorporate everything we had learned so far about forensic investigation. This was our final project, to replace a mid-term exam. In the run up to it, we had to select a fairytale (I chose *Bambi*), and write at least three pages, double-spaced. When writing it, some part of the story had to be turned into a murder investigation. We had to incorporate details from every unit we had studied so far to the point where we could solve the murder. When we had written our paper, we had to transform it into a slideshow that, when printed, looked a lot like a children's book. We had to use colors and pictures to represent the sequence of events. This was particularly enjoyable because it was a highly enjoyable class, the material was gripping and engaging, and I especially love Disney movies. My teacher thought of a good, rigorous way to incorporate everything we had learned thus far to create a rigorous, but fun, project. It took a lot to create something that was factually accurate, mimicked the movie, and was visually appealing, but the process was a lot of fun!

Creative Work as a Source of Pride and Ownership

Lessons with an arts component challenge students in a different way than their more conventional schoolwork does. They encourage them to use their imaginations and to literally think differently. Girls describe feelings of pride and accomplishment after completing these mind-stretching tasks. Lisa, a 12th grader, provided the following description of a ceramics class.

Design Technology with Ceramics

For me, one of the most rewarding and engaging projects I've embarked on in recent years was the design technology project in my ceramics class last year (11th grade). The goal of the project is to transform real-life objects into clay replicas, imitating the features and qualities of the object as accurately as possible. . . . I chose a shoe designed by Alexander McQueen, one of my favorite designers. The main challenge of the project was that because Alexander McQueen's designs are often exaggerated and eccentric, this shoe featured an eight-inch stiletto heel and an odd, curved, hoof-like front. My ceramics teacher and I worked for weeks to copy the shoe and though at times it seemed like it would not be possible, we managed to recreate it. . . . Although I could not have completed this project without my ceramics instructor, I accomplished a lot more than I thought I would be able to on my own as well.

It is striking how important this accomplishment was to Lisa. Working with the help of the teacher did not affect her feelings of pride in completing the difficult task. Indeed, Lisa's collaboration with the instructor seems to have enhanced her good feelings about what she learned.

In another example, Ms. Cook describes how her students found their math assignment, which incorporated art, challenging but ultimately an effective learning experience that blended geometry and creativity. Ms. Cook assigned her students the task of transforming a miniature candy wrapper to a larger size to scale. At first, the students were excited about the project, but then they soon realized how much effort the assignment would take. After a week of multiple student-teacher meetings with different students, they came to better understand how to break the assignment down into manageable pieces and make connections between how math influences art and how art can be incorporated into math.

In both this example and the one preceding it, students and teachers alike tell us girls find those types of lessons not only daunting but also fun and compelling. Doggedly working on the task (and, when necessary, getting strategic support from their teachers) gives the girls an important sense of accomplishment. Again and again, we read descriptions of students coming out on the other side of a difficult learning experience with a newfound knowledge of their growing capabilities as learners as well as with product of which they were proud.

We surmise that some of the feelings of accomplishment growing from incorporating arts into ordinary classroom lessons may be attributable to a new sense of ownership students develop for their work. Writing a play based on a novel or a fairytale to demonstrate one's mastery of forensic principles forces girls to get their hands dirty working with the subject matter. They then came to think about what they have learned in an entirely new way.

Teachers accomplish this didactic turn in different ways. One instructor, Mr. Larsen, describes having his students create a morning news show about a Middle Eastern country. The students are required to produce a story about a current event in a country of their choice. In teams, the students have to research the topic, write a script, and create a brief video about it. They also have to conduct an interview with a key, relevant newsmaker in their region.

Certainly, writing a script and acting it out allow students to express their creativity. But, beyond that, the assignment also requires a degree of collaboration and group work in which students are in charge of making decisions in order to move all elements of their effort forward. Finally, concluding their projects with an actual video embodies all their learning and provides them with an audience for their efforts.

Choice

It is important to reiterate that giving girls choice around the topics they study as well as in the ways they can execute assignments fosters their sense of ownership. In one example, Alexa, a ninth grader, specifically points to the fact that she had freedom to compose a book of poems she had written in any way she wished as the motivating factor for her interest in the assignment. Alexa goes on to comment how "being independent is an important factor that makes class more interesting." She truly appreciates that she could include any type of illustration and had creative control over the order in which she presented her poems.

This element of choice and self-direction is a theme that runs through several of our findings, of course. It can be an important part of personal relevance in learning and there are aspects of it in many of the descriptions of class discussions, multimodal projects, and hands-on activities. It is a central characteristic of creativity, since by definition, inviting students to be creative allows them to use their imaginations.

Creativity in the Twenty-First Century: Making Movies

Movie making is a particular form of art that girls find compelling and experience as a welcome supplement to their usual curricula. In addition to being a source of creative expression for them, making movies embodies the larger twenty-first-century context in which the students are learning.

Due to the evolution of computer software and other technology, the ability to make a film is now a skill that students often develop as part of their broader, out-of-school experience. These girls are happy when they discover it also is sometimes taken up by their teachers. Girls write appreciatively about assignments in which they make movies. And once again, it is another vehicle that allows them to make choices when creating their final products and, from that, gain a sense of genuine ownership over their work.

Creating Political Commercials

One of the most engaging and interesting experiences I have had in my years at my school was in my eighth-grade American Government class. We were given the assignment to create our own political commercial using the techniques of propaganda we had just learned in class. I thought this was a very engaging and fun experience because my friend and I decided we were going to "run against each other," so I was in some of her commercials and she was in some of mine. . . . I liked how we could film outside of the class, and one of my most vivid memories was when I took a camera to my figure skating lesson and part of my commercial included a segment of me spinning. I loved the fact that we could do virtually anything we wanted with our commercial, while still follow-ing the guidelines of having at least three forms of propaganda in our commer-cial. —*Angela, Tenth-Grade Student*

Angela's vignette makes it clear how much having the freedom to do her commercial any way she wanted meant to her.

In another example, a video project developed by Ms. Lopez, a high school Spanish teacher, not only highlights the various choices that students can con-trol when creating a movie but also illustrates how making one is inherently multimodal. Ms. Lopez discusses how she assigns her students the group project of making a movie in the style of a reality TV show such as *Fear Factor, Top Chef,* or *The Biggest Loser.*

In the project, students are required to use elements of creativity at every step from writing, to acting, filming, and editing. They also are required to work collaboratively in teams—a pedagogical practice that appears over and over as an important dimension of engaging girls in powerful ways.

Teachers who ask girls to make movies recognize that beyond fostering a sense of ownership, it, as with other forms of creative expression, promotes richer, more complex learning.

Videos to Celebrate National Chemistry Week

Each year in chemistry the students celebrate National Chemistry Week (NCW) held at the end of October. For the lesson, I propose a bunch of different cat-egories of demonstrations or materials that the students can use. Some of the categories have been fire, polymers, Halloween chemistry, acid-base indica-tors, explosions, magic tricks, pressure, and dry ice. The only requirements are that they work in groups of three to four members, they have a written script approved before they film, and their video must include an explanation of all of the chemistry seen in the film.

The students are given two class periods to work on the demonstrations and filming together at school and usually then need to edit the final version on their own. The in-class work is always a crazy time for me with everyone working on a different chemistry experiment.

Once the students submit their videos, we watch them in class and vote on the best ones, which are presented to the entire high school during a morning assembly. Also during that week, the students make small posters to hang up around school to display the theme of NCW and to show people some of the ways that chemistry affects their daily lives. The girls always are very excited to show what they have learned with the rest of the school and are particularly proud when their video is chosen for the assembly. —*Ms. Bradley, High School Science Teacher*

This vignette captures how layered and complex many of the lessons are that teachers and girls describe. The National Chemistry Week assignment links the girls' work to a theme-based national event. It therefore is meaningful in a much broader context than just their class. It requires students to work in teams to creatively describe a chemical phenomenon. The assignment also asks them to publicize the theme to a greater audience, and it enables them to choose among their creations to show to the whole school. In this example, we can see easily how girls would come to feel pride in their work and in their growing understanding of the subject.

Of course, making movies requires certain technological resources that not all schools or students may have. Even without access to school-based computers or cameras, however, over 80 percent of high school students had smartphones by 2015 and the percentage is growing yearly.[4] Still, even when they do not have such devices, teachers can capture the important qualities of the movie-making in other forms of collaborative, creative projects that students present, be it a play, comic book, or diorama.

Making creative activities a part of lessons is a source of motivation, engagement, and excitement for students. Girls welcome the opportunity to express themselves in a variety of modes. These experiences of creative thinking and doing are often nested within larger multimodal projects. But students also value the arts—fine arts, music, acting and drama, creative writing, and movie making—for their own sakes.

Arts matter whether they are used to promote learning in traditional subjects or are taken up directly in dedicated courses. Whether "for its own sake" or in the service of a separate learning goal, students enjoy being artistic. Incorporating creativity and the arts enriches learning, helps girls develop of sense of student ownership over their work, and constitutes a vehicle for them to express themselves in ways that other, more conventional modes of learning—such as listening to a lecture or studying for a test—simply do not permit.

LEARNING OUTSIDE OF THE CLASSROOM

A Trip to the Chesapeake Bay

One memorable experience in class that I had was when, in sixth grade, we took a trip to the Chesapeake Bay. We had been studying all about the bay's ecosystems in science, and this was our culminating project. The trip was three days and two nights, which meant that we did not explore the whole bay, but we had enough time to learn much more about it. My actual science teacher was not on my island, but she had organized the whole trip, so my memories were due in part to her work. During the trip, we spent most of our time on a boat, traveling to various islands and educating ourselves firsthand about the bay. We asked our very limited neighbors about how living on the bay affected their lives, and each student grew closer to her peers as we bonded in various group activities. It was a great learning experience because I felt that it was a more relaxed environment than everyday life at school, so no one was afraid to ask a question about what we were seeing. Overall, the trip was very engaging and I truly believe everyone learned more about themselves, each other, and most importantly the Chesapeake Bay. —*Sarah, Seventh-Grade Student*

Recall that in our study we asked participants to tell a story about a class experience that was especially interesting, engaging, memorable, or motivating to them. We elaborated by saying they could describe a particular lesson, unit of study, or choice of text or subject matter, a class activity or exercise, a project or assignment. When given this open-ended prompt, quite a few girls wrote about experiences that took place outside of the classroom.

These descriptions include a large range of activities running from listening to speakers to being involved in athletics or other extracurricular activities to going on field trips. An overarching theme of these descriptions, whatever activity the students describe, is that they foster and enhance relationships. These responses feature stories of encouragement and support from peers and adults during trying circumstances. They include tales about situations in which girls see they are contributing to a greater good and therefore feel worthwhile as a growing person. Overwhelmingly, they involve getting to know classmates and teachers more deeply.

Sarah's trip to the Chesapeake Bay illustrates the combined benefits of relationship building and meaningful learning. She describes how her three-day adventure gave her and her classmates the opportunity to learn about ecosystems firsthand and how a significant part of the experience involved the bonding that occurred among the girls; bonding that grew out of various activities that were a part of the trip.

Field Trips as an Extension of Classroom Learning

Many field trips take advantage of local resources (the proximity of the U.S. Capitol, the Metropolitan Museum of Art, other local museums, seaports that offer ecological tours, as well as local rivers, and even restaurants where employees speak foreign languages). A few involve travel and opportunities to do local, national, and even international service connected with classroom studies. Field trips that supplement science, history, literature, and the arts are most frequently mentioned, but trips supplementing classes in foreign language and government also occupy the imaginations of some girls.

Here, Lauren, a 12th grader, describes the power of a weekend trip to a local river. She makes clear how layered the experience was, citing the teacher's enthusiasm, the fact that it involved hands-on participation in a real experiment, and the impact their work will have on the broader community.

Surveying Aquatic Organisms

My teacher is a very enthusiastic and engaging person, so any project with her is an adventure. . . . One weekend she took a few students, including myself, on an optional field study in a river a short drive from the school. Because there was such a small group of us, we were able to take part in every step of this specific study. Though it was really cold that day, we were all trudging through the water collecting nets full of sediment and organisms, which we collected and identified. This particular experience was so memorable because it was hands-on and different. We actually were helping out with a statewide survey of aquatic organisms. It was nice to be able to get off campus and do real fieldwork as opposed to lab work. I had never done anything of this sort, but I thoroughly enjoyed running around the woods with my classmates.

In another example, Mary, a 12th grader at a different school, talks about how her teacher used the Metropolitan Museum of Art to reinforce what she was learning about art history. By bringing the material to life, it helped her remember it, piqued her excitement, and increased her understanding. Mary describes how the experience of seeing the art at the museum, "helps to make it much more real and alive than if we were learning straight from the book. It does not just help me remember a specific piece but also in understanding the overall concepts of the unit." Mary concludes by saying, "These visits help to keep me engaged. Getting out of the classroom makes the material less dry."

While the Metropolitan Museum of Art is a world-renowned institution, field trips do not have to be to famous locations to capture girls' imaginations. In the next example, tenth-grader Elisa talks about how a class trip to her teacher's house affected her. Here the intimacy of being at the teacher's home, the study of women, the carefully constructed hands-on tasks the girls had to perform, and the bonding it led to all add up to a memorable experience for her.

Colonial Life in the Present Day

In my history class our teacher of "U.S. Ladies" (a class about women in the history of America from Natives Americans to nowadays) took us out to her house to experience life at the colonial times for woman. We went down there by car at seven o'clock at night, and we had several workshops to complete: make fire,

make butter out of cream, make a candle out of melted wax, and finally cook
gingerbread. The butter workshop was very fun to do and it bettered our classmate relationships. Our teacher guided us through all the process, and we really
enjoyed ourselves. It was entertaining combining also the educative aspect of
what we learned; it was the first time of my life school was such fun!

Finding Inspiration in Assemblies and School Meetings

Even something as apparently mundane as whole-school assemblies can have
an important impact when the school offers speakers who have very high pro-
files with the girls or who address issues of special relevance to them. Christa,
an 11th grader, wrote about how former child soldier and renowned hip-hop
artist Emmanuel Jal electrified the school community when he visited and
how his presentation taught her an important lesson about herself as a learner.

Learning from Guest Speakers

A few months ago, Emmanuel Jal visited our school and told us his story. In the
one-hour presentation, we sat in the audience in awe by his stage presence and
excitement. He told his stories through raps and music that he wrote himself. It
was different than what I've typically experienced at my school during assemblies. Usually, the speaker stands in one place on the stage and talks about a topic
for what feels like hours. This was one of the few assemblies where my thoughts
didn't wander and I didn't have trouble keeping my eyes open. He knew exactly
what to do to intrigue the students and draw their attention. He told us to dance
when the music came on, and we all smiled and swayed while he preached his
story. This experience taught me that I learn and pay attention more effectively
when I'm actually interested in what is being told. Emmanuel's story inspired
me and made me want to do more to help child soldiers. He proved that anyone,
even from such a terrible background as his, can turn their life around and make
a difference. This experience was something I'll never forget.

Speakers who addressed the specific interests of girls and women captivated students too. In the following response, we see how an impressive
feminist speaker made a difference to the way Rita, an 11th grader, began to
think about herself:

Being Encouraged to Take Risks

The other day a speaker visited our school whose advice was especially memorable to me. I took notes throughout her speech, for I found the information
incredibly valuable. She told us to do something every day that we were afraid
to do and always take risks. She also told us that generally we notice our own

mistakes more than others do. She really encouraged us to verge out of our comfort zone and embrace new opportunities. I found this advice helpful because I typically hold back when a situation makes me uncomfortable or nervous. From now on I'll try to let go of this anxiety, because of her instructive words. Although this was not a classroom setting, I realized that at any other school I would not have such an enlightening experience. The speakers our school generally acquires have excelled as women in society and are predominately feminists. At a coed school, a speaker would not target the obstacles that women face in our current-day society.

In describing this inspirational speaker, Rita traces the woman's impact to the fact that she had already made her mark in her field and that she addressed issues of relevance to women that Rita believes she could not have talked about in a coed school. Further, Rita was open to being touched by the speaker's message about getting outside her comfort zone and taking risks because of the authority she ascribed to her.

Other girls also write about the impact of speakers who talk about issues of special relevance to women. Among the many topics the girls referenced in the study were talks about rape, alcoholism, good nutrition, and the Dream Act.

Fostering Class Cohesion through Field Days and Field Trips

Girls appreciate whole-school field days as well as whole-class activities that are explicitly designed to foster group cohesion and bonding. Several girls from one public school talk at length about "Contest," a daylong set of events pitting 9th and 12th graders against 10th and 11th graders. Ellen, a tenth-grade girl, reports:

School "Contest"

One memorable experience in school was Contest. At my school Contest is similar to what would be homecoming at other schools. Our 9th graders and 12th graders pair up against our sophomores and juniors. We partake in obstacle courses, an indoor hockey game, and perform a dance, step, and cheer to gain the most points possible. It's very memorable for me because it was the first time I felt like I actually belonged to my school (as a whole). It was so much fun and so overwhelming to see everyone enjoying themselves and getting along.

Other students talk about events that are designed to create cohesion within grade levels of both middle and high school. In one example, Vivian, another tenth grader, describes a four-day retreat full of activities designed to build trust and teamwork. She goes on to reflect that while her class had been close before, the series of team building, zip lining, and lifting her classmates into rope webs further enhanced their bonding.

Equally important are the life lessons that can be gained in these school-wide events. Becca, an eighth grader, highlights that in her description of a class trip:

Developing Trust through Bonding

When my class went on the outdoor education trip, I was not excited at all. I didn't think that I would like my group, and I was afraid that the group leaders would be very mean. I was so wrong about everything. I realized during this trip that there can never be a bad group because you should make the best of what you have, which is something that my school has taught me. I went on all of the most challenging courses that were possible because I knew that I could trust everybody who was with me.

Becca came away understanding how risk-taking is tied with trust, and trust was in part dependent on what she made of her group experience.

Stacy, a ninth-grade girl from a different school, similarly reflects on these lessons—common ones girls draw from these bonding trips—and also explicates how support for risk-taking from peers and friends enhanced her confidence as well as strengthened her relationships:

Repelling Off a Cliff

During our eighth-grade class trip our class was given the opportunity to repel off a cliff. Many of us were nervous, including me, about this task. We did not have to repel down the cliff if we didn't want to, but I chose to do it anyway. I normally didn't do many things like this. But as I was repelling down the cliff with my best friend encouraging me along the way, I felt very motivated that I could accomplish anything, and after that day with my class I feel much more confident and brave about things that I do.

Overall, girls' stories about field days and class trips designed to create cohesion within and across grade levels show they typically accomplish even more. They turn out to be surprisingly fun. They help girls see teachers in a new light and make them more "real." The experiences can foster risk-taking and courage. They build girls' confidence. And for some girls, they lead to a new gratitude for simply being amidst the beauty of nature.

The girls also made it clear that these out-of-class experiences can also be effective methods of reinforcing, enlarging, and enhancing classroom studies. When well prepared for them, students often come away with much better understandings of what they had been learning in class.

Academic trips give the girls a vivid new sense of the topic, how important the study of it is to the real world, and sometimes even how they can contribute to addressing the issues evoked by the topic. Girls often are inspired to study further and learn more. Just as important, girls appreciate their bonding effects. They come away from them feeling more connected to their classmates. They deepen existing friendships and encourage new ones.

Such bonding is the central purpose of many of the class-based, grade-based, and school-wide excursions. Whether at public, independent, or religiously affiliated schools, girls love the connections that they make with their peers and teachers on these adventures. And adventures they are. Those that test the girls enable them to take risks that stretch them and leave them returning to school with a greater sense of possibility. Supported by peers and teachers, they can grow in unanticipated and exciting ways. Further, they often come to see their teachers in a new and more vivid light.

Multilayered Experiences and Opportunities for Learning

This chapter first and foremost illustrates the layered nature of the experiences that students engage in that result in meaningful learning. The lessons, activities, and projects that students describe display how the multiple components of quality teaching can come together to create memorable lessons. The narratives also echo the larger ideas that frame our overall findings for this study. The descriptions that reflect teachers' thoughtful preparation of classroom structures and lessons, with the goal of promoting girls' engagement in the material, illustrate just one dimension of how much teachers matter in creating unique learning experiences.

Girls relish the fact that they can collaborate with one another, whether through group projects, teaching one another in class discussions or presentations, or coming together in school-wide competitions. All of these experiences help develop relationships among girls that enhance their learning experiences both in and outside of the classroom.

Part of the draw of the collaborative work and the fostering of relationships is that they enable girls to come together around topics that they care about. It is important for girls to see themselves reflected in the material that they are learning and to be able to make connections between what they study in the classroom and the broader topics of women in society, current events, and social justice.

The variety of lessons that students describe highlight how much they will embrace a curriculum that is rich and varied. Something that stood out to us as we read through the narratives was how intentionally teachers integrated different disciplinary subjects and modes of learning. Girls were not only asked to solve particular problems but also were tasked with developing and designing products or presentations that communicated the intricacies of their learning from working out the solutions.

The activities girls and teachers describe in this chapter highlight the growing framework of "design-make-play"[5] that is capturing the attention of educators, policymakers, and business executives alike. This framework aims to combine real-life problem-solving with the investigation and analysis of how things work. The design-make-play framework seeks to ensure that students derive pleasure from what they are learning and creating; that is, from the knowledge they are actively constructing. We discuss this framework in more detail in chapter 8.

Girls respond to work that is challenging and meaningful to them. They welcome having freedom in the classroom and the ownership of their learning that comes with being able to express their creative sides, having the power to make decisions about the focus of their research project, and feeling safe to express their personal opinions with their peers. We see how excitedly girls engage in multimodal and hands-on lessons that often include elements of creativity, technology, and creation.

Taken together, the stories we describe in this chapter reveal the wide variety of discussions, hands-on activities, multimodal lessons, and creative projects that girls find engaging and significant both inside and outside of the classroom. Their voices, combined with the reflections of teachers, come together to create a powerful narrative of what effective, memorable, inspiring, and meaningful learning looks like for girls in the twenty-first century.

KEY IDEAS

What Teachers Can Do to Effectively Implement These Activities:

- Class Discussions and Debates:

  - Instruct students on the elements of effective class discussions: how to take turns, defend your ideas, listen respectfully, and respond constructively to others' ideas.
  - Give your students the chance to lead discussions themselves.
  - Remember, while discussions are the norm in many literature and history classes, there are opportunities for them across the curriculum, including in math and science classes.

- Help students use class discussions to debate and solve complex math or science problems, to brainstorm solutions to academic or real-world challenges, and to debate ethical or philosophical questions in a variety of fields.

- Multimodal Projects:

  - Develop lessons and units that use several kinds of elements. A well-crafted multimodal project can contain almost all the qualities and activities of effective learning in a single experience.
  - Employ multimodal projects to allow students choice and deep involvement in a project as they work individually or collaboratively to direct their own learning.
  - Give students opportunities to be creative and to present their learning to others.
  - Be prepared to expend the time and effort to design and shepherd students through multimodal lessons. Our findings show this will pay off for you and your students.

- Hands-On Learning:

  - Set up hands-on learning experiences in ways that connect the course material to the students' lives in authentic ways.
  - Try to develop them in ways that are within your students' zones of proximal development, that is, push them beyond what they already know without making the task so difficult that they shut down.

- Creativity:

  - Find ways to get your students to use art in their assignments. The arts are very important to a society as well as to an individual's development and growth.
  - Give your students the opportunities each year to create "art for art's sake": to paint, build, draw, dance, sing, play an instrument, act, or otherwise create as a way to express themselves and to appreciate the arts.
  - Look for ways for students to learn and represent their learning through writing a poem, drawing a picture, or acting out a skit.
  - Bring opportunities for creativity into the classroom to help enliven it, to make it fun, and remember.
  - Art is a powerful learning tool, often cementing facts and concepts into students' heads in ways that traditional studying may not be able to.

- Out-of-Classroom Experiences:

  - Support field trips, outside speakers, and school-wide bonding events. They can play an important role in girls' school careers. These experiences are almost always memorable and can serve a variety of functions.

- Remember, too, relationship building among your students and between them and you is crucial for fostering a productive learning environment in your classes. For these reasons, support well-designed out of class experiences to foster learning within the class and across the school.

What Parents Can Do to Support These Types of Learning:

- This chapter is focused on classroom activities, but parents should consider the key elements of them to support their daughters' learning outside of school.
- Make sure your daughter has appropriate and important choices at home.
- Your daughter should be encouraged to think about what she wants to learn and how she can best demonstrate that learning.
- Take time to understand and support your daughter's passions. If she claims to not have them or not know what they are, help her find them.

NOTES

1. *The amazing Harkness philosophy.* Phillips Exeter Academy website. Exeter, NH. 2015. Available at: http://www.exeter.edu/admissions/109_1220.aspx.

2. Sadker, David, and Karen R. Zittleman. *Still failing at fairness: How gender bias cheats girls and boys in school and what we can do about it.* New York: Simon and Schuster, 2009; Neilson, Benjamin R. "The Shipley School 9th grade transition study: An exploration of gender in independent school practice." January 1, 2005. Dissertation available from ProQuest. Paper AAI3175650.

3. Palincsar, Annemarie Sullivan, and Ann L. Brown. "Interactive teaching to promote independent learning from text." *The Reading Teacher* 39, no. 8 (1986): 771–77; Rosenshine, Barak, and Carla Meister. "Reciprocal teaching: A review of the research." *Review of Educational Research* 64, no. 4 (1994): 479–530.

4. Piehler, Christopher. "Survey reveals students' mobile device preferences." *The Journal; Transforming Education through Technology.* 2015. Retrieved from https://thejournal.com/articles/2015/09/21/survey-reveals-students-mobile-device-preferences.aspx.

5. Honey, Margaret, and David E. Kanter, eds. *Design, make, play: Growing the next generation of STEM innovators.* Abington, UK: Routledge, 2013.

Chapter 4

The Importance of Teachers

She Made Me Excited to Go to Math Class Every Day

In the beginning of ninth grade I was very discouraged about algebra. I don't particularly like math. I thought I was bad at math and that my first year in high school math would be horrible. I told my new math teacher that I hated math and that I was really bad, but my teacher didn't think so. She told me that I wasn't bad at all, and by the end of the year I would believe that I was good too. When my teacher told me that, I thought she was saying that just to be nice, but throughout the year she taught me in a way that made it easier to learn. She made learning math more fun and made me excited to go to math class every day. All the years I've taken math, I haven't liked each one, but I will remember this year and my teacher because it was the one year I not only did good at math but I liked it. *—Erin, Ninth-Grade Student*

While there is no doubt that effective lessons require a good teacher, we did not expect, when we began this study, that so many of the students' responses would focus so intently on their instructors. After all, we did not ask about teachers. Our survey prompt specifically asked about class experiences. In our instructions to the students we suggested that what they chose to write about "might be a particular lesson, unit of study, a choice of text or subject matter, a class activity or exercise, or a project or assignment." However, after examining and organizing our data, we found that the single largest category of response from students was about teachers. Almost 20 percent of the responses from the girls focused on a particular teacher instead of a particular lesson.

We poured over our data and asked what it was about these teachers—and their teaching—that so inspired the students. What was so effective and memorable about these instructors? We found that student responses

69

about teachers focused on one or both of two categories: the pedagogical and the personal.

We quote Erin to open this chapter because it is such a good illustration of the two major ways that girls identify how teachers are key to their classroom experience. First, girls are sensitive to and appreciative of how a teacher approaches her or his work. This includes the choices the teacher makes about the content and structure of the lessons as well as the attitude that she or he brings to the job. Erin describes how her teacher "taught me in a way that made it easier to learn" and "made learning math more fun and made me excited to go to math class every day."

While Erin does not elaborate on the techniques that her teacher used, she is clear that the teacher was teaching in a way that entirely changed how she felt about the subject. Other responses provide more detailed examples of how teachers' knowledge, passion, organization, teaching philosophy, and instructional choices are tied to instruction that resonates with students.

The other central finding that emerged was the importance girls place on positive relationships with their teachers. Erin, the reluctant math student, illustrates beautifully how influential her teacher's faith in her ability was in helping her to believe in herself and develop a level of comfort with the material that she had not had before. Many girls told us that a personal connection with a teacher made all the difference in how they viewed themselves as students. These connections build students' confidence and are often the pivotal factor causing them to love subjects that they had previously disdained or flat-out rejected.

LOVING THE JOB

The students in our study clearly articulated how important it is to them that teachers are invested in their profession. This comes through in their descriptions of teachers' knowledge of the subject matter as well as in how they demonstrate a passion for it and for teaching generally. Research by other education scholars supports the notion that students grab on to a particular subject when their teachers are enthusiastically invested in the curricular content.[1] This makes perfect sense; if teachers are not interested in what they are doing, it is hard to imagine that their students will be.

In their narratives, girls rave about the teachers who are masters of their subject area. Many reference, as in this example from twelfth-grader Rachel, the teacher's intelligence and long teaching experience:

Teaching with a Sparkle in Her Eye

My teacher had been teaching at our school since my mom attended when she was in high school, yet she never lost the sparkle in her eye that she got from teaching. She always engaged us, even if we didn't want to be. A specific time that describes her utter adoration for the subject is when we were doing a lab about plant cells. The class was looking at small samples of different plants through a microscope. My teacher was fascinated every time she looked at all the different plants. "Look how beautiful it is, can you believe how complex and intricate it is!" She beckoned us to be as fascinated with the wax cuticle of a mesophyte as much as she was. And with time, we did come to appreciate how interesting what we were studying really was. Her excitement made me want to be just as excited.

In another example, a student praises her teacher's passion for the subject matter and enthusiasm for teaching and describes her teacher as "terrifyingly smart," because of her vast and deep knowledge of U.S. history. Another student comments on how her teacher's enthusiasm for teaching about Chinese soldiers in the Communist army came through in the teacher's sharing of captivating details about the soldiers' lives. This exciting retelling of a particular story from history led the student to become "engrossed" in learning about the topic.

These examples show that it is not enough for teachers to know their curricular content inside and out; effectively communicating love for the subject and for teaching is important as well. Girls find themselves interested, motivated, and engaged when teachers are able to blend their own excitement for their subjects with their knowledge of them. That is especially true when the teachers also find ways to make personal connections to their students by sharing appropriate aspects of their lives with them.

The girls frequently brought up how hearing teachers' stories and experiences helped to motivate them, especially when they were not feeling particularly confident or engaged in their work. Casey, an eighth grader, describes it this way:

Showing Your Appreciation for Girls' Struggles by Sharing Your Own

In French class of my current grade (eighth), we always have a very fun time. We laugh a lot, which makes everyone a little more engaged in class. During one class, while some people were having a tough time checking homework, my French teacher made a "French" sarcastic but funny remark, making the whole class laugh. Then she began to tell us a story about her as a kid in the French system, how she had to do a terrible math packet during the summer. It was really helpful to know that our teacher knew how we felt when we were having a tough time. She said that she had to push through just like we have to. Then I was energized and motivated to do my French work.

What draws Casey in is the fact that she feels that her teacher can relate to her. The French teacher's story is one that makes her seem human in the eyes of her students. Rather than standing in front of the room as an aloof expert who seems to have everything figured out, Casey's teacher gives the girls a glimpse of her own development and how she also struggled to stay focused on schoolwork when she was their age. Instead of frustration, the teacher shows empathy, which goes a long way with Casey.

In another example, a teacher's sharing of an exciting childhood experience accomplishes the goal of making her ninth-grade student, Marie, excited and interested in the class material:

Childhood Discoveries

The class experience that interested me the most was in a social studies class. My teacher is a great teacher and is amusing, which I think makes everyone enjoy listening to her. She also told us a story about when she was a child and was digging in her backyard and came across a Viking ship! I absolutely adore history, partially because of my excellent teacher and also partially just because history interests me. I am interested in many subjects but history has always been my favorite. I most definitely think having an amusing teacher helps everyone get interested and excited about the topic.

Other students described how teachers brought in pictures or told stories from travels to make an English or history lesson come alive. Once again, teachers' personal stories, whether descriptions from their own school days or from other experiences related in some way to the lesson, helped girls feel connected to them and therefore to the content at hand.

In other narratives, teachers' personal sharing was reflected through class discussions of particularly polarizing subjects. Some students noted how important it was to them when their teachers took a stand on a controversial topic and shared their opinion of it. This is the case in the following vignette that tenth-grader Lisa shared:

Opinions on Controversial Topics

Ms. Stein is particularly rewarding to have as a teacher because she is not scared to mention her opinion while giving the scientific facts in her argument. Many teachers will not discuss creationism or other controversial topics, especially since we attend a nondenominational school, but Ms. Stein always shares her opinions, which ends up making the discussion or debate more diverse, and several different opinions are shared.

Lisa's appreciation of Ms. Stein stems from her observation that her teacher seemed willing to go where many other teachers won't in classroom discussions. When Ms. Stein bravely shared her opinions about controversial topics, she was not only introducing students to her personal perspective and ideas but also modeled courage and gave her students the opportunity to get to know her on a deeper level.

As many of these examples have already highlighted, teaching with humor and a sense of fun can be very effective. While some students wrote about how funny a teacher might have been generally or what an enjoyable place the classroom was, many also connected the importance of fun and humor directly to learning.

Students describe how their teachers' sense of fun enabled them to become more engaged with something they previously feared or disliked. In addition, in all of the following examples students note the importance of a teacher's choice to use humor not only to convey a concept but also to make a connection with the students. The teacher ninth-grader Brooke described accomplishes this by bringing into the class amusing material that extends beyond biology.

Bringing Pop Culture into the Classroom

In ninth-grade biology class, my teacher gave us activities with different pop culture references such as *Harry Potter*, *Toy Story*, and Justin Bieber. It was funny, it kept us engaged, and really showed she cared as a teacher. It was still relevant to the subject, but it made biology more relatable and put it into an everyday situation. It was a helpful way to keep us motivated. Plus, at the end, she put a video of a celebrity singing about biology. Bringing pop culture into class keeps it fun. Plus, it showed me that my teacher really wants to make an effort to connect with us. Now I feel like I can talk to her about anything, both for in-school and out-of-school reasons.

Aisha's sixth-grade history teacher made class fun by dressing up and acting out different representations of what she was trying to convey to the girls.

Acting the Part in History

I remember in sixth-grade history, this was one of my favorite memories. I didn't really like the teacher, but on this day she was wonderful. We were learning about China, and she said we would have a "guest." She left the classroom, changed into a costume and came back in dressed, and acting, like a person with these different beliefs. She acted out the parts so well and never broke character. It was funny and engaging, and stuck in my brain.

In our last example, Irene, an 11th grader, describes how humor and fun can also happen outside of the classroom walls:

Getting Down and Dirty with the Kids

Well, on field day all of our teachers interacted with us by playing volleyball. We had extra fun, some students decided to play with the teachers, as students started seeing teachers play with great smiles and full of joy, more students joined and played volleyball with us. Gladly, it was a large group. We were screaming with joy, having our own group team dances. We all got to know how our teachers really are, and they are truly funny and amazing!

Pedagogical Content Knowledge

While students do not use this term, the qualities they appreciate in their teachers fit well into what educational researcher Lee Shulman[2] describes as *pedagogical content knowledge* or PCK. The idea behind PCK is that it is not enough for teachers to merely know the material they are teaching; they must also master how to communicate that knowledge to students. In classrooms that bring together students from different social backgrounds, orientations to learning, and levels of confidence in a subject, a teacher who is strong in PCK approaches her or his work with creativity and flexibility in order to reach all of the students.

When the girls described teachers who showed unflagging commitment to making sure all of the students understand the lesson and who demonstrate an ability to answer girls' questions satisfactorily, they are describing teachers with high levels of PCK. They are also describing teachers who understand that different students, with different kinds of social identities, may come at the material with unique perspectives. Teachers who have strong PCK and a keen appreciation for differences rooted in children's complex social identities will be most likely to reach most girls.

Another way of thinking about PCK is through the lens of what education scholar and researcher Christopher Emdin calls "reality pedagogy." In his TEDx talk,[3] Emdin describes reality pedagogy as "teaching and learning based on the reality of the student's experience." In the examples in this chapter we see teachers connecting with students by reflecting on their own experiences as young adults. We also see teachers incorporating current pop culture elements into their lessons in order to make them more interesting to students. And we see teachers laughing with and playing sports right alongside their students. All of these examples reflect how teachers bring together their knowledge of the material with their understanding of their students' lives in order to promote student learning.

A teacher well-versed in PCK tends to demonstrate the qualities that we've been describing in this chapter: possessing an excellent command of the material, showing passion for teaching and for the subject, ensuring that every student understands the lesson at hand, and putting himself or herself personally into the lesson. When all of these elements come together, it can make for an incredibly powerful learning experience. Alex, writing about her physics teacher, captures several dimensions of his mastery of pedagogical content knowledge. Her teacher uses a variety of effective pedagogical tools, engages the students' curiosity, and above all emphasizes student understanding.

Having Him as a Teacher Completely Erased All My Fears

I remember being nervous about taking physics my senior year as I had no idea what to expect. However, having Mr. Wilson as a teacher completely erased all my fears with his energetic lectures, crazy mnemonics, and prioritization of students fully understanding concepts (not just memorizing formulas). Here is one example of an event that particularly fascinated me with physics. My fellow students and I were learning about waves, and Mr. Wilson told us about a technique that a certain type of spider uses in order to survive: it will dig a relatively deep hole for itself, surround its opening with several rocks, and connect strands of webs from itself to each one of the rocks. When an ant or other sort of prey barely touches one of the rocks, the spider will sense the vibrations through the strand and will leap out of the hole with incredible speed to catch its prey—and the spider knows exactly which rock the poor creature touched. Mr. Wilson then proceeded to show us this amazing type of behavior in a short video.

Audrey, describing her experiences with her art teacher, gives us another perspective on her teacher's PCK.

Passion, Deep Knowledge, and Enthusiasm for Art

Earlier this year, during my senior year of high school, I enrolled in the elective art history class, and I was really looking forward to it, because it was with one of my favorite teachers. Not only was she easy to talk to, invested in her students' success, and extremely intelligent, but she also truly loved art and helping others be passionate about art as well. An instance that is most memorable to me is when we were discussing an abstract work by Paul Gauguin with so much symbolism in the work it made my head spin. But Ms. Chambers really got us engaged in a discussion when she assured us that we were quite capable of dissecting the painting and discovering its meaning and cultural significance as a class.

One of the things that I realized that day was how effective she was as a teacher because she truly had confidence in us as students. She would often give us long and difficult readings or quotations from art historians and artists to read and understand for homework. When we were finished with them, she would set up an online forum in which we would discuss aspects of the article that we found interesting or even disagreed with. For these assignments, I felt that I was being treated as an adult because Ms. Chambers truly wanted to hear what I had to say, and I felt that my opinions and thoughts were really valid. In a similar sense, she fostered class discussions and encouraged us to state our observations about a work of art, no matter how trivial or basic they may seem. I have learned so much from her: how to be a better writer and thinker, and how to appreciate art more thoroughly. And most, importantly, I learned that a good teacher is encouraging of her students in the way that she interacts with them; that is, when a teacher challenges her students, it shows utmost respect for them and shows them that you are invested in their success.

Audrey's description of her teacher is a beautiful illustration of a teacher with PCK. She describes Ms. Chambers as being: easy to talk to, invested in her students' success, intelligent, passionate about her subject, engaging, reassuring, and confidence-building. Ms. Chambers also shows her students respect and sets high expectations for them.

Reading descriptions of inspiring teachers such as these is uplifting. Teaching is a difficult job that has become only increasingly daunting over the past few decades. Many teachers rightly feel overworked, underpaid, and unduly burdened by the demands of a bureaucracy of testing and regulations. When teachers maintain their passion for their field of study and for sharing it with young minds, the results are inspiring. Who wouldn't want to be in the kinds of classes the students described previously? The teachers are able to take their students on a journey of learning and discovery that the girls will likely carry with them for years to come.

The teachers we have described demonstrated their passion for teaching in numerous ways: wowing students with their mastery of the material, revealing personal connections to the subject matter, and bringing humor and unbridled enthusiasm into lessons. In each instance, however, they also were demonstrating to the students that they cared about them.

Our stories show that having strong PCK is a necessary condition of excellent teaching. But it is not sufficient. The relationships teachers develop with girls are essential too. We term these "personal" connections (as opposed to the pedagogical, or learning-centered, connections described earlier). Of course, these two types of connection—impassioned teaching and genuine concern about students' lives and achievement—tend to go hand in hand.

LOVING THE STUDENTS

As we read through the responses from girls that centered in some way on a teacher, it was clear that, for many of the girls, it was how the teacher treated her that made all the difference in her learning. Child psychologist James Comer wrote, "No significant learning occurs without a significant relationship."[4] A great deal of research, including ours, has revealed that a relationship with a teacher is often the decisive element that allows a student to thrive in a class. Teachers' empathy and warmth consistently have been shown to correlate with improved academic performance. Conversely, and unsurprisingly, conflict with teachers is associated with poor school outcomes.[5]

The research of Nel Noddings[6] and other education scholars helps illuminate the factors that contribute to strong student-teacher relationships. In particular, Noddings' notion of an "ethics of care" highlights the importance of human beings' relationships within educational settings.

A key component of Noddings' theory is that caring requires that the "carer" truly engage with the person about whom he or she is caring to understand and respond to the person's needs. To demonstrate an ethics of care, teachers cannot simply prepare a lesson plan and present material to their students without regard for who those individuals are and what they need. Excellent teaching that demonstrates caring requires close knowledge of one's students, both as scholars and human beings.

We saw an ethic of care playing out in our study in the ways that teachers demonstrated their concern for their students' well-being both within and beyond the walls of the classroom. In a variety of ways, students described how they feel cared for and supported by their teachers, which in turn motivated them to work to the best of their ability in class, on homework, and on outside assignments.

Some girls wrote about a specific teacher who worked with them one-on-one as they struggled to master new material or complete a challenging project. Some talked about the personal attention they received outside of class, often during the teacher's office hours or conference periods.

An ethics of care is predicated on a deep knowledge of the individual and her needs. These needs will differ from student to student, of course. It is vital that teachers are aware of and sensitive to girls' race, social class, and personal circumstances, as well as to their particular learning issues. They should also consider how those characteristics interact within the individual and how they cause other students to respond to them. Teachers who are invested in an ethic of care are flexible and responsive to their girls' multiple identities and backgrounds.

Individual teachers, and schools as a whole, need to ask themselves if they are prioritizing the development of these relationships. Much research supports the notion that the emotional and interpersonal demands of school are often more important to children and teenagers than the academic content.[7] A teacher's ability to get to know and support a student as an individual as well as a learner can often make all the difference in that student's education and, more broadly, in her overall development. Callie's story about her ninth-grade math teacher captures this well:

Making Time for a Struggling Student

One time, I was struggling deeply with math. My math teacher was up to her
ears in papers (it was just that time of year). I came to her room at the regular
office hour time but stayed much later than anyone else. As she was getting up
to go home, she saw the look of panic in my eyes. Immediately, she put down
her bag and tutored me for another half hour. . . . My teacher's dedication has
always impressed and encouraged me.

In addition to reports of individual out-of-class help from teachers, students
also wrote about teachers who provided them with personalized academic
help during class time. Girls talk about being coached through a difficult art
project, receiving customized explanations when they did not understand a
particular concept, and having in-depth discussions about an emerging thesis
for a research paper. In these moments students reported feeling energized by
the individualized academic support they received from their teachers.

Other responses described times when girls would meet weekly with their
teachers about subjects or material that they found particularly daunting. In
this example, Claire, a sixth grader, talks about how her teacher's varied
approaches to preparing for tests helped her to learn the material and have
fun at the same time:

Creative Study Sessions

In Ms. Lear's fifth-grade history class we were studying for a test. She hosts
special study sessions on Mondays before tests for the students that would like
to attend. She helps the students with any questions, and they are expected
to take notes. One study session she let all of the girls play Jeopardy on the
SMART Board. Another creative study idea is when she asked volunteers to act
out the roles of famous historic people or scenes. The study sessions were very
helpful to the students when learning the material and taking tests.

In another example, tenth-grader Valerie explains how group study sessions with her classmates and a welcoming teacher not only helped her to
learn the material in chemistry class but also made her feel more comfortable
reaching out to other teachers for help when she needed it. She concludes by
saying, "Not only was I more interested in the topic of chemistry, one of my
favorite classes but I also learned that meeting with a teacher to stay on top
of assignments really helps. . . . This class and Mr. Davis have taught me to
meet with a teacher whenever I have any question and to stay on top of all
my assignments in order to succeed in a class."

Students often credit regularly scheduled sessions such as this with helping them grasp challenging material, particularly in subjects that they did not

consider their strongest. As we will discuss in more detail in chapter 8, math and science are two subject areas in particular where girls feel less confident compared to other subjects. For this reason, developing supportive and positive student-teacher relationships is particularly important. When teachers make the time to offer academic support they send a powerful message to their students.

For other students it is the emotional support that makes the biggest impression on them. Of course, academic support and emotional support are not mutually exclusive. In many cases it is the combination of the two that has an important positive effect. This is most often seen in a teacher's unwavering belief in a student's ability to achieve. Here, Natalie, an 11th grader, describes how her teacher changed how she thought about herself.

Those Simple Words Were Pretty Life-Changing

I finally came in to meet with my teacher one-on-one after she had told me to many times. She simply told me that she knew I had it in me. Those simple words were pretty life-changing. I could tell by her care and the time she took to meet with me one-on-one every week after that first meeting that she wanted to see me do well, and she thought I could do well. . . . I began to love Spanish and ended the class with a B+. The teacher, who at the beginning I thought hated me, really admired my growth, so she put me into the honors Spanish class for my sophomore year. I had her as a teacher again, and because of her motivation, three years later, I'm now in Honors Spanish IV. I'm light years away from how I began freshman year, and she reminds me of that. She reminds me of how proud I should be . . . she advises me and motivates me to keep going with Spanish. I wouldn't be anywhere close to where I am without her guidance, passion, support, and belief in me.

In other examples of connection and emotional support, students described teachers who related to them as individuals and took the time to get to know them beyond their performance in the teacher's class. Bella, a twelfth grader, explains how she appreciated her poetry class because of the effort her teacher made to get to know her, and through that process, how she, Bella, got to know herself better as well. In describing an experience in which she shared a poem she had written, she wrote, "He not only raved about it in class; he mentioned my poem in conference with me and expressed his excitement for my newfound poetic voice. . . . His interest in my work and his interest in getting to know me better as a person allowed me to become a better poet and inspired me to be more interested in myself."

Students described teachers who had helped them during difficult times, whether in a moment of frustration with a difficult task, an awkward social interaction with an assigned partner on a project, or a drop in academic performance after a traumatic life event. Other students appreciated teachers whom they felt were invested in their learning and success beyond merely the grades they receive in the class. For example, Courtney, a ninth grader, shared a moment that she experienced in class that she would never forget:

A Powerful Life Lesson

When I first started high school at the beginning of this year, I came into Western Civilization having almost no background knowledge. I remember stepping into the class and thinking, "What am I getting myself into?" I felt myself getting nervous that all the other students in the class knew so much more than I did and that I was going to fail. I had always had this failure to believe in myself and have confidence, and I assured myself that I would not be able to make it out alive. It wasn't until about three weeks into school in late September that I realized something. My teacher had called on me for an answer, and like always, I doubted myself and started my answer with, "Well, I'm not sure if this is right, but . . ." She stopped me mid-sentence and said, "Never say that in my class again. If you don't have confidence in your answer, no one else will." This was the first time anyone had really pointed me out on my insecurities, and although it felt strange at the time, I would thank my teacher for that moment for the rest of my life. I'll admit that I've definitely said that more than one time this year, but when I do, I always remember that special moment. I may not feel confident in my answers or always know the right things to say, but confidence is key to my success. Even though I am only a freshman and still learning the ropes of not only school but also life, I know that this experience will carry me on when nothing else will.

Teachers can also make girls feel cared for as individuals by making sure their classrooms are welcoming places and also ones in which girls feel they are respected and challenged. For students this often translates into feeling treated as an adult or an equal. Justine, a ninth grader, recalled how her eighth-grade history teacher connected with the class.

She Talked to Us Like We Were Adults

When I was in the eighth grade, I could surely say that I had the most amazing teacher in the entire world. She taught the eighth-grade history class and never failed to make class interesting. It was not as though she was trying really hard to be funny or make class enjoyable for us, I suppose it just came naturally. I think the reason why the majority of us performed so well in her class was because she treated us like we were kind of, in a way, her friends, but at the same time talked to us like we were adults and instilled a great sense of responsibility into each of her students. . . . My advice to teachers is to make a balance between treating their students like friends as well as like mature adults. This doesn't make a student feel too "free" in class, but (at the same time) doesn't make them feel babied or feel as though the subject that they are learning is actually the most pointless piece of knowledge in the world.

Some people may hear that a teen wants to be thought of as an adult and assume she is resisting authority or overstepping bounds. The responses from students praising teachers for treating them with respect and as adults, equals, or even friends, instead reveal classroom environments in which students rise to the respect given to them. The girls in our study wrote eloquently about being asked for their opinions, of taking ownership over their learning, and of then achieving more than they ever thought they could. This response from Patricia, a ninth grader, includes many of those elements:

Classroom Discussions in an Environment of Respect

In eighth grade, I was taking a class called American Studies. It was really interesting and I was highly engaged during the 80-minute sessions. I think it had to do greatly with my teacher. He was unusual in that he took everything we (the class) had to say seriously no matter what it was. The discussion was my favorite part of the class. It was not the teacher who would decipher the text to us but rather our own peers. We would build on each other's ideas and come to understand the text on our own. When we did not reach the conclusion he meant for us to, then he would ask us questions that would eventually lead us to it. He treated us like adults. He would listen intently to what each of us had to say.

It is quite telling that Patricia finds it *unusual* that her teacher took what she and her classmates had to say seriously. As more teachers communicate to girls, both overtly and subtly, that they truly respect and take their opinions seriously, it is likely that more girls will take themselves seriously as learners and sources of knowledge.

TEACHING STUDENTS, NOT LESSONS

Girls thrive when they are taught in a way that recognizes their own human-ity, importance, and sense of self. Through the reciprocity of warm, caring relationships with their teachers, they stop being passive recipients of infor-mation. In the process, they gain self-confidence and a sense of themselves as competent students and knowledge makers. Pedagogy that "humanizes"[8] students emphasizes how meaningful learning occurs at the intersection of cognition and emotions. This pedagogy draws on three different elements: the development of meaningful relationships, the presence of material that is relevant to girls' lives, and the opportunity for students and teachers to have a reciprocal transfer of knowledge rather than having the teachers situated as the sole experts and holders of information.

The teachers the girls describe in their vignettes enact all three of these elements. They foster relationships beyond the traditional teacher-student interactions and support student development beyond academics to help girls thrive in school. They put girls at the center of their learning, valuing what they have to say and how they make meaning. Finally, they ensure that the material is often relevant to the girls' lives. Truly meaningful learning occurs when teachers bring these elements together. This is especially true when there is both an intellectual and an emotional component to the engagement between teachers and students.

When teachers are working to understand their students emotionally and intellectually, it is important that they appreciate their unique needs. Here it greatly helps to consider girls' class, race, and sexuality as well as other dimensions that are integral to girls' social identities. Especially when the teacher is distanced culturally in some way from a student, it is important that he or she work to understand the challenges and needs of that girl and to find ways to forge a connection with her.

Humanizing pedagogy[9] also requires that teachers examine and reflect on their own multilayered identities in relation to that of their students. These differences and similarities can influence factors in the classroom such as how teachers and students communicate with each other, present and understand emotional expression, and even resolve conflicts.

As we saw in chapter 2, the importance of making learning relevant to girls' lives cannot be overstated. Real engagement at school occurs when the subject matter has demonstrable real-life connections and students are shown how it is applicable to their lives either at present or for their future education or careers. When teachers know about how their students live, what matters to them, and what struggles and triumphs they are experiencing, they can craft relationships that will foster learning and inform the teacher's own curriculum design and teaching.

Teachers must ensure that their students are engaged co-creators of knowledge. Humanizing pedagogy promotes the whole development of young people by creating conditions in the classroom that encourage students to fully use their talents and capabilities.

When girls are given such opportunities, they are working toward their own sense of mastery by realizing that *they* can be sources of knowledge rather than just relying on their teachers, books, or Internet sources as the authority on what is true or right. Ideally, teachers will act more as guides or facilitators of their students' growth than as the gatekeepers of knowledge. True learning is about student growth, not merely an accumulation of facts.

MAKING THE CONNECTIONS IN THE CLASSROOM

It is clear that enacting a humanizing pedagogy in the classroom asks teachers to structure their lessons and teach in a particular way as well as developing closeness with their students. As the girls report, teachers who bring to their classrooms a deep level of knowledge and passion for their subject matters are best positioned to engage their students. They not only communicate their own love for the subject, but they structure lessons that require their students to co-construct knowledge through active rather than passive learning.

Such teachers will also communicate to their students that they believe in them as learners, see them as capable individuals, and respect them as fellow scholars. The examples we included in this chapter had many illustrations of ways that teachers cultivated these relationships and positive interactions.

Students easily pick up on and interpret those teachers' verbal and nonverbal cues related to closeness and caring. Nonverbal cues include increased eye contact, smiling, positive head nods, reducing the distances between teacher and student, more direct body angles, more touch, and greater vocal variation.

Verbal cues that convey teacher presence and engagement include teachers' use of humor, self-disclosure, complimenting of students' performance, the use of inclusive pronouns, confirmation of others' statements, and the use of names and other informal forms of address.[10]

Again, we want to stress that it is important that teachers get to know their students. These are general suggestions that tend to cultivate closeness, but, again, it is important that teachers gauge students' reactions and adjust behaviors as needed to connect with individual girls.

Getting to know students well takes effort and time, but the rewards are great. By offering welcoming and supportive after-school help sessions, attending student performances or athletic events, and remembering details about girls' lives, teachers show that they care about their students and are interested in them.

In the classroom, crafting assignments that allow and encourage students to bring in their personal interests is not only engaging but also creates opportunities for teachers to learn more about their students' lives and passions. Finally, and perhaps most important, simply listening to students and showing them that they have been heard can be a powerful source of connection.

Of course, relationships go both ways. As teachers begin to get to know students, their students get to know them. We have already seen how meaningful it is for girls when teachers share their opinions or tell stories from their lives.

In many cases students also draw a connection between their learning and their appreciation of their teacher's humanity. Teachers who bring their passion and personal connection to the classroom are able to reach students far more effectively than those who hide any personal connection to their work or, worse yet, have no true connection either to the joy of what they do or to their students.

We are not suggesting that it is possible for every teacher to develop a close relationship with every student. Some teachers will naturally connect with certain girls at a deeper level than others. Girls will also have different types of relationships with different teachers. We do believe, however, that teachers' behaviors in the classroom can generally bring them closer to most of their students. They can do this by employing the techniques we've highlighted in this chapter: showing dedication in their preparation for class, revealing passion and interest in the subject matter, demonstrating respect for students, and altering their teaching to respond to students' learning needs.

In addition to a general closeness and sense of mutual respect between students and their teachers, it is our hope that every child at any given school will have a strong interpersonal relationship with at least one or two adults, be they teachers, aides, counselors, or learning support personnel.

School administrators and department heads need to find a way for staff members to communicate about their students, particularly those who are struggling in some way and do not appear to be connected to an adult. Teachers and others who interact with such students should share information and make sure that there is someone at the school each girl can trust and turn to – and maybe, as important, someone who turns to the girl.

KEY IDEAS

What Teachers Can Do to Engage Students Pedagogically and Personally:

- Show your passion for what you are teaching. Talk with your students about why you have pursued the field you are in, why it matters to you, and why you believe it should matter to them.
- Use humor in the classroom. Find ways to bring joy into your lessons and your teaching.
- Within the bounds of good judgment, let students see you as a person. Talk about your own experiences as a student.
- Share your opinions on important topics, but in ways that make it clear you respect opinions different than your own.

- Learn all you can about how your students learn and what matters to them. You can gather data from their mistakes as well as their correct answers, from your observations, and simply by asking them.
- Make time for students during class and after school. While we know teachers have many demands on their time and energy, spending it this way can reap great rewards.
- Communicate to your students that you believe in them and help them believe in themselves.
- Use positive reinforcement as frequently as possible when you can ground it in students' actual behavior. Positive feedback is much more effective than negative reinforcement.

What Parents Can Do:

- Encourage your daughter to reach out to teachers or mentors if she is struggling academically with a subject or concept.
- Debrief her after she gets support and discuss with her how it went.
- Coach her if she talks about struggling with a teacher—she doesn't have to connect with every adult in the school, but it is helpful if she can work on a strained relationship.
- Pay attention to what your daughter says about her relationships with teachers and be concerned if she does not seem to have made any connections to any of them.
- Bring your concern about a lack of connection to the school head or counselor and see if it is confirmed.
- Work with the school and your daughter to figure out how the school may facilitate at least one important connection.

NOTES

1. Patrick, Brian C., Jennifer Hisley, and Toni Kempler. "'What's everybody so excited about?': The effects of teacher enthusiasm on student intrinsic motivation and vitality." *The Journal of Experimental Education* 68, no. 3 (2000): 217–236; Kunter, Mareike, Yi-Miau Tsai, Uta Klusmann, Martin Brunner, Stefan Krauss, and Jürgen Baumert. "Students' and mathematics teachers' perceptions of teacher enthusiasm and instruction." *Learning and Instruction* 18, no. 5 (2008): 468–482.

2. Shulman, Lee S. "Those who understand: Knowledge growth in teaching." *Educational Researcher* 15, no. 2 (1986): 4–14.

3. "Reality pedagogy." Dr. Christopher Emdin TEDx Talk at Teachers College, Columbia University (2012). Retrieved from https://www.youtube.com/watch?v=2Y9tVf_8fqo.

4. Comer, James P. "Schools that develop children." *The American Prospect* 12, no. 7 (2001): 30–35.

5. Roorda, Debora L., Helma M. Y. Koomen, Jantine L. Spilt, and Frans J. Oort. "The influence of affective teacher-student relationships on students' school engagement and achievement: A meta-analytic approach." *Review of Educational Research* 81, no. 4 (2011): 493–529.

6. Noddings, Nel. *Caring: A relational approach to ethics and moral education.* Berkeley, CA: University of California Press, 2013.

7. Noddings, Nel. *Caring: A relational approach to ethics and moral education.* Berkeley, CA: University of California Press, 2013; Raider-Roth, Miriam. *Trusting what you know: The high stakes of classroom relationships.* Indianapolis, IN: Jossey-Bass, 2005. Reichert, Michael, and Richard Hawley. *I can learn from you: Boys as relational learners.* Cambridge, MA: Harvard Education Press, 2014.

8. Bartolome, Lilia. "Beyond the methods fetish: Toward a humanizing pedagogy." *Harvard Educational Review* 64, no. 2 (1994): 173–195; del Carmen Salazar, María. "A humanizing pedagogy: Reinventing the principles and practice of education as a journey toward liberation." *Review of Research in Education* 37, no. 1 (2013): 121–48.

9. Bartolome, Lilia. "Beyond the methods fetish: Toward a humanizing pedagogy." *Harvard Educational Review* 64, no. 2 (1994): 173–195; del Carmen Salazar, María. "A humanizing pedagogy: Reinventing the principles and practice of education as a journey toward liberation." *Review of Research in Education* 37, no. 1 (2013): 121–148.

10. Christophel, Diane M. "The relationships among teacher immediacy behaviors, student motivation, and learning." *Communication Education* 39, no. 4 (1990): 323–340.

Chapter 5

Why These Lessons Work

In chapters 2 and 3 we describe the almost 2,000 narratives we received from teachers and students and relate them to important theories of curriculum design. In chapter 4, we show how much value girls place on strong relationships with their teachers as well as how central teachers are to the effectiveness of great lessons.

The stories teachers and students tell are often striking and sometimes moving. They consistently reflect the sound tenets of a constructivist-based[1] Maker[2] curriculum[3] and relational teaching.[4] A constructivist-based curriculum emphasizes how children develop (construct) their understandings through experience and reflection. In our study, girls described how doing hands-on activities, crafting multimodal projects, actively experimenting, and discussing their findings with peers deepened their understanding of the class material in ways that simply reading from a book or listening to a lecture could not.

The Maker Movement is closely aligned with constructivist learning in that it promotes a "design-make-play" approach to teaching classroom subjects. In chapter 8, we will discuss the Maker approach in detail, particularly in regard to how it can engage girls' interest in STEM subjects. For our purposes here, it is enough to say that when girls have to engineer objects and then make them and when they play with materials, their learning is enhanced and their ownership of their knowledge is increased.

The narratives we received also revealed how relational teaching—the intentional development of meaningful connections between girls and their teachers through a variety of strategies—made girls feel valued and cared for in their classes. Careful examination suggests that there are underlying principles that unite the lessons we studied and help explain how they combine to produce effective teaching for girls.

The students' and teachers' stories about inspiring lessons and the activities that constitute them, together with the students' stories about how much teachers matter, reveal an undeniable connection to the developmental needs of girls. The participants' narratives reflect a picture of girls as highly complex individuals who require much more than academic information to develop in ways that prepare them for the demands of a constantly changing, global twenty-first-century world.

Without understating the importance of helping girls acquire disciplinary knowledge, if they are to grow into inquisitive, competent, self-confident, lifelong learners, great teaching also must be designed to maximize their human development more broadly.

Psychologist and school consultant Michael Thompson captured this challenge in his compelling book, *The Pressured Child.*[5] Thompson talks about the large divergence between how most adults understand school and how children experience it. For adults, what is essential is what Thompson calls "The Lesson"—the daily substance of what teachers try to get children to learn. Parents and teachers want students to master the subject matters of history, English, math, physics, chemistry, and foreign languages so they are prepared to move on to college. When parents ask their children, "How did school go today?" they usually have in mind their experience of the multiple lessons they have encountered.

Figure 5.1. "The Lesson"

Thompson maintains that most adults fail to think beyond this view of schooling. He argues that what children face is much more complicated than simply learning the material taught. Yes, they are trying to learn their subjects, but to become successful adults they must also learn how to "do school"—to understand their singular, individual approaches to learning, while simultaneously managing the expectations of their parents, the demands of their teachers, the rules of school, and the complex and ever-changing social relationships among their peers.

Thompson calls this "The Strategy" and argues that to be fully successful, each child must develop one unique to herself that enables her to navigate the broader challenges of school. Many of these challenges lie outside of the gaze of adults. Yet meeting them and mastering them are central to children's well-being.

To succeed in school and beyond, a student must become proficient in "The Lesson" and "The Strategy." Mastering the former often depends on developing the latter. Further, these skills simply constitute but two parts of the broader set of developmental tasks students must accomplish to become self-confident, capable, productive adults. Drawing on Thompson, Figure 5.2 captures our take on the challenges that students face.

In schools, much of the learning about "The Strategy" takes place outside the conscious awareness of adults. In a truly effective school, teachers will address "The Lesson" while *simultaneously* recognizing that children need to learn strategies for how to manage their learning (metacognition) as well as their interpersonal relationships. We believe the elements of great lessons that our research has unearthed cover all of these areas of growth.

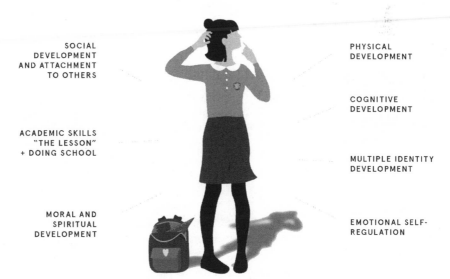

SOCIAL DEVELOPMENT AND ATTACHMENT TO OTHERS

PHYSICAL DEVELOPMENT

COGNITIVE DEVELOPMENT

ACADEMIC SKILLS "THE LESSON" + DOING SCHOOL

MULTIPLE IDENTITY DEVELOPMENT

MORAL AND SPIRITUAL DEVELOPMENT

EMOTIONAL SELF-REGULATION

Figure 5.2. What Kids Must Accomplish in School

In the rest of this chapter we examine in turn each of the developmental tasks girls must master to flourish as successful young women. We then illustrate how the components of effective teaching practices our research uncovered contribute to girls accomplishing one or more of them.

THE DEVELOPMENTAL TASKS GIRLS MUST ACCOMPLISH

There is no one agreed-upon list of developmental tasks children need to master in order to grow into competent, well-functioning adults. Developmental psychologists include somewhat different categories in their accounts. Careful reading of major theorists, as well as of lists of developmental tasks put out by universities and state departments of child development,[6] indicates that their understandings overlap considerably and cover very similar territory. We have modeled our discussion on Thompson's framing of the tasks while modifying it to be inclusive of other theorists' views and what we have learned from working with many girls in various kinds of schools over the years.

Of course, to some extent, these categories are arbitrary in that there is a great amount of overlap among them. None of the tasks stands in complete isolation from the others. They are interrelated and support each other. Nonetheless, we find it helpful to separate them because girls will develop some skills more easily than others and certain areas of development will be more or less pertinent to their lives at different times and in different situations. By somewhat artificially isolating the different components we, and other developmental theorists, hope to provide a framework for considering whether girls are being properly supported as they grow from infants into mature, capable, and emotionally secure adults.

Task 1. Cognitive and Academic Development: Mastering "The Lesson" and Learning to Learn

First on the list of developmental tasks girls face are the traditional requirements of being a student: demonstrating mastery of the material taught in school. We know that adolescent girls looking ahead to successful careers must learn "The Lesson," the substantive, discipline-based knowledge presented in every class. If they are to feel good about themselves and experience success in school, they must master various subject-matter disciplines.

Acquiring and applying this knowledge requires girls to learn how to approach new material with confidence, stay interested and engaged, and employ their curiosity. Ideally, they will develop a positive approach to learning and an understanding of their strengths and challenges as learners. These are not simple matters and take years of progressive effort to master.

Girls' academic capacity depends, in large measure, on their growing cognitive abilities. From middle school through high school they typically experience a profound change in their ability to think abstractly. Beginning as infants, they are constantly engaged in trying to figure out how the world works. As they go through adolescence they expand their abilities to coordinate abstract ideas, to envision possibilities, and to invent hypotheses.

Given appropriate opportunities to explore and test their hypotheses, girls enhance their learning and increase their abilities to plan successfully. They also begin to learn and apply new decision-making skills in which they weigh their thoughts and emotions, seeking an appropriate balance for different circumstances.

Acquiring these key cognitive abilities on their journey through primary and secondary school helps girls learn *how* to learn their school subjects. A primary task of cognitive development at this stage is for girls to gain a meta-understanding of their thinking and how they learn best; to think about their thinking—precisely the skill they need both to master academics and to do school successfully. An equally important developmental task, however, is to look at the world with more awareness. This includes recognizing the status of and expectations for girls and women.

Girls generally are expected by people in our society to be organized and well behaved in the classroom. Teachers and parents may expect them to be able to focus and stay on task better than many boys can. They are expected to be cooperative and quiet. These expectations, of course, can be burdensome for girls for whom staying quiet, focused, and organized in class does not come easily.

In addition, even while managing the "model student" expectation placed upon them, girls also often encounter negative stereotyping and lowered expectations in certain academic subjects. Neuroscientist Lise Eliot describes the cultural barriers that girls in the United States must contend with around the negative perceptions of their innate abilities connected to science, technology, engineering, and math. Differences in the types of toys that girls are encouraged to play with and the levels of positive reinforcement they receive when interested in STEM subjects tie into the subtle, negative lessons that girls learn about gender and these fields.

The internalization of the stereotypes that boys are naturally better at math and science than girls causes girls to have less confidence in their abilities, particularly as they enter adolescence. These lowered expectations can, sadly, translate into poorer performance on tests or into eschewing entire fields of study. To thrive in school, girls must be made aware of the existence of these gendered stereotypes and encouraged to pursue their academic advancement based on their own personal abilities and desires rather than on the expectations of others (an imperative we take up in chapters 6, 7, and 8).

Task 2. Mastering "The Strategy"

As Michael Thompson describes it, being successful in school requires not only memorizing facts, mastering disciplinary areas, and developing the ability to think abstractly, but it also involves figuring out the rules of classrooms, gyms, cafeterias, playgrounds, hallways, and the administration. It requires learning good time management as well as discerning what each teacher wants and how to meet his or her expectations. And students need to do this in ways that maintain their own sense of integrity.

Girls must discover how to manage each teacher's and administrator's authority while simultaneously developing their own. And they must do this within the context of rich, complicated social relationships among their peers. Indeed, if girls are to flourish, they also must learn how to manage group and inter-group relationships and acquire conflict resolution skills. With peers, this involves learning about and negotiating multiple social hierarchies while maintaining their own sense of self and well-being. With adults, it involves understanding the complexities of students' institutionally subordinate positions while hopefully learning to negotiate with grown-ups to establish positions of relative autonomy and equality.

While girls are engaged in learning this complex set of skills, they must simultaneously figure out how to assume increasing responsibility for themselves. They must take on more roles; participate in and maybe run various organizations; do outside jobs; and, ultimately, learn all that is necessary to prepare themselves for taking a productive place in the labor force.

More broadly, girls must discover how to meet their commitments to their families, their schools, and their communities. They need to learn to be good citizens in each of these domains. They must accomplish all of this while negotiating gendered norms about how to dress, act, be a friend, and participate in class. In a society in which "acting like a girl" is an insult, what does it mean to be appropriately feminine but not weak? This is a complex question for most adults and one that girls must answer more or less unconsciously as they develop their identities and places within their school community.

Task 3. Moral and Spiritual Development

As girls grow cognitively, they begin to acquire the capacity to question the beliefs of early childhood and to develop their own morals, values, and standards, related to but uniquely differentiated from those of their parents, their schools, and their places of worship. They begin to ponder their place in the universe, considering their relationship to nature, to mortality, and to the possibility of their connection to a higher being.

For girls, this meaning-making often develops within the gendered (and raced and classed) context of how society defines "good girls" and "bad girls." In her work about adolescent girls, scholar and girl activist Rachel Simmons[7] has found that they often struggle with the notion of perfectionism—getting good grades, always smiling, and always doing the "right" thing. Her research argues that this striving for inevitably unattainable perfection creates a situation in which girls may become confused about who they are and what they truly believe.

Simultaneously, as girls become involved in the internal work of deciding what beliefs and ideas will guide their lives, they also begin to gain a broader, more complex, and sophisticated understanding of justice and fairness and come to care for others in more altruistic, less self-centered ways. This area of development is highly related to girls' broader social development.

Task 4. Social Development

From the very beginning of their lives, girls must learn attachment and intimacy. As much research has shown, if children lack secure attachment to their parents or other caregivers, they are destined to live lives fraught with interpersonal risks. Early attachments prepare girls for learning how to make and keep friends and to establish trusting relationships with adults.

In their young childhood and preteen years, children tend to base friendships on mutual interests and then, as the girls become adolescents, relationships become rooted more in shared feelings and understandings. Girls learn how to give and get support from peers and adults. But merely forming connections is not enough.

To establish and maintain necessary social relationships, girls must learn successful conflict resolution skills. This is complicated by their need to figure out how to negotiate their own unique sense of femininity and gender. As we described in chapter 2, Lyn Mikel Brown and Carol Gilligan[8] have found that a central part of adolescent girls' social development is a push-pull that girls feel in maintaining their existing relationships with others while also staying true to their own voices. Brown and Gilligan describe this experience of adolescent girls as being at a "crossroads" between moving away from being girls and moving toward becoming women while discovering and then navigating the societal pressures of girlhood and womanhood.

Girls' ability to stay connected while representing what is central to them—that is, maintaining their authentic selves—develops sometime during middle school as they begin to acquire more complex levels of perspective taking. When they have learned to assume the role of another person with whom they are engaged, and simultaneously hold their own perspective, they can begin to use both to appreciate others and to resolve contentious situations. These skills are crucial to resolving disputes and misunderstandings.

Task 5. Emotional Self-Regulation

Of course, relating to people, communicating well, and effectively managing academics all depend on girls' ability to manage themselves well. They must learn to regulate their increasingly complex emotional experiences, feelings, and impulses. This includes handling and expressing romantic feelings, sexual desires, and intimacy.

Developmental researchers have written about the complex landscape that girls must navigate when it comes to making decisions about which emotions they should express, and how and when they do it. Girls must contend with stereotypes of being too emotional and risk being labeled as "aggressive" when demonstrating feelings of frustration or anger.

When girls choose to express their emotions fully, particularly those emotions that may be thought of as "unfeminine," they risk pushing others away and damaging some relationships. All of these skills related to emotional self-regulation involve assessing, judging, and managing risk-taking while relating to others. This means girls must discover how to express their own feelings accurately while understanding and responding appropriately to the feelings of others.

Girls also need to become progressively more responsible as they acquire and learn to effectively handle new roles and responsibilities. This involves developing autonomy from people while staying connected to them. It also means honing their decision-making skills by learning to weigh both their emotional reactions and their intellectual understandings of themselves and others. In short, it means developing their emotional intelligence so they can know and master themselves while coming to understand and work well with others.

Task 6. Language and Literacy Development

Social relationships depend, in large measure, on learning to communicate clearly with others while maintaining self-regulation. Most girls are proficient at expressing themselves verbally by the time they reach middle school. But there is much more to learn. Becoming a successful teenager and adult depends on increasing levels of sophistication in engaging in conversations, understanding levels of discourse, and "reading" between the lines.

Girls also need to learn to write effectively. Whether speaking or writing, they must learn to draw on facts to make their case, to argue logically, and to successfully express their ideas. Their interpersonal power depends to some degree on acquiring an adult vocabulary and appreciating the effective and appropriate uses of slang. One central outcome of all this is gaining the confidence to speak in public to ever larger and more demanding audiences as well as to communicate in writing to different kinds of people.

Girls today are coming of age in an era in which social media and technology are quickly becoming the dominant modes through which we communicate. As girls navigate through social media sites such as Twitter, Facebook, Snapchat, and others, they are consistently bombarded with powerful messages about politics, race, gender, sexuality, and social class, just to name a few. In this day and age, it is not enough for girls to know how read and write when engaging with these mediums but to do so with a growing awareness of the public nature of their work. Not to learn this is to put themselves at risk of exposure and even exploitation.

One of the tasks of adolescence, then, is to be able to examine media with a critical eye in terms of how girls and women are portrayed, while also learning how to effectively communicate their ideas through various technologies and social media. Young women who are part of a marginalized group because of their race, ethnicity, class, or other relative difference face additional layers of complexity when navigating the ways they both are allowed and expected to portray themselves.

All girls and women must do this in a virtual world that can be particularly vitriolic toward their sex. Women who present their ideas online, be they bloggers, academics, gamers, or journalists, face far more harassment and abuse than men do – and often of a harsher and more threatening type.[9] Young women who participate in social media must develop skills that support them in navigating through and deciding how to respond (or not) to this common backlash.

Task 7. Physical-Athletic Development

Of course, all the development girls are undergoing within their minds and hearts takes place within their growing bodies. To become fully competent, they need to sharpen their fine and gross motor skills, increase their coordination, and continually maintain their overall fitness. They need to gain an increasing sense of strength and self-control. Physical development also requires that girls learn to adjust to their sexually maturing bodies while discovering their sexuality.

Though not all girls are athletes, they all need to work on their athletic skills, including disciplined training. Many care about athletics and must work to become competent in individual or team sports. Whether or not they are athletes, girls must come to terms with competition (which is also an important part of social development and acquiring a sense of competence), and learn to collaborate effectively with teammates.

Thanks in large part to the passage of Title IX in 1972, adolescent girls today grow up in a time where their athletic pursuits are encouraged, and most can take advantage of athletic opportunities that were not previously available. Research has found that girls' participation in team sports not only increases their self-esteem but also contributes to the development of more supportive peer relationships, stronger social skills, and higher academic achievement.[10] Girls' participation in organized sports is also an important vehicle for developing leadership skills. Active involvement fosters determination, self-discipline, time management, and sensitivity to the needs of others.[11] All of these elements are skills that help girls along a positive developmental trajectory.

However, even while the landscape is improving in terms of opportunities for girls to participate in sports and to accept all kinds of bodies, our society is still bombarded with unattainable expectations for women's appearance. Ultra-thin models and Photoshopped images of celebrities surround us. Magazine covers, billboards, TV commercials, and movies communicate to girls which forms of beauty are valued in our society, leaving out girls who may not possess the traits of thin bodies, straight hair, and lighter skin.

Girls are susceptible to accepting these images as reasonable standards by which to judge themselves. Physical development, therefore, is closely linked with identity development. Ideally, part of a young woman's growth includes the ability to accept and love her body and to separate her self-worth from how closely her appearance adheres to an idealized conception of the female form.

Task 8. Identity Development

Becoming one's own self involves coming to terms with multiple layers of identity. Girls have to discover who they are and to become comfortable with it. This is a complex and challenging undertaking, as people add to and change some aspects of their identities from the time they become cognizant of themselves as individuals to the time they die.

Adolescence is the time when girls first become acutely aware of themselves as individuals, separate from their families, and begin to craft who they want to be. They must learn and then come to terms with the fact that they have multiple identities; they are girls of a certain race and class, of a certain ethnicity and family history, of a certain religion or ideology, of a certain set of skills and challenges. Each of these identities becomes more or less salient depending on the social contexts in which they find themselves.

Learning to manage multiple identities, that is, knowing what to put forward and what to keep in the background under what circumstances, as well as learning to collaborate with people with different multiple identities, is a major dimension of situating oneself comfortably in the world. Indeed, developing positive feelings about the various dimensions of their identity is central to girls' ultimate happiness. Developing a sense of individuality through them and as well as a sense of connectedness to others who are developing their own sense of individuality through their own identities is one of the fundamental challenges girls face as they go through school.

GREAT LESSONS AND STRONG RELATIONSHIPS FOSTER GIRLS' DEVELOPMENT

These eight developmental tasks make tremendous demands on girls as they grow up. It is our job as parents and educators to guide and assist them on their journey to being capable, confident adults. The stories that the teachers and students tell about their most memorable lessons share the quality of helping girls' developmental growth in one or more of the eight areas.

Given the levels of support children need as they learn and grow, it isn't surprising that such a relatively large portion of the girls in our study name their teachers specifically, more than any single type of lesson or style of teaching, as central to their learning. Developmentally, girls need strong, caring connections with at least some teachers to bind them to work and school as well as to foster their social development more broadly.

Girls need to trust adults enough to be able to discover their own voices, test limits safely, and learn that they can have some reasonable degree of influence over their environments. To grow academically they also need at least some teachers who are excited by their subjects and some too who know their academic areas so deeply that they model for students what knowing means.

Developmentally, girls need to form intimate relationships not just with adults but also with peers: to learn to work and play with them successfully and to figure out how to manage the ups and downs that are an inevitable part of any friendship. Girls' participation in team projects, group activities (including whole-school field days), outdoor explorations, and adventures where they must depend on each other to learn and to succeed clearly foster their interpersonal skills and help them build multidimensional relationships with each other. These also enhance their physical development: girls love the challenge of rope courses, outdoor orientations, and other "Outward Bound" kinds of activities they experience in some schools.

Meanwhile, the discussions, debates, and collaborative activities girls prize foster their language development and help them learn how to influence their peers and gain confidence around engaging in public discourse.

Because such work always involves figuring out how much to say, how much to dominate, and when to accede, when to follow, and when to lead, they also help girls hone their social development and their self-management skills.

Girls' academic development, as well as their "learning to do school," is clearly fostered by several of the highly regarded kinds of lessons we discerned in both the girls' and teachers' narratives. Lessons that are clear, orderly, and build on each other bolster girls' understanding of disciplinary structures and ways to master them by promoting learning how to learn. Hands-on and project-based lessons require them to experiment and experience firsthand how to construct knowledge as well as to learn how knowledge is constructed.

Such experimentation promotes cognitive development. As cognitive psychologist Kurt Fischer is fond of saying, "Brains grow by being stretched; the more they are used the more capacity they develop,"[12] a sentiment strongly supported in Lise Elliot's work on brains and gender.[13]

Finally, lessons that enable girls to connect with topics they care about deeply do more than engage them actively in the subject; they can also foster their moral development. Whether they explore the plights of girls and women across the globe, find ways to improve recycling within their schools, lobby local politicians about the quality of their local lake as a habitat for wildlife or national politicians about the need to curtail climate change, they are sharpening their understanding of what they value and finding ways to influence others about it. In the process, girls also are clarifying their own senses of self; they are working on their identity development.

These opportunities for both moral and spiritual development are furthered when their teachers ask big questions about what girls value, about how people make meaning of their lives, about how to come to terms with the evil they see or read about every day. When girls can debate about these kinds of issues in lively and challenging ways, they are helped to learn who they are while coming to know and appreciate who their classmates are as well.

Of course, most effective and motivating lessons enable girls to work on several developmental tasks at once. Readers who skim back through the examples we have given in chapters 2, 3, and 4 will discover how well the skills, knowledge, and caring of teachers, the qualities of lessons, and the kinds of activities we identified all provide pathways for helping girls master them.

We have selected three examples that demonstrate the direct way academic lessons can help girls in multiple areas of development. In the first story, Ms.

Vaughn, a high school teacher, captures how her lesson can promote moral and language development as well as cognitive growth:

Environmental Impact Project

I co-teach a semester-long environmental science and policy course for 11th- and 12th-grade students. In this course, we have had one to two major assignments each semester that ask students to carefully examine a specific way in which they or their school impacts the environment (such as water use, transportation, electricity use, etc.), quantify their impact, and come up with a specific proposal to improve [the situation]. . . . These projects have been excellent learning experiences for the students. They get to choose a topic that is interesting to them and study it deeply enough to understand the many environmental impacts of the activity (such as the impacts of driving cars, maintaining athletic fields, installing solar panels at the school). They gain an awareness of the many ways in which their lifestyles impact the environment. Most students have never been asked to think about environmental impact in this way, and they are often surprised to learn about their individual roles, and how easy it is to make important changes. They get excited about what they learn, share it with their friends and family, and also feel pride and accomplishment when their work results in a change at the school.

From a developmental perspective, the girls' moral beliefs guide their individual selections of topics. They must think about the personal and societal impact of the issue they have picked. Then, using the science they are learning, they are asked to develop written arguments to effectively persuade school authorities to alter school practices.

In the next example, Cynthia, an eighth grader, discusses the powerful influence her seventh-grade life science class had on her:

Taking Learning in Our Own Hands

I am a very academically motivated girl. I excel in all classes, but the class that motivated me to set such high standards was my seventh-grade life science class taught by Ms. Landry. It was not only the teacher that motivated me but it was also the method of teaching she brought. This particular teacher would metaphorically dangle a star above our head and our job was to do our best to reach it. Every time we had Ms. Landry we would do lab. However, it was not the lab that produced a sense of motivation and interest in me, but it was what the lab taught us. A typical lab in Ms. Landry's class had structure. The structure goes as follows: introduction, hypothesis, materials list, procedure, accept or reject your hypothesis, conclusion, and questions. Ms. Landry gave us the guidelines and we received the responsibility of creating our own introduction, hypothesis, etc.

Because we were able to have the responsibility to take learning into our own hands, I was able to create my own experiments, questions, and answers. I was able to discover information on my own and learn to answer my own questions. Along with learning new concepts, I was able to learn the importance of critical thinking and individuality. Now in eighth grade I have moved beyond just the classroom and taken that self-reliance I learned last year into my own hands. I am an extremely ambitious girl with a dream to become a pediatric orthopedic surgeon specializing in engineering. This way I will be able to create my own healing techniques and rehabilitation apparatuses to provide for my patients in need of medical attention. I hope to one day create a new method of healing that will be faster and prevent further injuries.

Ms. Landry's teaching fostered Cynthia's cognitive, academic, and identity development. Challenging her to create, develop, and execute her own experiments enabled her to try out ideas, implement them, and then experience the results as feedback about her hypotheses; it actually helped her develop her own knowledge—to construct her own understandings. By Cynthia's own testimony, this process not only taught her the focal concepts of the course but also sharpened her critical thinking.

The way Ms. Landry structured the class also strengthened Cynthia's self-confidence as well as her sense of herself as a budding scientist with a dream of becoming a physician. Teaching like this not only helps girls learn subject material but also imagine themselves and their futures in bigger, more exciting ways.

In the last example, Grace, a high school student, writes about the important effect a school trip had on her entrance to a new school. In a very straightforward fashion she reveals how the school's efforts to orient new students made her feel much more comfortable and connected to the school.

Outdoor Education Trip

I came to [this school] in seventh grade and I was very nervous. All of my friends were going to the public middle school for my district, and I was the only one going to an all-girls school. The seventh grade was going on a class trip called Outdoor Ed. Outdoor Ed was a bonding experience for everyone. At first, I did not want to go. I was terrified because I knew no one, and I was going to be in a cabin with girls who had been at the school since lower (elementary) school. I begged my parents to let me skip, but they told me that I would have a great time once I went. My class went to Outdoor Ed and on the bus I sat with my mentor, whom I became good friends with. Everyone talked on the bus and I started meeting everyone; it felt great! I started talking to a girl on the bus, who I found out knew one of my family friends. Once we got to Outdoor Ed, I went to my cabin and all of the girls were very welcoming. I talked to all of them and had some of the nicest conversations that I will remember. The girl on the bus who knew my family friend was also in the cabin next to mine. All of the girls I met would hang out with me during the different activities throughout the two days. From dinner to s'mores by the fire and long chats, I knew that this trip was worth it. Although I was very nervous to go on the trip, I am thankful that I did because I met some of my best friends on Outdoor Ed and without them, I wouldn't have nearly as many memories at my school as I do now. I am thankful that [my school] encouraged all of us to go on the trip and bond because it is a great feeling to meet new friends.

Other narratives tell similar stories of the importance of outdoor education adventures, particularly for new students. They often included repelling challenges and rope courses that teams of girls had to accomplish together. Girls reported that these physical adventures fostered "safe" risk-taking that tested their endurance, helped them overcome their fears, and fostered bonding within the class. Such curricula promote girls' social, emotional, and physical development in ways that also help them move forward successfully as a class new to the school.

Having read through our analyses of narratives about memorable lessons and effective teachers and seen how well they foster all eight dimensions of girls' development, it would be reasonable to wonder how gendered they are. We take up this vital question in chapter 6.

KEY IDEAS

We describe eight major areas of adolescent development:

- Cognitive and academic development: Mastering "The Lesson" and learning to learn
- Mastering "The Strategy" for success as a student: Learning how to navigate the social, emotional, and organizational challenges of school
- Moral and spiritual development
- Social development
- Emotional self-regulation
- Language and literacy development
- Physical-athletic development
- Identity development

While both boys and girls must grapple with these tasks, there are unique aspects of each related to girls' gender and identity as young women. We take these up in chapter 6.

Effective and engaging lessons not only impart content knowledge but also help students develop in one or more of these areas.

Strong relationships with teachers and peers are also central to girls' personal growth and development.

NOTES

1. Dewey, John. *Democracy and education.* New York, NY: Free Press, 1966; Piaget, J. *The child's conception of the world.* Lanham, MD: Littlefield Adams, 1951; Vygotsky, Lev. "Interaction between learning and development." *Mind and society.* Cambridge, MA: Harvard University Press, 1978: 79–91.

2. THE MAKER: An aspect of teaching focuses on the pleasure that comes from building and creating a product. Students who take on the identity of makers like to explore, tinker, and collaborate to create innovative new machines, models, and materials.

3. Honey, Margaret., and David E. Kanter. *Design, make, play: Growing the next generation of STEM innovators.* New York, NY: Routledge, 2013; Halverson, Erica R., and Kimberly Sheridan. (2014). "The maker movement in education." *Harvard Educational Review 84,* no. 4 (2014): 495–504; Kafai, Yasmin B. "Learning design by making games." *Constructionism in practice: Designing, thinking and learning in a digital world* (1996): 71–96; Maker's Movement. http://makerfaire.com/maker-movement/.

4. Raider-Roth, M. B. *Trusting what you know: The high stakes of classroom relationships.* San Francisco, CA: Jossey-Bass, 2005; Reichert, M., and Hawley, R. *I can learn from your boys as relational learners.* Cambridge, MA: Harvard Educational Press, 2014.

5. Thompson, Michael, with Teresa Barker. *The pressured child.* New York, NY: Ballantine Books, 2004.

6. Havighurst, Robert J. "Research on the developmental-task Concept." *The School Review* 64, no. 5 (May 1956): 215–223; Fischer, Kurt W., and Arlyne Lazerson. *Human development: From conception through adolescence.* Freeman, 1984; Steinberg, Lawrence. *Adolescence,* McGraw-Hill, 2014; https://www.bestbeginningsalaska.org/activities-resources/child-development-areas; http://teachingcommons.cdl.edu/tk/modules_teachers/documents/5dimensionsdoc.pdf; http://hrweb.mit.edu/worklife/raising-teens/ten-tasks.html.

7. Simmons, Rachel. *The curse of the good girl: Raising authentic girls with courage and confidence.* Penguin, 2009.

8. Lynn Mikel Brown, and Gilligan, Carol. "Meeting at the crossroads." Cambridge, MA: Harvard University Press, 1992.

9. Fenaughty, John, and Niki Harré. "Factors associated with distressing electronic harassment and cyberbullying." *Computers in Human Behavior* 29, no. 3 (2013): 803–811; Henry, Nicola, and Anastasia Powell. "Beyond the 'sext': Technology-facilitated sexual violence and harassment against adult women." *Australian & New Zealand Journal of Criminology* 48, no. 1 (2015): 104–118.

10. Pedersen, Sara, and Edward Seidman. "Team sports achievement and self-esteem development among urban adolescent girls." *Psychology of Women Quarterly* 28, no. 4 (2004): 412–422.

11. Hart, Lawrence, Juneau Mahan Gary, Christie Creney Duhamel, and Kimberly Homefield. "Building leadership skills in middle school girls through interscholastic athletics." *Greensboro, NC: ERIC Counseling and Student Services Clearinghouse. ERIC ED* 479832 (2003).

12. Fischer, Kurt. "Mind, brain, and education: How cognitive & neuro science can inform educational practice" (paper presented at the Annual Round Table of the Center for the Study of Boys' and Girls' Lives, Bryn Mawr, PA, 2008).

13. Eliot, Lise. *Pink brain, blue brain: How small differences grow into troublesome gaps—and what we can do about it.* Oneworld Publications, 2010.

Chapter 6

Gender in the Classroom

In chapters 1 to 5, we have shared what we learned from girls and their teachers about motivating lessons, engaging approaches to teaching, and the importance of deep relationships. We have explained the connections between adolescent development and great lessons. Astute readers have likely been asking themselves: "Are these findings truly gendered?" "Don't boys value relationships as much as girls?" Our answer is largely: Yes! While we did not study boys, our colleagues Michael Reichert and Richard Hawley[1] did, and the findings in their book, *Reaching Boys, Teaching Boys,* correspond very closely to ours.

In this chapter we first look at why the way we typically think of boys and girls at school is outdated and problematic. We show how common assumptions about girls' and boys' abilities are actually false and damaging to their schooling experiences. We then recommend a much more nuanced and, we believe, useful and effective way to think about gender at school.

This book is about our study of girls in girls' schools. We are no way implying, however, that girls categorically learn in different ways than boys do. In fact, based on our research and a large body of supporting evidence, we reject entirely the notion of there being a "girl brain" and a "boy brain" when it comes to learning. Part of what inspired us to write this book was our dismay with widespread notions regarding sex-based differences in how students learn and about the purported existence of teaching techniques that cater to brains that come from either "Mars or Venus."

Yes, bookstores contain many guides that claim to have uncovered sex-based brain differences in learning styles. The authors of these works argue for what they claim are the best brain-based strategies for teaching boys or girls. A large body of scientifically rigorous research, however, refutes claims of any reliable, broadly applicable sex-based difference in how students prefer to take in information and learn. We'll say that again: *most research shows that there are no significant sex-based differences in how boys and girls learn.*

In our study of students and teachers in girls' schools, we found that the girls and their teachers generally described the same elements that make lessons exciting and motivating as the boys and their teachers in our colleagues' study did. Again, we certainly are not arguing that there are no differences between boys and girls. However, the reality is that while boys and girls are different in many ways, there is little credible evidence that their *brains* and *learning styles* fundamentally differ.[2]

That is not to say that gender is not incredibly important. Almost universally, the first question anyone asks when someone has a baby is: "Is it a boy or a girl?" Gender is a central, perhaps *the* central, identity shaping an individual's life from day one—or even earlier if parents chose to know their infant's sex in utero.

All societies have deep and abiding gendered behavioral expectations for children. Boys and girls tend to wear different clothes, have different hairstyles, and be given different toys to play with. In the United States, this trend has been accelerating in recent years.

In the 1970s, a much smaller percentage of toys sold in America were directly marketed to either boys or girls[3] compared with today. Similarly, clothing and hairstyles were far more gender neutral than they are now. Walk into a Toys "R" Us today, and you will find different areas devoted to boys and girls featuring vastly different kinds of toys. You will find the same segregation in the children's departments of clothing stores. And when the retailer Target decided in 2015 to stop identifying toys, bedding, and other children's items by gender there was an outcry by many who felt passionately about the need to enforce these divisions.[4]

In addition to gendered norms for what children play with and how they dress, we have many gendered behavioral expectations for children. We tend to expect boys to be very active, loud, and rowdy. We tend to assume that girls will be quieter, nurturing, and focused.

Minor differences in averages between the groups (boys on average are slightly more physically active than girls, tend to throw balls farther, and the like) lead to sweeping generalizations despite the fact that individual boys and girls fall along a wide and overlapping range of what is normal.

People both notice and are told about minor differences in the averages between the groups and this then tends to reinforce their own expectations. When grandma sees one toddler grandson about to jump off the kitchen table she is likely to say, "He's such a boy!" When his twin brother is sitting quietly in the corner looking at a book, she is unlikely to make the same remark.

There is also a certain amount of self-confirmation and regulation that happens with stereotypes. If six out of ten boys in a group are jumping around and playing superheroes, the other four boys in the group are more likely to go along and try to be interested in those activities as well—even if they would rather be reading or drawing.

Years of research has shown that brains exhibit great neural plasticity; that is, the ability to change over time based on external stimuli. This means that male and female brains often do begin to differ over the course of a lifetime based on different behaviors, actions, and lessons boys and girls repeatedly experience or engage in.

The result is that minor average differences in infants' brains, coupled with at times extreme differences in what boys and girls are exposed to, can lead to differences in brain development, some of which may be gendered. Neuroscientist Lise Eliot[5] explores these differences that emerge from the intersection of nurture and nature in her book *Pink Brain, Blue Brain*.

However, even with the existence of neural plasticity and the divergence that may emerge in many boys and girls and men and women over time, the way they learn best still has not been shown to be meaningfully different. Indeed, in hundreds of studies on sex differences, conducted over many years, few significant differences have been found.[6] As Eliot explains, there is "surprisingly little solid evidence of sex differences in children's brains" despite the existence of external behavioral differences.

Identifying (and being identified) as a boy or girl or as a man or woman is a huge part of every person's life experience. Like race, gender is a component of who we are that affects how others see and judge us as well as how we make sense of the world and our place in it. From a very young age, children recognize gender in themselves and others and it shapes what they do and how they think.

Thus, we do not dispute the importance of gender; of having a sense of self that is connected to being a boy or a girl (or to having a sense of gender fluidity). Quite the contrary, since gender is such a central part of who we all are, we think it needs to be discussed and explored in schools and society more often, and in much more sophisticated ways, than it currently is.

The interconnected influence of innate biological factors and socially influenced cultural factors affect us every day: in the types of games we play, in our tastes in reading and clothes, in the language we use, and in myriad other aspects of our lives. In school, it affects the choices students make about what to read and which classes to take, what games to play, how they think about themselves and their abilities as learners, and what they imagine their futures will be. It affects equally how parents, other children, and teachers view and interact with them.

So, yes, certainly there are differences to be found across groups of boys and girls. Go to an elementary school playground and you'll probably find more boys engaged in large-group, active play (though there will be plenty of girls in the mix as well).[7] You will probably see more boys in detention. There will be many more girls signed up for ballet after school and many more boys in karate.

These differences, though absolutely important to children's development, are highly socially influenced and largely contextual. The differences vary from schoolyard to playground to street to home. Go to a neighborhood full of children and many of the separations one observes in the school yard disappear.[8]

GENDER AND LEARNING

While such contextually shaped differences in boys and girls are important, they don't mean that male and female children categorically learn in different ways. Indeed, a preponderance of evidence shows that the capacity of boys and girls to learn, the ways that their brains function at the neurological level, and how they mentally develop are not very different at all.

One can be forgiven for finding it hard to believe that girls and boys generally learn in the same ways. We are inundated with messages that they are fundamentally different creatures. These messages are found on TV and in the movies, in newspaper headlines, on talk shows, and in the comments of parents at the playground.

There are best-selling books based on the alleged fundamental differences between boys' and girls' brains and learning styles. Take this quote from *Strategies for Teaching Boys & Girls*[9] by an author who has made a career of stressing boy-girl differences. In it, Michael Gurian and his colleagues sum up the general position that girls and boys have different brains and different ways of thinking and learning.

> Exciting research into the living brains of males and females has shown us not only that boys and girls are different at the organic level but also that how they learn includes many differences, from the day they are born.[10]

Unfortunately, Gurian makes claims such as these without providing references to back them up. While he offers a few references to works that were influential in helping him develop his directives for schools, he does not provide a list of scientific citations upon which he draws these bold conclusions.

Leonard Sax, another prominent author who endorses brain-based differences and gender-based teaching, similarly makes bold claims without providing research evidence to back it up. For example, in his very influential book, *Why Gender Matters*,[11] he argues that a tomboyish girl "probably has more in common with [a very feminine girl] than she has in common *with her brother or any other boy* [emphasis added]."

Sax is arguing that two very different girls are going to have more in common with each other than they are with any boy. This is a radical—and ultimately unsupportable—statement. On almost any of the hundreds of variables researchers have measured comparing boys and girls, the *within-group* differences between girls (or between boys) are far wider than the separation between the averages of the two groups.[12]

Though Sax makes a point in his book that he will provide citations and evidence to back up all of his claims, there are many important statements, such as the one discussed previously, for which he provides no supporting evidence. What is more, even the research studies he does cite are frequently problematic.

One of the main claims in Sax's book is that girls hear better than boys do and that this has serious implications for their experiences in school and how they should be taught. He cites several different studies of auditory processing and tone sensitivity, but, when one *actually reads the sources* he is using, one finds that he is cherry-picking results, making connections the studies do not support, and even misinterpreting or erring in what the articles actually say.[13]

Authors like Sax and Gurian go out of their way to insist that they are not trying to limit or pigeonhole boys and girls, but the overall message of their books is that boys and girls are vastly different when it comes to learning. A teacher or a parent should realize (so their books suggest) first, that there are essential differences in boys' and girls' brains and, next, that these differences have serious implications for how they should be taught.

A careful reading of the evidence Gurian and Sax use to support their assertions reveals that they tend to both overstate small differences and to misrepresent data. A fair-minded, broader reading of the research literature strongly suggests that claims of differences *at best* underappreciate the similarities of boys and girls.

Decades of research on boys and girls and how they learn, process information, and grow intellectually have found no consistent, statistically significant differences between them. Those who promote boy and girl learning styles most often base their arguments on studies that find minor average between-group differences in girls and boys.

The problem with building an argument on such differences is that those who do so ignore the actual distribution of findings across the two groups. When the averages in each group are relatively close, the results from all of the subjects in the two groups tend to fall along strongly overlapping bell curves. This is the case in practically every study of boys and girls where some amount of difference is found.

To explain this in more concrete terms, we'll use height. Men are, on average, taller than women, but of course adults of both sexes grow to a wide range of heights. Thus, while the average height of men in the United States is roughly 5'9", and the average height of women is roughly 5'4", most men and women will either be shorter or taller than those heights.

Height differences across populations fall along a normal distribution and form bell curves; the highest point of the curve reflects the median height. Half of the population would fall along each half of that median. If you chart the bell curve of men's heights and women's heights on the same graph, you will find a large overlap. There are plenty of men who are less than 5'9" tall and plenty of women who are taller than 5'4". A very small number of men would be on the very farthest right end of the graph, representing the very tallest of the tall heights (in this case approaching 8 feet). Similarly, the extreme end of the left side of the graph would include a handful of women. The, middle portion of the graph, however, would include both men and women because it represents the substantial range of heights that they share.

When we say, "Men are taller than women," we mean that their average or median height is greater, not that every man is taller than every woman. Imagine that we drew a line between the median heights of men and women on a graph, say at around 5'6½", and everyone on the left side of the bell curve had to shop for clothes in a women's store and everyone on the right could only go to a men's clothing store. Obviously, there would be a lot of people unhappy with their clothing options.

To reiterate, men and women's height differences are statistically significant though there is great overlap among them. When you start to look at distributions of mathematical ability or age of speaking first words, or expressions of empathy or developing fine motor skills or hundreds of other measures, the differences—again even when statistically significant at all—are almost always very slight and not useful for making assumptions about individuals.

Sadly, this reality doesn't stop people from looking at a slight statistical difference between boys and girls and declaring that boys are a certain way and girls are another. The implication of such an assertion is that almost all of the individuals in each group do something in a way that closely resembles others in their group. What happens, then, to anyone who falls along the opposite sex's side of the bell curve? Too often the implication is that something must be wrong with that person.

The SAT provides another useful example of the overstated absurdity of many claims about gender differences. For decades the mean score of boys on the math portion of the exam has been statistically higher than that of the girls. A number of theories have been proposed to help explain this discrepancy, including the fact that a larger number of girls than boys (including girls who may not be college bound or taking advanced math classes) take the exam each year, yielding a lower average for girls as a whole.

Too often the simplistic takeaway from this mean difference in scores has been: "boys score higher on the SAT math exam than girls do." The reality is, once again, that when you look at a bell curve of the distribution of scores, you see that there is vast overlap in the scores of boys and girls.

We find it downright startling that anyone can look at the science on how girls' and boys' brains develop and learn and try to put them in two discreetly different camps. No one, we hope, would look at data from the SAT and say, "Well, boys scored higher on average than girls, so let's put all of the boys in the school in the advanced math class and all of the girls in the remedial one." But this is pretty much what the available literature on teaching boys and girls separately because of brain differences is trying to do: take the existence of a very small average difference between the two groups to justify putting girls and boys in two separate buckets when it comes to teaching.

Overlapping bell curves don't make good headlines. Many people prefer simple, clear-cut answers—especially ones that conform to their preexisting beliefs. Thus we "know" that girls talk sooner than boys, and boys are better than girls at spatial rotation tasks. Nuanced measures finding a slightly better performance by girls or boys *on average* too often result in a widespread belief that you shouldn't expect your young son to be talking yet or that there's no chance your daughter will be good at engineering.

This brings us back to Leonard Sax's assertion that when it comes to developmental measures—such as elements of hearing and sight—a girl is going to have more in common with *any other girl than with any boy*. For that to be true, the distribution of findings for boys and girls would have to form *completely* separate bell curves. That is just *not* the reality. It does no one, especially girls, any good to pretend that in learning they are separate species from boys; that they are utterly unlike each other.

When it comes to learning multiplication or comprehending the facts of a history lesson, there is no evidence that boys and girls should be in two different groups any more than children of different races should be. *That does not mean, however, that gender does not matter*. As we have noted, gender, like race—and other key aspects of an individual's identity—is very important to a person's experience both in and out of the classroom.

This means it is vital to consider gender in constructive ways when designing lessons—ways that do not limit any individual with biased assumptions. What we want to stress is that when teachers and administrators are thinking about their students' genders, they should be thinking about uncovering bias, dismantling stereotypes, promoting a healthy classroom culture, and building relationships with and among students. What they shouldn't do is make assumptions about whether any particular child is going to benefit from a particular pedagogical device or strategy solely based on his or her biological sex.

THE REAL POWER OF GENDER AT SCHOOL

Among the hundreds of narratives we received from girls about wonderful lessons, there were many that spoke directly to how gender affected their experience in the classroom. As we discussed in chapter 2, certain types of lessons were effective in part because of their relevance to the girls' identity as girls. The most obvious examples of this were found in lessons that addressed the study of women and girls explicitly, such as those focused on current events involving the experience of women refugees or those about the research of important female scientists. Teachers should look critically both at individual lessons and their curriculum as a whole, asking themselves if what they are teaching will resonate with all of their students.

This always means taking into consideration their students' genders. We were inspired by a recent news story about an 11-year-old Black girl, Marley Dias, who started a campaign to get books highlighting children of color as the main character donated to her school so that she didn't have to be always reading about "White boys and dogs." This student was able to voice her dissatisfaction with a curriculum that was ignoring her identity as a Black girl. She had a legitimate desire to see her experiences represented in the literature her class studied.[14]

Even when the subject matter of a particular lesson is not directly tied to a female protagonist in a novel or a particular woman from history, there are ample and, as our data suggest, necessary opportunities to make important connections to gender and to girls' senses of self. When a teacher sets out to teach in a way that respects students' identities and provides opportunities to help their academic and personal development, there will be authentic and personalized learning. This learning includes recognition of who the girls are and what they want from their lives.

Girls' identity *as girls* matters to them. They respond to opportunities to think about girls and women in their various subjects. They respond positively when teachers create safe spaces in which to discuss delicate topics such as those involving sex, violence against women, or the place of women in religion.

Despite such testimony, one might ask if such a focus could be counterproductive. Indeed, in discussing our research, we are often asked whether focusing on gender might actually represent a step backward given that girls and boys are now much more equal in their opportunities and prospects. Just as there are opponents of "PC culture" who argue that we should strive to be colorblind rather than acknowledge the unique experiences of people of color and the powerful ways that race and ethnicity affect our society, some people similarly argue that we should be "gender blind" and that pointing out that boys' and girls' lives are different may actually be regressive.

Such reactions are problematic in two ways. First, students are aware of their gender and that it affects them every day. Ignoring gender does not make it irrelevant; it only eliminates opportunities to address it constructively and use it to promote learning in the classroom. Second, much evidence suggests that we have a long way to go before girls and women have gained equality in our society—certainly in terms of pay and in obtaining leadership positions in business, politics, and beyond.

We launched our study to find out from teachers and girls what they saw as the most memorable lessons. We wanted to uncover the types of teaching that gets girls excited about learning. By and large, what we found was that what girls view as engaging and motivating lessons actually reflect good educational practice that would inspire any student. But, it also became clear that girls' identities matter and that good teaching includes an explicit gender consciousness.

By gender consciousness we mean possessing an active recognition of the ways that gender affects our lives. For teachers this means realizing that students have a sense of gender that guides how they interact with the world around them and that also affects how others respond to and treat them.

It also means recognizing that, along with race, ethnicity, religious background, sexuality, and socioeconomic status, gender exerts a powerful influence on the paths our lives take. Even now, as we move well into the twenty-first century, being a girl or a woman too often still means being subject to lowered expectations and double standards.

To engage and motivate girls fully, we need to address the challenges they continue to face. It should be a tenet of our educational system that we work to undo bias and inequality in the lives of all our students. For girls, this means addressing ongoing sexism and lack of equal opportunities they may face.

We write about these challenges with full understanding that they may not apply to every girl all the time—in fact, they likely do not. Girls in different parts of the country, with various racial, ethnic, and socioeconomic backgrounds, at different types of schools and with different home lives all have their advantages and challenges. However, all girls, no matter their circumstances, still tend to encounter two major barriers to academic success: negative stereotyping and overt harassment.

CHALLENGES GIRLS AND WOMEN CONTINUE TO FACE

Stereotypes are universal. There is no one who can be entirely free of harboring them and there is no group that escapes having some applied to it. That doesn't mean that we should stop striving to reduce their detrimental effects.

Stereotypes are likely a result of the human brain's attempt to make sense of huge amounts of information by employing overly simple categories in order to respond to the large numbers of different kinds of people we all encounter. Unfortunately, stereotypes can turn negative and limiting. What's more, they can be invisible, even to one's self.

Researchers at Harvard University using the *Implicit Association Test* have been able to demonstrate racial bias in laboratory experiments. This bias often exists even in people who emphatically deny harboring any preferences for Whites over Blacks and who are in fact, quite troubled to find that they exhibit them. In their book about stereotypes, two of the developers of the test, Mahzarin Banaji and Anthony Greenwald, write about how even best-selling author Malcolm Gladwell, whose mother is a multiracial Jamaican woman, discovered he had a pro-White bias. Of course, he found this very distressing.[15]

Taking part in a study is one thing, but one may ask if these stereotypes manifest themselves outside of the laboratory. The answer is without a doubt, yes. Study after study confirms that, while often slight or subtle, stereotyping permeates our society, often in harmful ways.

Many negative stereotypes about girls and women remain firmly in place. On both a conscious and subconscious level, people often expect women to be less capable and less intelligent than men, especially in mathematics and scientific fields. Often they are thought to have worse leadership skills[16] and to be overly and sometimes inappropriately emotional or abrasive.[17] Anyone who argues that such sexism ended years ago need only look at Corinne Moss-Racusin and her coauthors' 2012 study of gender bias in STEM careers.

In a randomized double-blind study ($n = 127$), science faculty from research-intensive universities rated the application materials of a student—who was randomly assigned either a male or female name—for a laboratory manager position. Faculty participants rated the male applicant as significantly more competent and hireable than the (identical) female applicant. These participants also selected a higher starting salary and offered more career mentoring to the male applicant. The gender of the faculty participants did not affect responses, such that female and male faculty were equally likely to exhibit bias against the female student. Mediation analyses indicated that the female student was less likely to be hired because she was viewed as less competent.[18]

It is important to underline the fact that female faculty members in this study were just as likely to be pro-biased toward the "male" candidate as their male peers. If you asked them if they were biased against women, they would undoubtedly argue that they are not. The professors in the study assumed that they were fairly assessing the "hirability" and salary worth of the candidate in front of them, regardless of whether the applicant had a male or female name. When their responses were analyzed, however, the imaginary candidates had far more success when they were presented as male. It is likely that most faculty members in this study feel strongly that it is important to increase the number of women who enter STEM fields. But when they were tested, their hidden biases emerged. It is not hard to imagine the ways that biases such as these compound over time to greatly affect girls' and women's experiences and ultimate success both academically and professionally.

The negative stereotyping and unequal treatment of girls in comparison to boys have been found in a number of different areas. Parents tend to speak to their sons more about money and finance than they do to their daughters—and trust them financially more as well.[19] Parents and teachers talk to girls differently about computers[20] and math[21] than they do to boys.

In one experimental study, mothers of 11-month-old boys and girls were asked how steep an incline their son or daughter would be willing to climb down.[22] On average, the mothers of boys thought their babies would make more attempts and climb down steeper ramps than did the mothers of girl babies. Across the findings, the mothers of boys consistently overestimated how well their sons crawl and how steep a ramp they would tackle, while the mothers of girls consistently underestimated their daughters' abilities. In reality, infants' motor skills do not differ by sex at that age.

In another study, this one involving men and women in advanced science courses in college, male students consistently overestimated how well their fellow male students were performing in the class and guessed that they had higher grades than their female peers who were actually performing and scoring better.[23] In this instance, the women in the study did not exhibit sex bias, ranking their classmates' performance fairly accurately regardless of sex.

One must ask what the long-term effects are of being consistently underrated (for girls) and overrated (for boys). Again, it is important to note that these biased actions are largely invisible—typically to the one making the sexist assumptions and often to the one on the receiving end of them as well. This invisibility makes negative gender stereotyping all the more insidious.

Equally distressing as the ongoing and widespread gender bias against women is the internal stereotyping that they do to themselves. There is strong research evidence showing that girls who internalize negative stereotypes about themselves do worse in areas in which they are expected by the stereotypes to do poorly. This is especially likely to happen when the part of a person's identity that is associated with a negative stereotype is "activated" or brought to their mind before a test.

Claude Steele, one of the foremost researchers on what is called "Stereotype Threat Theory" designed with his coresearchers a test to explore women's negative stereotypes about themselves and mathematics. In one experiment, a randomly selected group of women were told that the results of a difficult math test they were about to take showed clear gender differences. These women scored worse than a random group of women who were not told females tended to score poorly on the test. When girls and women internalize the idea that they won't be good at something because of their sex, it can become a self-fulfilling prophecy.[24]

In addition to the quiet sexism that often plays out due to stereotypes, girls and young women are frequently the subject of overt sexism and harassment. In a study we conducted in an elite private school, we saw such behavior firsthand when some boys at the school repeatedly degraded girls in the classroom and literally told them to hush when they tried to participate in class discussions. Teachers colluded in this behavior by simply not noticing it, though it was quite apparent to our observers. We have observed this type of behavior repeatedly in classrooms across a spectrum of schools.

Girls and women of color, and those who are set apart from the majority ethnically, religiously, or in terms of their sexuality or gender status too often face further hurdles of bias and harassment. Not only do girls of color report higher rates of sexual harassment and bullying in school than their White female peers but also stereotypes attached to girls of color as loud, unruly, aggressive, and hypersexual lead to a hyper-policing of their behaviors by teachers and administrators in an attempt to make them more "ladylike."

Recent reports by the African American Policy Forum and by the National Women's Law Center (NWLC), in addition to the NWLC's #LetHerLearn campaign highlight how girls who attend schools with zero-tolerance disciplinary policies often find themselves in a no-win situation. The zero-tolerance policies have little effect in stopping the harassing behaviors, and instead, the girls themselves are the ones who get in trouble and are often faced with suspension when they try to defend themselves.

Clearly, as a society we still have a long way to go to reach full gender equality. Our study suggests that acknowledging and honoring girls' gender in the classroom is one way to promote equity. This can be done by helping them think about what it means to be a woman in the twenty-first century and how their gender affects them and their interactions with others.

Our study demonstrates that talking about gender and its role in our society and girls' lives leads to better relationships, a deeper connection to classroom material, and stronger connections to school. This, in turn, should lead to greater success in their studies and beyond. It will benefit not only individual girls but also our society as a whole. In a truly equitable world we would have access to the participation, competencies, and skills of all members of our society. To accomplish this, classrooms need to become much more gender conscious and proactively support equality in expectations and opportunities for students.

THE NEED FOR GENDER CONSCIOUSNESS IN THE CLASSROOM

Over the years, we have spent a great deal of time in both coed and single-sex settings, and we have observed that schools, with some notable exceptions, tend to take one of two approaches regarding the gender of their students. Some try to ignore or erase its existence as much as they can. The other, less common approach we have seen is limited to certain single-sex schools and coed schools with single-sex programs that tout the importance of gender for the wrong reason: they claim to employ brain-based curricula that support how boys and girls learn and argue that they can apply specific pedagogical approaches benefiting that sex. We fully support differentiated instruction for different kinds of learners, but, as we have argued, there is no reliable evidence that any broadly applicable differences in how boys and girls learn exist.

There is another, more constructive way of approaching gender in schools. Gender is important and should be acknowledged and accounted for – not to put students in particular boxes but to better understand and support them as complex individuals. This can be accomplished by schools becoming responsibly gender conscious. In chapter 7 we explain more fully what we mean by gender consciousness and, using examples, show how it can be integrated into any subject.

KEY IDEAS

- There are no broadly applicable brain-based differences in how boys and girls learn.
- People who advocate for teaching to the boy or girl brain tend to take the existence of minor average differences between boys and girls to mean that the two groups are entirely separate.
- Gender does matter, but not as a way to know exactly how any individual child learns best.
- Gender is extremely relevant in our society, and bias and sexism against girls and women still exist.
- Teachers need to acknowledge the importance of gender (and other aspects of identity) in students' lives in and out of school.

NOTES

1. Reichert, Michael, and Richard Hawley. *Reaching boys, teaching boys: Strategies that work—and why.* San Francisco, CA: John Wiley and Sons, 2010.

2. http://languagelog.ldc.upenn.edu/nll/?p=166; Fischer, K. W.. "How Cognitive & Neuro Science Can Inform Educational Practice." Address to the Annual Round Table of the Center for the Study of Boys' and Girls' Lives, 2008. Available at: www.csbgl.org; Eliot, L. Pink brain, blue brain: How small differences grow into troublesome gaps and what we can do about it. Boston, MA: Houghton, Mifflin, Harcourt, 2010.

3. Sweet, Elizabeth. "Toys are more divided by gender now than they were 50 years ago." *The Atlantic* (December 9, 2014).

4. Rhone, Nedra. "Target's Gender Neutral Signage Is a Plus for Consumers." *Atlanta Journal-Constitution.* http://www.ajc.com/news/lifestyles/shopping/targets-gender-neutral-signage-a-plus-for-consumer/nnKWy/.

5. Eliot, Lise. *Pink brain, blue brain.* Houghton Mifflin Harcourt, Boston New York 2009.

6. Hyde, Janet Shibley. "The gender similarities hypothesis." *American psychologist* 60, no. 6 (2005): 581.

7. McGrath, Daniel J., and Peter J. Kuriloff. "Unnatural selection on the unstructured playground." *School Community Journal* 9, no. 2 (1999): 41–65.

8. See Barry Thorne's carefully observed seminal work, *Gender play: Girls and boys in school.* Newark, NJ: Rutgers University Press, 1999.

9. Gurian, Michael, and Kathy Stevens. *Boys and girls learn differently: A guide to teachers and parents.* San Francisco, CA: Jossey-Bass, 2010.

10. Gurian, Michael, and Kathy Stevens. *Boys and girls learn differently: A Guide to Teachers and Parents.* San Francisco, CA: Jossey-Bass, 2010.

11. Sax, Leonard. *Why gender matters: What parents and teachers need to know about the emerging science of sex differences.* Broadway Book, NY, 2005.

12. Hyde, Janet Shibley. "The gender similarities hypothesis." *American Psychologist* 60, no. 6 (2005): 581.

13. http://languagelog.ldc.upenn.edu/nll/?p=171. From the blog of Mark Liberman, Christopher H. Browne Distinguished Professor of Linguistics at the University of Pennsylvania.

14. Fish, Amy. "Making Afro-Urban Magic: Zetta Elliott discusses the barriers to black children's authors and writing the realities of black kids." *Transition* 121, no. 1 (2016): 70–80.

15. Banaji, Mahzarin R., and Anthony G. Greenwald. *Blindspot: Hidden biases of good people.* New York, NY: Bantam, 2016.

16. Johnson, Stefanie K., Susan Elaine Murphy, Selamawit Zewdie, and Rebecca J. Reichard. "The strong, sensitive type: Effects of gender stereotypes and leadership prototypes on the evaluation of male and female leaders." *Organizational Behavior and Human Decision Processes* 106, no. 1 (2008): 39–60.

17. Johnson, Stefanie K., Susan Elaine Murphy, Selamawit Zewdie, and Rebecca J. Reichard. "The strong, sensitive type: Effects of gender stereotypes and leadership

prototypes on the evaluation of male and female leaders." *Organizational Behavior and Human Decision Processes* 106, no. 1 (2008): 39–60; Snyder, Kieran. "The abrasiveness trap: High-achieving men and women are described differently in reviews." *Fortune Magazine* (2014); Heilman, Madeline E., Aaron S. Wallen, Daniella Fuchs, and Melinda M. Tamkins. "Penalties for success: reactions to women who succeed at male gender-typed tasks." *Journal of Applied Psychology* 89, no. 3 (2004): 416.

18. Moss-Racusin, Corinne A., John F. Dovidio, Victoria L. Brescoll, Mark J. Graham, and Jo Handelsman. "Science faculty's subtle gender biases favor male students." *Proceedings of the National Academy of Sciences* 109, no. 41 (2012): 16,474–16,479.

19. T. Rowe Price. Eighth annual parents, kids & money survey. Accessed March, 2016; Lynsey K. Romo & Anita L. Vangelisti, Money Matters: Children's Perceptions of Parent-Child Financial Disclosure. *Communication Research Reports* 31, no. 2 (2014): 58.

20. Cooper, Joel, and Kimberlee D. Weaver. *Gender and computers: Understanding the digital divide*. Mahwah, NJ: Lawrence Erlbaum Associates, Publishers, 2003.

21. Gunderson, Elizabeth A., Gerardo Ramirez, Susan C. Levine, and Sian L. Beilock. "The role of parents and teachers in the development of gender-related math attitudes." *Sex Roles* 66, no. 3–4 (2012): 153–166.

22. Mondschein, Emily R., Karen E. Adolph, and Catherine S. Tamis-LeMonda. "Gender bias in mothers' expectations about infant crawling." *Journal of Experimental Child Psychology* 77, no. 4 (2000): 304–316.

23. Grunspan, Daniel Z., Sarah L. Eddy, Sara E. Brownell, Benjamin L. Wiggins, Alison J. Crowe, and Steven M. Goodreau. "Males under-estimate academic performance of their female peers in undergraduate biology classrooms." *PloS One* 11, no. 2 (2016): e0148405.

24. Spencer, Steven J., Claude M. Steele, and Diane M. Quinn. "Stereotype threat and women's math performance." *Journal of Experimental Social Psychology* 35, no. 1 (1999): 4–28.

Chapter 7

Practicing Gender Consciousness

To create a gender-conscious, inclusive, and empowering institution, teachers and administrators must critically examine activities within the classrooms as well as the school environment as a whole. We provide several recommendations for becoming more gender conscious as an organization. We focus these suggestions on maximizing success and opportunities for girls but firmly believe that these strategies will be beneficial for all students within a school.

A useful first step for schools is to conduct what we call a gender audit. These audits can take many forms. We recommend some combination of a school-wide climate survey of teachers and students combined with focus groups and a review of school practices. The Center for the Study of Boys' and Girls' Lives (www.csbgl.org) has been using a reliable and valid Comprehensive Assessment of Student Life (CASL) for years. It has proved a very useful way to assess students' scores by gender, race, and social class on a set of dimensions ranging from students' perceptions of the degree of faculty support to their evaluation of stress and anxiety and peer relations. Other well-regarded comprehensive school climate surveys are readily available.

The goal of the audit is to get the opinions of students, teachers, and administrators regarding gender within the school community and to combine that with data on school leadership, grade point averages, extracurricular activities, and other measures of girls' involvement and success at the school. Here are some important questions for administrators and other school leaders to ask in an analysis of school practices and climate:

- What is the ratio of male to female teachers at this school?
- What are they teaching?
- What is the gender makeup of the administration?

- What are the course-taking patterns in high school of girls compared to boys?
- Are any girls experiencing harassment?
- Are girls' sports and any other gender-divided activities supported by the school community similarly?
- What are the common assumptions that teachers and students have about boys and girls in the school?
- Has the administration ever done focus groups with girls to ask how about their experiences in the school?

These questions should be asked about the boys in the school, too, if it is a coeducational school.

Some of the questions require only a quick look at school records to find answers. Others will require discussions and possibly surveys or focus groups. For example, determining if students are being harassed can be assessed only partially by school records of reported harassment. Administrators and teachers must talk to each other and to girls in small groups or through surveys to try to uncover bullying or harassment, which far too often goes unreported. The National Center for Safe Supportive Learning Environments has an excellent compendium of surveys that can be used to assess various aspects of a school's culture and the health and well-being of students.[1]

Collecting the data is not enough, of course. If a school discovers that its advanced math classes are highly skewed to male students or if girls' sports are largely ignored by the school community, the next difficult step is figuring out how to address the problem. We recommend a task force made up of students, teachers, and administrators that can come together with the goal of recommending action steps to improve girls' experiences at the school.

At the classroom level, there is much that teachers can do to incorporate positive gender consciousness. It begins with systematically acknowledging gender as something that affects students' lives both internally and externally. Being gender conscious as a teacher means understanding that gender is a salient part of students' identities and should not be something that limits their participation in the classroom or the possibilities for their futures. It means acknowledging that stereotyping and harassment exist and that it is imperative to combat them by bringing them out in the open and addressing them. It means offering opportunities to all students without making assumptions about what their abilities or interests are.

Gender matters to all individuals and is relevant in most interactions in our society. Of course, incorporating gender consciousness into one's classroom will mean different things depending on the grade level and subject matter taught as well as the gender composition of the class. In some cases, there are steps teachers should take depending on whether they are in a single-sex or coeducational classroom. Most of our recommendations, however, can be used in either setting. Here are some broad areas for teachers to think about and some specific examples.

CONSIDER THE PARTICIPATION OF STUDENTS IN THE CLASSROOM

Is there a gender dynamic contributing to some students not volunteering answers or participating in discussions? A great deal of research has shown that human perception can be flawed. This holds true in the classroom. While teachers may have a sense that girls are participating equally or feel that they know which students are asking the most questions, we find that it is a good idea to have one's lesson recorded or observed by someone taking notes to get a more accurate picture. Teachers can even enlist students as statisticians to track participation of classmates.

Teachers should be paying attention to where students sit if they are allowed to choose their own seats, which students volunteer to answer questions or pose their own, and how other students respond when their peers speak up. It is crucial that teachers determine if girls in their classrooms are being silenced or if they are silencing themselves.

While a classroom might have some very confident and outspoken girls, teachers need to be alert to the girls who do not feel that they may fully participate in the classroom. This silencing can be the result of poor relationships among boys and girls, but it can also result from the ways teachers ask questions and organize lessons. For example, teachers who ask questions of the entire class often elicit many more comments from boys. Teachers who go around systematically when questioning get much more balanced results.[2]

PAIR AND GROUP WORK: IS ONE SEX DOMINATING?

Teachers need to listen in when students work together in pairs or small groups. Are girls typically taking on the "secretary" or "notetaker" role? Sometimes a few boys will take over mixed-sex groups and dyads, though this is not always the case. It is important that teachers pay close attention to grouping patterns. Further, if students are working in teams, it is important to try out different patterns, sometimes giving students the choice of teammates and sometimes assigning them.

Teachers should be alert to which groupings are working best and which are problematic, not just in terms of student behavior and the students staying on task, but in terms of girls' participation and their ability to take on leadership roles within the group. Students can be asked to provide confidential feedback about their teams. Teachers can then use the data for finding the grouping that works best to be able to structure group work so that all students participate fully in the activity.

LESSON CONTENT

Teachers must ask themselves whether the experiences of women and girls are being represented in their lessons. No matter the subject, girls need to understand the participation and contribution of women in that area and to see themselves in any future role they may wish to pursue. Students should also be given opportunities to respond to world events, history lessons, literature analysis, art projects, and other assignments on a personal level. As we discussed in chapter 2, relevance is hugely important to girls. They should be encouraged to examine how their gender (as well as socioeconomic background, race, religion, and any other important aspect of their identities) informs their understanding of the subject matter.

To engage girls fully, teachers must provide safe spaces to discuss difficult or delicate subjects, particularly those involving sex, violence, and women's rights. Middle and high school students are capable of discussing and even debating controversial or charged topics, but frameworks for respectful listening must be established.

While we know that many girls thrive in single-sex environments, we do not believe that separation of the sexes for most education is necessary. However, when discussing sensitive topics in school, including sex education and discussions about the status and treatment of girls and women, there may be a place for segregating boys and girls and allowing them a chance to speak in single-sex groups.

Much of the work of creating a gender-conscious classroom will be done by the teacher beforehand in lesson planning. Much of it may also be invisible to the students. Teachers may be actively creating a gender-conscious classroom when they choose a theme for a lesson, arrange the desks in a certain way, encourage a particular student to speak up, and allow room for dissenting voices.

Students may never realize what strategies are at work. We do not feel that it is important to overtly remind students of their genders. They are well aware of it and most have been since they were toddlers. What it does mean is putting extra time and thought into how one organizes a lesson, structures a class discussion, selects texts, and dismantles negative stereotypes about what girls can and cannot do.

Here are some examples of what lesson plans for the gender-conscious classroom can look like. They are not intended to be step-by-step guides but rather ideas that may serve as inspiration for teachers as they examine their own curricula and pedagogy.

Tenth-Grade World History and English Literature Unit on World War I

A tenth-grade history teacher in a coeducational classroom is teaching the first lesson on a unit about World War I (WWI). The unit is designed to correspond to the students' English literature unit on twentieth-century British literature. It is the second semester of the school year and classroom routines are well established.

The teacher begins with a short lecture reintroducing how things stood in Europe geopolitically at the turn of the twentieth century. She asks the students questions about material they've previously covered, making sure to call on both boys and girls who raise their hands. Several minutes into the lesson, the teacher notices that one of her students, Jasmine, hasn't raised her hand at all during the lesson and invites her to participate.

She chooses not to put the student on the spot with a right/wrong question but offers a more open-ended question about a subject the class has discussed at length. "Jasmine, what can you tell me about British Imperialism during the reign of Queen Victoria?" Jasmine offers her thoughts on the matter, bringing up some of the points the class had debated a few weeks prior. The teacher builds on the issues Jasmine introduces and reminds the class of the multiple ways Queen Victoria influenced world history.

The teacher goes on to introduce the main historical figures the class will be studying as they learn about The Great War. In addition to world leaders and generals—all male—the teacher includes women important to this period, especially the critical role that female nurses played. She also introduces Dr. Elise Inglis, a Scottish doctor who worked on the front lines, and Flora Sandes, the only British woman to officially serve as a soldier in WWI.

In each day's lesson, the history teacher makes sure to teach not only about the major events—battles, treaties, advances in warfare—but also about the effects on the day-to-day lives of the citizens of the participating countries, noting the ways women participated and the ways that all of the citizens in the involved countries were affected by the war and related world events.

In their English literature class, the students will be studying poems from this period by both men and women. In a culminating project designed by the teachers together, the students will create wartime scrapbooks. They will choose six important dates between 1914 and 1918 and write a news article and corresponding diary entries for each date.

They are encouraged to base the diary entries on versions of themselves living approximately 100 years prior in the United States, England, or France. How would their lives be affected? How would their sex, race, or religion affect their experiences during the war? How would their families be affected?

The history teacher has incorporated gender consciousness into her lesson and the overall unit in multiple ways. She makes sure that all of her students are participating in class discussions and also brings Jasmine into the discussion when she seems reluctant to raise her hand to volunteer. She makes sure to do so in a way that does not put Jasmine on the spot.

In addition to discussing the most well-known historical figures associated with WWI, all of them male, the teacher makes sure to discuss groundbreaking and heroic women who participated both at home and on the front lines. The English teacher similarly made sure to include excellent examples of poetry from The Great War written by both men and women.

When students are discussing the poems, the sex of the poet is one of many facets of class discussion. The teachers encourage the students to think about how the poet's life may have influenced his or her writing.

The final project for the combined history/English unit includes an element of deep personal connection and relevance, requiring that students consider their lives today and how they would have been different a century prior.

Twelfth-Grade AP Physics Experiment about Mass versus Weight

The teacher begins the class with a brief discussion about an assigned lesson the students watched at home on their computers the night before. After watching, the students had to complete a problem set. If they had any questions or needed clarification about this lesson or the problem set, they e-mailed the teacher. Without noting who asked the questions, the teacher reviews answers and asks if anyone needs further explanation.

The teacher has found that when the students are able to send in their questions ahead of time—and anonymously as far as their peers are concerned—she tends to get far more participation than she had in years past when she had merely asked students to raise their hands in class if they were confused about something. Once the new material and homework has been reviewed, the teacher moves on to the day's experiment.

For this activity the teacher lets the students break into groups of four of their own choosing. In her ninth-grade earth science class she tends to put the students into pairs or groups herself to make sure no students are left out and that the very rowdy kids don't wind up all together, but she has found that her twelfth graders are good about getting into groups quickly and working diligently. In addition, whereas her younger students tend to segregate by sex or simply choose to work with their friends, her senior students are savvy enough to know that it's a good idea to be on a team with their peers who are strong academically.

Before passing out the experiment guide she asks the students to assign themselves numbers 1 through 4 in each group. At each step of the experiment, each person will have a particular role. In this experiment the students will be building a ramp and timing three different vehicles as they descend it.

The students have used power tools to build in AP Physics once before, so with a short reminder of the safety rules, the teacher sends them to the worktables in the back half of the room. The teacher has ensured by the way she wrote the experiment instructions that all four members of the group will share the work ahead. Previously, she had too often found that the boys tended to use the tools, and the girls almost invariably became the scribes in the group.

The teacher is constantly striving to communicate to all of her students that they are young scientists with unlimited potential. She works hard to create an environment in which all of her students feel included and able to participate. The teacher feels that she achieves many benefits with the "reversed classroom" approach to new material.

Though her school has been encouraging more girls to take AP Physics, the class still has a 2:1 ratio of boys to girls. In traditional lectures and problem set discussions, she has found that the female students can become quiet as a few outspoken boys dominate. With the reversed classroom lesson, all of the students have time to take in the material, work on the problems, and submit their questions for review. She similarly removes opportunities for a few students (most typically boys) to dominate by assigning roles in the experiment instructions.

The teacher goes out of her way to mention the work of both female and male physicists and engineers when she discusses the real-world applications of what the students are studying. On one wall of the classroom the teacher has a poster of the 2013 NASA astronaut class, which included for the first time an equal number of men and women.

For this teacher, gender consciousness manifests itself in the organization of her lessons more than in the content. Drawing on knowledge of how women are often marginalized in STEM classes, as well as on her own observations in her classrooms, she has structured her homework assignments, direct instruction, guided practice, and experiments so that all of her students are able and encouraged to participate fully.

Tenth-Grade Art Lesson on Perspective Drawing

The art teacher starts with a brief history of the use of perspective in painting, focusing on the Renaissance painter, sculptor, and engineer Brunelleschi. Using the room's SMART Board, he shows additional examples of the early use of perspective from Masaccio and other Renaissance masters. He intentionally includes the female Renaissance painter Sofonisba Anguissola among his examples. He then goes into a technical description of how to create the illusion of depth in drawing, introducing students to the concepts of vanishing points and horizon lines.

The teacher then shows examples of perspective in more recent art, not only pencil drawing and painting but also sidewalk art and graphic design, again including both male and female artists' work. The class has previously discussed the role of women in art—both as artists and subjects of art. The class also considered the reasons so few women were able to become professional artists until relatively recently.

After the lecture and some examples of how to find the vanishing point in a room, the teacher has the students get their drawing pads and rulers and sketch the classroom. After twenty minutes they have peer critique. The teacher has devised a rotating pairing system in which all of the students will critique one another by the end of the semester.

As the students pair off to give each other feedback, the teacher reminds them that a good rule of thumb is "two positives and a challenge." He walks around the room listening in on discussions and helping direct the students to give useful critiques. For homework, the students are instructed to draw their bedrooms using the elements of perspective drawing.

The teacher demonstrated gender consciousness in many ways in this lesson. He made sure to include both male and female artists in his examples. He has previously acknowledged and discussed with his students why so few professional artists were women historically. When his students paired up to give peer critiques, he made sure to monitor the discussions. He was alert to students who were either too overbearing and negative or those too reluctant to offer an honest assessment.

By rotating the class, the teacher made sure that students didn't work with their friends all the time. Finally, by having the students draw their own rooms as an assignment he is making the assignment relevant to their lives. Finally, he has set it up so students will be able to discuss how different students expressed their central identities.

Ninth-Grade French Lesson on Gender Pronouns

The students are in their second semester of French and have been introduced previously to the main French pronouns. The lesson today will go more in depth about gendered pronouns and especially about how they are used when referring to groups of men and women together or about people of unknown sex.

The high school the students attend requires two years of a foreign language: Spanish, French, or Mandarin. In the last few years, French has become more of a "girls" class as the teacher has had fewer and fewer boys enroll. To combat the notion that a language spoken by more than 200 million people should for some reason be identified with one sex more than another, the teacher begins every lesson with a brief film clip or song in French, almost always less than five minutes long. She selects news segments, children's shows, French versions of popular English songs and shows, YouTube videos, stand-up comedy, and more.

In addition to varying the type of media, she also includes segments from France, Canada, Haiti, Cameroon, and other French-speaking countries around the world. The students, new to studying French, do not understand most of what they hear, but the teacher nonetheless shows them "French in action" in as many contexts as she can. Her goal is to instill in her students the idea that French is a living language being spoken all over the world by myriad people, and is not simply a collection of lessons in a textbook.

The teacher also thinks very deliberately about the content of what she shows and who the speakers are. She pays attention to how many men and women are included in what she shows, as well as the races and ages of those represented.

The teacher frequently discusses her experiences growing up in France. She talks to the students about how their lives are the same and different from when she was a teenager several decades before in a foreign country. In the course of lessons on food vocabulary or formal versus informal forms of the address, the teacher will encourage the students to think about the ways that their lives and their language are rooted in a particular time and place.

Just as nationality, race, and socioeconomic status enter into the teacher's lessons about language, so too does gender. For example, she will point out ways that women and men sometimes use certain French words or phrases differently and encourages her students to think about why that is and whether it is problematic.

For the lesson on gendered pronouns the teacher begins by having the students talk and think about pronouns in English. With a little assistance, they are able to compile a list of the most common pronouns. The teacher then asks them about which pronoun they typically use when they do not know a person's sex. For instance, "If you see a doctor about that burn, make sure to ask *him(?)* if you should keep it covered." In this example, the teacher says that the sex of the doctor is unknown and asks the students if they should use "him" or not.

A discussion ensues, with most of the students saying that in English they would opt for the gender neutral (if grammatically incorrect) "them" in that case. Having reviewed pronouns in English and established the parameters of the debate about language, gender, and equality, the teacher moves on to French pronouns. She presents the standard French Academy grammar rules but points out common differences in usage in various French-speaking cultures. She also touches on the use of feminine versions of professions and titles. The class has a lengthy discussion about the pros and cons about various approaches.

The French teacher recognizes that our world is gendered and that language is a powerful force in our society. She encourages the active acknowledgement and discussion of the ways that language is constructed and the ways that we use it to reflect gender norms and divisions in the world.

Seventh-Grade Pre-Algebra Lesson on Ratios

The seventh-grade math teacher is introducing ratios to his class. He begins with a brief definition of what a ratio is and then asks the students to stand up and move around the classroom to compare different groups. In years past he has always used the ratio of boys to girls, but he has found his lessons more effective when he doesn't overtly separate the students by sex or emphasize their genders to them. Instead, he asks all of the students wearing blue jeans to go to one side of the classroom and those not wearing them to go to the other.

The teacher writes the ratio on the board, "16 students with blue jeans to 8 students without." He then has the students return to their seats and demonstrates how to reduce the ratio by the largest common divisor. After the students have taken notes on this, he has them stand up again. This time he asks students to separate based on if they are currently taking band, art, or drama as their elective. The students separate into three groups around the room and the teacher writes, "11:8:5" on the board. The students return to their seats and the teacher continues his lesson on three-part ratios.

At the end of the instructional portion of the lesson, the teacher asks the students to turn to a partner sitting near them and to take turns telling each other one important piece of information about ratios. The teacher uses this pedagogical technique frequently and the students are getting better at it. Doing this activity requires them to pay attention to the lesson, take good notes, distill what is most important, and communicate it to a classmate.

In the past, the teacher had gone around the room and called on students to provide the main takeaways, but he found that many of his students froze up. The activity works better in pairs, and when the students have been coached on how to do it. He is strict about the students only offering a single fact on each turn; otherwise he has found that some of his stronger students will repeat the entire lesson in one go.

After the students have reviewed the lesson in their pairs, they are given a worksheet on ratios for homework, which they begin to work on in the last few minutes before class is dismissed. As the students leave the classroom the teacher stands by the door, bidding them farewell and offering encouragement to each of them. "You rocked it today, Joel." "Thanks for asking that excellent question, Elle." "You were a great mathematician today, Chiara."

In this lesson, the teacher made a conscious decision not to single out the girls. He knows that as the girls approach adolescence many of them will begin to be less confident in class, particularly in math, and that they may have internalized a belief that they are just not good at it.

Instead, he purposefully chooses to have the students stand and mix themselves up for the demonstration in ways that blend the groups of boys and girls.

During the lesson, as he asked for volunteers to answer some of the sample problems he was writing on the board, he made sure to call on an equal number of boys and girls. He designed the reteaching segment so that the students were all required to participate equally, taking turns offering a single important takeaway about ratios.

Finally, the teacher interacted with all of the students as they left the classroom and made sure to give them all positive feedback, which is particularly important for his students, many of them girls, who have already decided that they aren't strong in math. His stated goal is for his students to achieve success in his classroom every day. Even if they are struggling with a concept or get things wrong on a test, he reminds them that working hard and trying again is always a victory.

This attitude is beneficial for all students, but particularly so for those who have math phobias or do not identify themselves as "math people." Too often this group includes a disproportionate number of girls. With subtle changes to the way he teaches and how he speaks with and interacts with students, this teacher is helping keep his reluctant math students, including the girls, engaged and enthused about their abilities in this field.

INTEGRATING GENDER CONSCIOUSNESS INTO THE CLASSROOM

These descriptions are meant to demonstrate the relevance of gender throughout the school day and across subject areas. Again, we do not believe that teachers need to address gender in every lesson, but over the course of a unit or year of study there are many occasions when the participation of women in historical events, the arts, or another field of study can and should be emphasized. If teachers want to make a big difference in girls' lives, they must work toward seamlessly creating an inclusive, unbiased, and supportive classroom that upends stereotypes and empowers them.

While teachers need not ask girls (or boys) to reflect on their gender identity daily, there are many occasions when teachers may have students think about how their lives have been shaped by certain events in history or what their lives may have been like had they lived in a different time or place. In addition, merely in the ways that teachers set up a classroom activity, arrange desks, or call on students to provide answers, they can encourage or discourage the participation of girls.

Finally, to maximize relevance, teachers should openly encourage students to bring their personal lives into their studies. Students do not exist in a vacuum while doing schoolwork. The world around them and their prior experiences all influence their participation and how they approach assignments.

Creating a gender-conscious school and classroom is not a onetime endeavor. Being gender conscious means creating an environment that consistently acknowledges the power of gender in our lives and makes space for students to discover how their gender affects them and their learning. It means confronting and hopefully dismantling internal and external stereotypes and biases. It means recognizing that there are innumerable ways for students to "do gender" and that we shouldn't force expectations upon any members of the school community.

Fostering gender-conscious classrooms also means recognizing that girls have other important social identities. Since they have racial and ethnic and social-class backgrounds that interact with their genders, it is important that teachers create environments in which girls can explore their identities, how they interact in different contexts, and how all of this affects them. Letting them explore their own histories in relationship to the topics under study is one very good way to do that.

More broadly, we should encourage girls to follow their own pursuits and permit their curiosity to develop and grow wherever it takes them (and in coed classes we need to do that with boys too). A few decades ago, many schools didn't even allow girls to take advanced math and science classes. Today, there is a growing national focus on the importance of having women enter STEM fields. Hopefully, in the future we will have gender parity across all academic fields, and all students will pursue the path and career best suited to them. A wonderful vignette from a high school student in our study describing an activity from her science class captures the kind of outcome we are advocating for all girls:

Women in Science and Engineering

One classroom experience that I felt especially engaged in was in an elective that I took in the WISE (Women in Science and Engineering) program at our school in my junior year. The class was called Projectiles. The day that

I especially liked was when I was working with my partner on our 5-foot tall trebuchet that we would design to launch [a] pumpkin [as far] as possible for a competition. Our teacher taught us on that day how to use the drill without puncturing a hole on any organ parts of our body. We were wearing goggles, measuring out inches, feet, and angles. There was sawdust everywhere and there was a fluster of activities that was fun and very engaging. I remember my partner and I especially had trouble with our angle measurement, and we ended up having to redraw and revise our models several times. But we were enthusiastic. We felt like we were six-year-old kids building houses with LEGOs and cards; only at that time we were experimenting with professional tools and making potentially destructive machinery.

It was a hands-on classroom experience like this that made me feel this is all what being in an all-girl environment is about. We can build and break things. We can map out plans, calculate measurements down to the hair, imagine and create according to whatever we envision, and not be underestimated because we are girls.

A NOTE ON MALE AND FEMALE TEACHERS

The data from our study did not reveal any consistent differences in the types of lessons male or female teachers described in their responses nor were students' responses about the lessons connected to their teachers' genders. However, that does not mean that the teachers' genders do not matter. Just as the girls' lives are affected by their gender, so too are their teachers'. Teachers, after all, are not robotic pedagogues; they are individuals with multiple identities and expectations and biases just like every other person.

As our study demonstrated, girls care about making personal connections with teachers. Indeed, forming connections with them seems half the battle in getting girls to actively engage in their studies. In gender-conscious classes, teachers need to carefully share relevant aspects of their own experiences about how gender shaped their career path or their understanding of a subject area.

Periodically, teachers need to find ways to acknowledge that their gender does affect their relationship with their students, just as their race, geographic background, and age may. One way to do this is by naming their own identity, for example, "As a Black man, my college experience was a certain way," or "as a woman who was an engineering major, I had the following experiences."

IDENTIFYING A GENDER-CONSCIOUS SCHOOL

Parents reading this are likely wondering whether the school their daughters attend (or where they were hoping to send them in the future) is gender conscious. They probably want to know how to determine if the school is committed to promoting girls' success or if it is rooted in outdated ideas about brain differences or complacent about pernicious stereotypes.

Evaluating a school's gender consciousness requires some legwork. We advise parents to speak to administrators and teachers about their views on how children learn. If they claim to know how to teach a "girl's brain," one should ask them what that means. Parents should try to spend time in the school if they can. How are students grouped in the classrooms? Is there a group of either boys or girls dominating class time?

Above all, we encourage parents to talk with their daughters. Ask them about their experiences at school. Look over their homework and lessons with them. Ask if they feel connected to the literature or history they are studying. Ask if they can see themselves as an engineer or author or pilot. If they say that math or science or any other subject just isn't for them, try to understand why they feel that way and help them find role models. Not every student will be interested in STEM fields for college or a career, but it is important to make sure that girls are not being denied access to those paths either overtly or subtly. Ideally, parents and educators will work together to acknowledge the powerful role gender plays in our society and in each individual's life while simultaneously confronting and thereby reducing sexism and negative stereotyping of girls.

KEY IDEAS

- Schools should conduct a gender audit of school climate and, if needed, form a task force of students and adults to address problems related to bias, stereotyping, harassment, and other unfair practices.
- At the classroom level, teachers should carefully examine student participation patterns, the dynamics of pair and group work, and their lesson content. Sometimes it is easier to do this by pairing up with other teachers and observing each other's classrooms.
- To make increasing the possibility of making a big difference in girls' lives, teachers should become gender conscious. Being actively gender conscious as a teacher means:

  - recognizing the importance of gender in student's lives;
  - confronting and dismantling biases, stereotypes, and harassment of girls wherever it emerges;
  - recognizing the multiple identities that students have and how those may intersect with gender in unique ways for different students; and
  - structuring lessons and interacting with students in ways that actively support and empower them to be successful across the curriculum.

NOTES

1 https://safesupportivelearning.ed.gov/topic-research/school-climate-measurement/ school-climate-survey-compendium. The National Center on Safe Supportive Learning Environments (NCSSLE) is funded by the U.S. Department of Education's Office of Safe and Healthy Students to help states and their local districts address issues of safety in schools. In particular, it works to help schools grapple with problems that affect learning such as bullying, harassment, violence and substance abuse, by providing funding for prevention projects. It also offers resources that help schools assess their climates around these dimensions.

2 Sadker, Myra, and David Sadker. *Failing at fairness: How America's schools cheat girls*. Simon and Schuster, 2010; Neilson, Benjamin R. "The Shipley School 9th Grade Transition Study: An exploration of gender in independent school practice" (January 1, 2005). Dissertations available from ProQuest. Paper AAI3175650.

Chapter 8

STEAM and Intellectual Risk-Taking

Although by many measures girls are doing better academically in math and science in middle and high school than they were even a couple of decades ago, they are still underrepresented in classes focused on computer sciences and technology. Their participation in these STEM fields dwindles dramatically in college.

This profound diminution directly contributes, of course, to the dearth of women pursuing STEM-related careers. Since these fields are both vital to the health of our economy and potentially lucrative for individuals pursuing them, this represents a serious loss for society and for women.

We have argued that gender consciousness in the classroom is important across all subjects and grade levels, but its need is perhaps most acutely felt in math and science classes. Gender consciousness is one way to help girls overcome the negative societal stereotypes they experience and sometimes internalize. Current research about girls and STEM also shows that they become much more motivated in scientific subjects and more likely to continue in scientific careers when their classroom environments are personally relevant to and nurture their curiosities—and when intellectual risk-taking is supported.

There is growing evidence, too, that integrating arts with STEM studies (popularly known as STEAM), as well as including designing, making, and playing within the STEM curricula, greatly enhances girls' interests in the fields. This recent literature and our findings from girls' schools reinforce one another and reflect the importance of finding new ways of teaching and supporting girls in these areas. These approaches not only directly impact girls but also contribute to the well-being of society at large.

There is no doubt that all of the elements we have explored that make a classroom environment safe, welcoming, and exciting are applicable to

STEM classes. Furthermore, the wonderful classroom activities that the teachers and their students described in their narratives can almost all be worked into an algebra or chemistry or computer science lesson.

By forming close connections with their students and fostering those classroom qualities and activities to which girls respond, STEM teachers are well on their way to connecting more girls to these fields. Unfortunately, even the most passionate and involved teachers providing the most engaging lessons are often not enough to overcome the persistent inner notion so many girls have that STEM careers are just not for them.

Educational researchers have used the metaphor "STEM pipeline" to refer to the ways in which the experiences children and young adults have with math, science, and technology influence their pursuit of college majors and careers in these domains.[1] From an extremely early age, children pick up on subtle cues about how they are supposed to behave and what is expected of them. We know that there is a large gender gap in the STEM pipeline. This gap begins early on and becomes increasingly apparent during adolescence, with girls tending to display much more engagement and confidence in subjects related to the arts and humanities compared to those involving math and science.[2]

In response to this trend, researchers and educators alike continue to search for teaching approaches and curricula that will increase girls' presence in this pipeline and their interest and confidence in STEM subjects.

ENGAGING GIRLS IN STEM

Sources of the Gender Gap in STEM

Girls and boys tend to take the same number of high school STEM courses (except for computer science classes, which are consistently boy-heavy). Their performance on homework and overall course grades in these classes tend to be equal to or even better than boys'. However, the relative equality of girls' and boys' course-taking patterns and GPA achievement in high school STEM classes does not translate to standardized test scores in those subjects, selection of college majors, or the workforce.

There is evidence that something social scientists refer to as *stereotype threat* is an important factor. As we discussed in chapter 6, an underlying fear of their (imagined) innate lack of ability in these fields may negatively influence some girls' performance on high-stakes tests, even when their classroom performance and GPAs demonstrate their strength and ability in those subjects.

As we discussed previously, researcher Claude Steele and his colleagues found that when college-aged women were primed about their gender before taking a math test (by telling the participants that the results of the test tend to illustrate gender differences in math ability), they underperformed relative to men. However, when women took the same test without being reminded of their gender beforehand, or were not led to believe that the test would reveal any gender discrepancies, they performed equally to men.[3]

This research goes on to show that when stereotype threat around math is regularly at play for college women, they tend to de-identify with math ("I'm just not good at math") as a way of protecting their positive sense of self. Similarly, even if they take and ace AP and other advanced math and science classes in high school, many girls will insist that they aren't "natural" scientists or mathematicians and will avoid those majors in college.

Thus, even while girls take high school math and science classes in the same numbers as boys (again, except for computer science), they do so with less confidence and fewer ambitions to pursue these fields in college.[4] It is becoming clear that parents and teachers will need to work hard to alter girls' self-perceptions regarding STEM.

Research shows that those girls who do maintain strong self-concepts in relation to STEM subjects do not appear vulnerable to stereotype threat and that they are more likely to pursue college majors and careers in those fields.[5] The fact that having a strong and positive self-concept seems to serve as a protective factor against stereotype threat and to promote a positive attitude for girls toward STEM raises the question of how parents and educators can engender and support girls' positive self-concepts in relation to these subjects.

Research into children's attitudes and beliefs about their abilities in different subject areas points to a strong correlation between the messages that girls receive about gender and STEM from their parents, teachers, and the media, and their corresponding decline in engagement and positive attitudes toward STEM subjects.[6]

For instance, studies have shown that parents tend to be more interactive with boys compared to girls when attending interactive science-related museum exhibits.[7] Further, U.S. parents, especially White and high-socioeconomic status parents, have been found to give less computer-related support to their girls than their boys.[8]

In addition, gender stereotypes often persist when portraying people in technical roles. For example, in a recent analysis, men comprised 75 percent of the people mentioned and portrayed in a computer magazine targeted toward educators.[9] These societal factors lead to a gender divide early on and serve as a seed for the increasing STEM gender gap as young people mature.

In a telling 2015 study, researchers followed three cohorts of male and female students in Israel to measure the effects of teacher biases on the students as they advanced through school. Using a variety of measures, the researchers found that many teachers demonstrated negative bias toward girls and math and this had a large effect on the girls' performance and course-taking later in school. The bias was partially measured by comparing scores on girls' and boys' blind and non-blind math tests. When teachers scored the tests with names removed, they graded the girls higher than the boys. When the names were on the tests, they scored boys higher than girls.[10]

In elementary school, boys and girls demonstrate similar levels of interest in math, science, and technology, but the ways in which they approach activities related to these subjects tend to be gendered. Boys, for example, *tend* to describe more STEM-related experiences with tools, use computers more at home and school and play more with electronic games. Girls, on the other hand, *tend* to describe STEM-related experiences that relate to such gender-stereotypic activities as gardening or baking. They also often describe less variety in the ways they use computers.

It is during the period of adolescence that the gender stereotypes associated with boys and girls related to STEM subjects seem to become pernicious and solidified. By then, a majority of boys and girls subscribe to the idea that the STEM disciplines are more for boys than for girls.[11] Many teenage girls internalize this message and begin to doubt their abilities in math and science, and they begin to report less interest in careers that are associated with those subjects.[12]

The combination of youths' efforts to define themselves in relation to various identities and the increased freedom they are given to select academic courses contributes to this increased gender differentiation in STEM engagement and pursuits. Girls' relative lack of interest and confidence at the high school level translates into a vastly lopsided course-taking pattern in college.

Data from the National Science Board[13] highlight the underrepresentation of women at the undergraduate level earning bachelor's degrees in STEM fields: engineering (eighteen percent), physics (ninenteen percent), and computer science (eighteen percent). At the doctoral level, women continue to be underrepresented (though they increase their relative percentages), making up just twenty-five percent of those earning degrees in engineering, thirty-three percent of those in the physical sciences, and twenty-six percent of those in mathematics and computer science.

The exception to this trend seems to be in biology and, not surprisingly given that, in matriculation into medical school. Women now make up roughly half of all medical school classes, but they pursue becoming doctors as a profession in smaller numbers than men. Indeed, across careers, women who graduate in STEM disciplines are less likely to work in their field of study compared with men. Only 26 percent of female STEM degree holders go into STEM fields, while 40 percent of men pursue those occupations.[14]

There are no definitive explanations for such attrition. There are indicators, however, that STEM departments and classrooms in colleges have male-dominated cultures and that this kind of culture persists into the workforce, contributing to women's flagging interest, even when they are otherwise well suited and well prepared for the fields.

Another alarming trend related to girls and the STEM pipeline is the lack of girls of color taking STEM-related courses at the high school and college levels. Not surprisingly, this arises from a lack of access to advanced courses in STEM subjects. Nationwide in the United States only 50 percent of high schools offer calculus classes and only 63 percent offer physics classes.[15] Additionally, 10 percent to 25 percent of high schools do not offer more than one of the core STEM classes, such as algebra I and II, geometry, biology, and chemistry.[16] Because girls of color disproportionately attend schools that are underfunded and under-resourced, lack of access to even introductory STEM courses already puts them at a disadvantage in having the academic background they need to pursue STEM careers.

A second component of the "leaky pipeline" for girls of color connects to stereotypes and assumptions around who STEM subjects are "for" and "not for." Here, too, negative stereotypes are a significant factor in dissuading girls of color from joining STEM-related extracurricular activities and taking STEM classes. Girls of color not only have the double burden of having to contend with negative stereotypes related to girls and STEM but also with negative stereotypes that question the abilities of people of color to be successful in these fields.

Getting more women of all backgrounds to major in STEM programs in college and to then pursue careers in those fields will involve changing cultural norms, attitudes, and assumptions on campuses and in places of business. Part of that change may feel a bit like a chicken and the egg problem; many of these school and work cultures will not truly change until there is a critical mass of women in these fields, but women may be disinclined to enter these fields until the culture has changed.

Change efforts, therefore, will not work if only focused on the workplace or the university campus. We must also work much farther down the pipeline and prevent girls in kindergarten, fifth, or twelfth grade from being turned away from entire fields of study in which they may otherwise thrive. We need to focus attention on how children experience math, science, and technology years before they ever think about their college major.

STEM in the Classroom

Educational researcher Diane Halpern and her colleagues have developed a five-part approach to work against the negative self-stereotypes many girls have about themselves and their abilities in math, science, technology, and engineering.[17] Happily, their recommendations fit closely with everything we found about engaging and motivating lessons.

They are:

Teach Students that Academic Abilities Are Expandable and Improvable

This recommendation advises that teachers—and we would advise parents as well—to emphasize that math and science abilities are not fixed, inherent traits. Rather, they are a set of skills that can be improved over time through practice and effort.

This recommendation draws on the work of developmental psychologist Carol Dweck[18] and her research-based theory of malleable intelligence. Dweck found that when students, even those who are high-achievers, view their cognitive abilities as fixed and unchangeable, they are more likely to be discouraged and to demonstrate less effort when they encounter challenging material. These students tend to be oriented around "performance goals" and are more concerned about appearing smart or intelligent than about learning.

Students who take on what Dweck calls an "expandable" or growth perspective about their abilities tend to continue trying even when met with setbacks or frustration. In contrast to students who believe in fixed intelligence, these students tend to pursue *learning* goals rather than performance goals. Such students focus on learning new material, and look to develop a working understanding of difficult material, even if the process of doing so reveals them struggling, and not necessarily appearing "smart."

Gender stereotypes about math and science are particularly pervasive because they often rest on the idea that math and science abilities are determined by biological traits: boys "naturally" having an edge over girls because they "are born that way." To the extent girls and their parents adhere to this view, it would make sense that their daughters would distance themselves from STEM subjects.

If girls have a fixed mindset when it comes to their abilities around STEM, they may be less likely to take on tasks where there is a potential for failure, and therefore a risk of not appearing able. However, if they have an expandable view of their intelligence, they will be more likely to embrace failure and uncertainty as part of the learning process, and not as confirmation of their lack of their abilities.

This suggests that teachers and parents who successfully encourage girls to undertake STEM subjects will work intentionally and persistently against fixed–mindset attitudes in children and teens. Teachers will organize their classes so that students "try and undergo," in John Dewey's term. They will encourage girls to experiment, see the consequences of their trials, and use those outcomes as feedback to support or alter their hypothesis, not judge themselves.

In our study, we saw teachers promoting a malleable or growth mindset with their students through the multimodal lessons and projects. Providing several different avenues through which girls could learn a topic gave the students the chance to approach the lesson with the mindset that practice and persistence pay off as a way to hone one's skills, rather than believing they have only one chance to get something right.

Provide Prescriptive, Informational Feedback

This recommendation advises that educators provide feedback that speaks to the strategies, effort, and learning process that girls engage in when completing math and science tasks. Research has found that students' beliefs about their abilities and their performance are positively affected when they receive feedback that goes beyond general praise or speaks merely about the students being intelligent and instead points to their specific actions.[19]

Prescriptive and informational feedback supports a malleable view of intelligence by providing suggestions that point to places where a student's thinking may have gone off track or how a student might use a different form of problem-solving to accomplish a task. This type of feedback offers a student the chance to engage in a learning process to figure out how to get to the answer rather than shutting down when she simply hears that her answer is wrong.

Such feedback is particularly important for girls in math and science classrooms because, as other research has shown, they tend to have low confidence in their math and science abilities, regardless of how well they may actually be doing in the class.[20] Giving girls specific, informational feedback tied to the process of understanding the task focuses their attention on what they can do differently to solve the problem correctly rather than attributing it to their lack of ability.

In addition to the type of feedback that girls receive, the frequency of how often they receive it is also important. Education scholars Myra and David Sadker spent over twenty years observing teacher-student and peer interactions in coeducational classrooms.[21] They found that boys tended to receive feedback (whether negative or positive) more frequently than girls.

The Sadkers attributed this to the fact that in classrooms girls often sit quietly and stay on task more than boys and, because of this, teachers assume that they do not need as much attention. The Sadkers also found that teacher bias extended beyond gender to include race as well—White boys received the most attention, followed by boys of color, followed by White girls, with girls of color receiving the least amount of attention overall.

Giving girls high-quality, consistent feedback, particularly in STEM classes, communicates to them that they belong in the class, that their presence is valued, and that they have meaningful ideas to contribute to the larger class. Our findings around the importance of student-teacher relationships in girls' lives illustrate how meaningful, and often life-changing, it is for girls to feel like they are seen as valuable members of the class by their teachers.

Expose Girls to Female Role Models Who Have Succeeded in Math and Science

As we've argued in chapter 6, part of the reason that girls lose interest in STEM subjects is the lack of visibility of successful women in those fields. The negative stereotypes about girls and women not having the ability to succeed in STEM can seem very real when there is no evidence provided to the contrary.

This recommendation suggests that bringing in classroom materials and inviting guests that illustrate how women are actively involved in STEM careers is not only a way to expose girls to a more realistic perspective of the outside world, but it also works against the phenomenon of stereotype threat. In line with our findings, having girls meet female role models in STEM careers shows them how science, math, engineering, and technology can be relevant to their own lives.

Furthermore, inviting women into the classroom who represent a variety of careers that require an in-depth knowledge of STEM subjects, such as plumbers, electricians, and carpenters, in addition to scientists, engineers, doctors, and the like, can show girls potential pathways to different careers where girls and women are often absent.

Additionally, organizations such as Black Girls Code,[22] and IGNITE,[23] movies that celebrate women in STEM such as *Hidden Figures* and *Contact*, and popular TV shows like *Bones* and *NCIS* can all be brought into the classroom as part of a curriculum that serves to normalize the presence of girls and women in STEM. Indeed, the excitement in educational circles generated by *Hidden Figures* points to ways such films may be used to encourage girls.

Provide Spatial Skills Training

This recommendation speaks to the research that suggests that another explanation for why there are gender differences on standardized tests is that boys and girls may approach solving test items differently. Researchers have shown that boys tend to solve math problems on an assessment more successfully when they are "highly spatial in nature."[24]

In a study of 24,000 ninth-grade students, boys performed better on the items that involved spatial processing, while girls outperformed boys on tasks that required memorization. There is evidence that the early divergence of girls' and boys' play activities contributes to the development of their spatial-processing differences.[25] For example, boys tend to more often than girls use tools, build with building sets, and do other tasks that help develop spatial reasoning skills.

Halpern and her colleagues' recommendation for special training for girls, like many of their other proposals, subscribes to the idea of expandable abilities. Spatial skills can be learned over time given consistent practice and reinforcement. Learning these skills has the potential to increase girls' confidence and sense of efficacy in the STEM subjects.

In chapter 3, we gave many examples of how hands-on and multimodal lessons and projects create opportunities for girls to practice and develop their spatial skills through the building, measuring, and creating. It doesn't hurt that girls report finding this kind of work engaging and memorable.

Create a Classroom Environment that Sparks Initial Curiosity and Fosters Long-Term Interest in Math and Science

To maintain girls' engagement in STEM subjects, educators should work to develop strategies and practices in the classroom that stimulate girls' interest and confidence. Halpern and her colleagues make a distinction between two types of interests that educators and parents should focus on.

The first type is *longterm*, meaning the interest is stable over time and often captures personal preferences about a particular topic or activity. The other type is *situational*, in which the interest often stems from curiosity in relation to a specific task or challenge. This recommendation suggests that educators and parents need to work to spark an initial curiosity in girls about STEM subjects. This curiosity may become a gateway to long-term engagement.

All of these recommendations are important, but this last one may be both the most important and the most challenging. How does one create a classroom environment that sparks initial curiosity and fosters long-term interest in math and science, especially in the teen years when girls' attitudes may be on their way to becoming fixed against math and science?

As we've noted, the messages that girls receive about STEM subjects start early and come from all different areas in their everyday lives. These messages often contribute to the STEM pipeline issue that we see farther down the road where girls are more likely to pursue activities and careers that have social and artistic elements rather than scientific ones. What does it take to reverse this track leading girls away from majoring in a STEM field?

Echoing what the girls and teachers in our study told us, Halpern and her colleagues recommend that educators and parents make classroom material relevant and show how the formulas, concepts, and processes that girls and young women are learning connect to their daily lives. They also advocate using group work, project-based learning, and creative approaches. These are all practices that we saw over and over again in the students' and teachers' responses.

Turning STEM into STEAM

When reading through the student and teacher narratives, we noticed a fascinating trend in their responses. The lessons that they described often contained opportunities for innovation and creativity through the incorporation of art into STEM subjects—an emerging curricular framework known as STEAM. Beyond bringing art into STEM subjects, what distinguishes STEAM from STEM is STEAM's emphasis on integrating different elements of the classroom into a series of lessons or projects.

Georgette Yakman describes the significance of this framework as bringing the study of STEM subjects into the context of the twenty-first century: "We now live in a world where you can't understand science without technology, which couches most of its research and development in engineering, which you can't create without an understanding of the arts and mathematics."[26] It is vital to stress Yakman's point, as it would otherwise be easy for people to dismiss the addition of the arts to STEM as pandering to children's interests that are stereotypically associated with girls, instead of understanding how it is becoming an essential part the way people are addressing scientific problems.

In our narratives, we see this integration reflected in the ways students move beyond completing isolated experiments in physics classrooms to creating musical instruments out of test tubes that then culminated in a concert performance with their teacher accompanying them on his guitar. We read about how students made claymation movies to illustrate the relationship between enzymes, digestion, and synthesis—once again moving past the typical worksheets and diagrams of science classes, and even beyond traditional experiments—to a more skills-integrating and interactive project.

Having artistic components as a part of their STEM lessons gives girls the opportunity to be creative and to express themselves in an academic area where that often has been absent. This seems to capture their attentions in ways traditional teaching of science and math have not. In the following example, Elizabeth, a middle school student from our study, writes about how meaningful it was to her to have art incorporated into her science class. In the assignment, the students had to use different colors to draw an animal. This, in turn, led the class to learn about light and infrared waves.

Learning about Light through Creating Animals

This year in science we had to make up a mammal, and it could be anything we wanted it to be. This project was not a very big project. It was only a short assignment that we worked on for a couple of days. This mini-project related to the lesson of light, and infrared, and how we can't see certain waves of light. I liked this project because we got to be creative and think of something that has never before been thought of. I think that it is fun when we get to use our creative side when we work on projects, like presenting skits or drawing pictures. Pictures also help me learn the lessons better because I like to visualize things rather than just listen to them being taught to me. I like it when we learn lessons and it has a story to go with it or a picture, something that I can take away from because it helps me imagine it better and therefore remember it. I understand this unit in science a lot better now that we did this project.

Elizabeth describes how having the opportunity to be creative in her science class is not only fun but also fosters a deeper understanding of the material because the creative components such as drawing pictures and creating skits align with her learning style.

Beyond the novelty of bringing creativity into STEM subjects, our findings suggest that STEAM in the STEM classroom has the potential to promote the long-term interests and engagement of girls in STEM subjects and STEM-related careers. An example of this trend is illustrated in this response of Leah, a high school student:

Being Inspired in Science Class

In environmental science, my teacher assigned us to create a video on population growth in various countries. I chose Senegal and spent a week researching the country's demographics, economy, and environmental degradation. I enjoyed this project because it was different than the usual lecture that I was accustomed to. The assignment allowed me to be creative and have fun, rather than making me write an essay and dread it. In my video, I had the opportunity to include images and footage from Senegalese broadcasts. Using multimedia enabled me to understand the effects of population growth on Senegalese society. After working on the video, I realized that I enjoy projects more than tests and essays. The project also gave me the opportunity to try documentary production, a job that never interested me before but that I now strongly consider as a career path.

Leah's example, Elizabeth's story, and others we see in our data highlight how the implementation of a STEAM framework in STEM classrooms creates a space for girls to explore their creative sides in subject areas where they may not have felt confident or that they belonged. Additionally, STEAM expands the ways in which STEM concepts can be taught so that girls with varying learning styles feel that they can access the material with deeper understanding.

Another framework emerging in K–12 schools that complements STEAM is the "design-make-play" approach. The goal of design-make-play is to encourage the interest and excitement of young people in STEM that will lead to a long-term appreciation and investment in scientific subjects.[27] This framework also pushes for the integration of science, math, technology, and engineering subjects to allow for as much creativity and innovation as possible.

Design takes the form of students learning how to identify a need or task, develop a plan for how to accomplish the task, and then figure out how to evaluate whether the plan worked. With design, students take on the empowering role of being problem-solvers and thinkers. Nina's description of a project in her physics class illustrates what the "design" component of the framework can look like:

Creating Circuits

Senior year physics has been an influential class for me. The unit on electronics done in the first semester was quite enjoyable because it was interactive, and I felt I was learning a lot. At first, I didn't really understand the material or how to set up the breadboard circuit in the right way. In pairs of two, each table used one of the circuit boards, some IC chips, LEDs, and plenty of jumper wires to follow the circuit diagram on the lab sheet. My partner and I worked well together and that was part of the fun I had during the unit. We were able to joke about our mistakes and come up with new solutions. Once I was taught the proper way to use the jumper wires, I was able to make great strides in my understanding. The atmosphere of the room was casual with each table working on their own board . . . our teacher was always available to help and make sure there were no large problems/things we were missing. By the end of the unit, I was able to set up the circuit with very little help from the instructor. I not only understood what the lesson was about on paper but I also had a bit of real-life experience to go along with it.

Nina's experiments with building circuits was not only a learning experience for her but also something that she found enjoyable. She and her lab partner were given the freedom to play around with different solutions, and didn't have the pressure of having to get the right answer the first time around. Aligning with the goal of the "design" element of the framework, Nina and her classmate enthusiastically became problem-solvers and were confident enough to take control of their own learning, something that is particularly important to enhance girls' confidence in STEM subjects. Highlighted by the popular Maker Movement,[28] the "make" aspect of the design-make-play framework focuses on the pleasure that comes from building and creating a product. Students who take on the identity of makers like to explore, tinker, and collaborate to create innovative new machines, models, and materials. Allyson's description of an egg drop competition captures the "make" element perfectly:

Finding Success in the Egg Drop Competition

The project I have chosen is the egg drop in fifth grade. What we had to do is make an egg carrier that would be dropped from the ceiling, with only a limited amount of supplies. It was fun because we got to work as a team and share ideas with each other. You had to drop it twice. The first time was with a small plastic cup, and the second time was without. Some of the supplies were a glove, cotton balls, paper, paper towels, and string. My group succeeded by putting the egg in the glove then in the cup. Next we used the string to make a parachute with the paper. Our egg survived! Next we had to do it without the cup. We made the glove full of cotton balls and made a hole in the middle. Then we put more on top. We closed the glove with a piece of string, and we still had the parachute. We dropped our egg and it still survived. We watched as other groups dropped and their eggs didn't survive. The next thing we had to do was make a commercial. We made our commercial like a woman going to the therapist because her eggs broke. Then we brought out the "Egg Protector 2000" and now everything was better. We ended the commercial with a catchy theme song, and that was also the end of our project.

Allyson's play-by-play account of her team's work during the egg drop competition reflects the exploration, collaboration, and tinkering characteristics of the "make" part of the framework. Each time her group encountered a new challenge, they took stock of the materials that they had available and altered their design so they could still protect their egg.

Allyson's engagement and excitement about her experience shine through in this example—she loves that she and her group were able to try out new ideas and ultimately be successful. This narrative also shows how being in the driver's seat when doing STEM-related activities can enhance girls' interest and increase their identification with STEM subjects.

The final component of the design-make-play framework is "play," where students are given the freedom to find joy in the process of exploring and inventing. Instead of focusing on getting the right answer or creating the perfect product, play emphasizes embracing creativity and exploring the multiple pathways that exist in the design-make-play process. Here Olivia, a twelfth grader, describes how being able to work out difficult concepts through hands-on activities helped her to understand the class material better:

Using Play-Doh in Calculus Class

My most memorable unit was one we just completed, about the definite integral and its uses. One of the concepts within definite integrals is its application in calculating volumes of the rotation of a given curve. This particular application can be quite difficult to picture on a 2-D chalkboard or SMART Board, so Mrs. Benson came into class the first day with a large shopping bag filled with individual cups of Play-Doh. Throughout the unit, which lasted about a week, we brought our Play-Doh to class each day and used it to visualize total volumes as well as the individual "slices" that make up the foundation Riemann sum from which we take the limit. This limit of a Riemann sum is the definition of the definite integral. Although this teaching tool may sound like a waste of time or particularly childish, it was a very effective way of illustrating a 3-D concept when other methods were not available. I enjoyed working with my hands, as I am especially creative, and believe that engaging my hands, not just my mind in class, allowed a particularly difficult topic and unit to be more interesting and easier to understand.

Olivia's example shows how being able to "play" can go a long way toward helping students grasp challenging concepts. Bringing Play-Doh into the lesson, as we saw Ms. Chase reference in our discussion of hands-on learning in chapter 3, can make new material more accessible and potentially less anxiety-provoking than if it were taught in a more conventional way. This "play" element of the framework is particularly important in working to combat the disengagement that leads girls to believe that science, technology, and math are "not for them."

Based on our findings and other current research, introducing arts and the design-make-play framework into math, technology, and science lessons has the potential to grab and sustain girls' interest beyond their middle and high school years. This can have the far-reaching effect of getting them into and then sustaining them through the STEM pipeline, with more girls ultimately choosing a college major and a career in fields that may have otherwise seemed closed to them.

INTELLECTUAL RISK-TAKING IN THE STEM CLASSROOM

In contrast to stories of stereotype threat and "going underground,"[29] in our study we encountered example after example of girls confidently participating in their math, science, and technology classes. The girls who chose to write about these classes were not afraid to share their ideas in class and try new activities where they might not be sure of the correct answer—in short, they were open to taking risks.

Education researcher Ronald Beghetto defines intellectual risk-taking (IRT) as "engaging in adaptive learning behaviors (sharing tentative ideas, asking questions, attempting to do and learn new things) that place the learner at risk of making mistakes or appearing less competent than others."[30] Developmentally, IRT in the classroom setting plays a significant role in adolescents' identity development by creating a space for them to engage in tasks that they feel are just above their current level of understanding.[31]

Drawing on Vygotsky's concept of Zone of Proximal Development (ZPD),[32] where students learn material that is just a bit above their current understanding, teaching that fosters IRT promotes learning and cognitive development in youth by asking them to stretch themselves intellectually and emotionally. It encourages them to try out new and novel ideas, to do thought experiments for which there are not necessarily easy answers, and to collaborate with others while going well beyond their current comfort levels. Undertaken successfully, this kind of teaching helps students deepen and expand their understandings about what they are studying, be it history, English, math, or any other subject.

For teenage girls, taking intellectual risks can be particularly daunting because of the ongoing societal messages telling them that their thoughts, opinions, and knowledge are not valued. At an early age, girls are typically rewarded for their docility and for quietly staying on task with their assignments rather than for exercising their intellectual curiosity. In too many cases this leaves IRT outside of their everyday experience in the classroom.

The behavior of staying on task and of trying to be a good student intensifies for many girls once they reach adolescence and it can transform into a fear of making a mistake and not being perfect. As a consequence, in the classroom the behaviors of sharing out new ideas, asking questions, and trying out new procedures without knowledge of how it could turn out become something that many adolescent girls avoid rather than embrace.

Fortunately, there is a growing body of research about how to encourage IRT. We are learning that when certain elements are in place, girls are more likely to risk a wrong answer and to more confidently engage with material that stretches them intellectually. These elements include promoting a sense of freedom to ask questions without the fear of being wrong and encouraging collaboration among peers.[33] Recall, that these are components that closely align with the findings from our own study.

Our research demonstrates that STEAM has the potential to encourage girls' IRT. The types of IRT that were identified most often by students and their teachers involved girls giving presentations to their peers about some kind of product they had created in a math, science, or technology class. The presentations often served as a culminating activity through which the girls could teach what they had learned to others, whether it was their classmates, their entire grade, the whole school, or their parents. In the following, Sadie's description illustrates the different ways girls can take positive risks in STEM areas through presenting on a research project:

Presenting a Research Project on Bioluminescence

In the second semester of seventh grade at [my school], the students are assigned a final project instead of final exams. The teachers leave the topic of each student's research project completely open, so they can experience learning in depth about a topic that truly interests them. Then each student is assigned an advisor based on their area of focus. For example, my faculty advisor was the science teacher as my topic of research was bioluminescence. They guided us through our initial research, and then turning what we found into a project we could use to teach others about our topic through visual, hands-on, or written means. At the end of the semester we had a fair for other middle school students, parents, and teachers where they could travel from project to project and learn about each child's topic. I found this project particularly engaging and motivating because the motivation wasn't getting a higher grade than your classmates, as it was a pass/fail project, but instead was about learning more about a subject that interests you and explaining your interests to others. Furthermore, it combined research with presentation, allowing students to present their ideas in new and creative ways to captivate their audience, such as I created a simulation where when the reactants in biolumines- cence met, a light would turn on. While I did partially enjoy the project because it was successful for me, I believe even if others weren't as interested in my project, I still would have found it a rewarding experience, as it presented the rare opportunity where I actually felt interested and motivated to complete my work.

Presenting to audiences of peers and teachers or even parents usually requires that girls open themselves up to outside reactions and evaluation. This adds both another layer to their risk-taking and another opportunity to get feedback that can foster further learning. Not only are girls taking the risk of presenting their ideas but are also often being evaluated by their peers, and sometimes parents, in a formalized manner.

An example of how IRT and student presentations can come together within the STEAM framework is illustrated by this narrative from Ms. Terry, a high school biology teacher:

Presenting about Protists

When teaching students about protists[34] and the characteristics of different protist groups in AP biology, I would present the material and then would ask them to write personal ads that would describe and highlight the characteristics that made each group different. They would have to synthesize the material and express it in a form that was unique and interesting to them. I gave them examples from a lesson that focused on describing different insect larvae phyla. We would go over the material together as a class, and students would evaluate each other's on the criteria of creativity as well as their ability to know which group of protists they were in.

Girls relish the kind of IRT involved when presentations and projects require them to be creative. They like expressing themselves in new ways and thinking about concepts from different perspectives. When projects are designed to be collaborative they also demand IRT, as girls must voice their opinions, delegate tasks amongst one another, and make decisions with the goal of completing the assignment.

In the following example, Ms. Washington, a high school biology teacher, describes how the "genethics" project she assigned presented opportunities for girls to safely take intellectual risks in her classroom:

Debating Ethical Issues in Science Class

In my introductory biology class, I give a group-based project that has many components. The project is centered on ethical scientific issues, which we call "genethics." The girls are broken into small groups that focus on one issue. Girls like to work in small groups and often find the dynamics stimulating. After the group work is complete, the girls engage in a debate in front of the rest of the class. It is important to give girls plenty of chances to further their public-speaking skills, and this is easily facilitated in an environment where there is familiarity and not intimidation. Young girls speaking to girls tend to be more comfortable than to a coeducational audience. As their confidence in public-speaking grows, they will be able to adapt to mixed audiences in the future. The girls are interested and engaged in the contemporary nature of the topic and thrive in collaborative units. Though some are apprehensive about speaking in front of others, they soon realize that the safety and warmth of the all-girl class-room provide a sense of security and help to build confidence.

Ms. Washington's assessment of how public-speaking opportunities are particularly important to girls' development reminds us that on entering adolescence, girls tend to silence themselves and "go underground" as a way to maintain their social relationships. In contrast, in Ms. Washington's classroom, girls were encouraged to confidently collaborate with and present to one another. The social relationships that girls develop and maintain are not based on their silence, but rather on their lively participation in carefully constructed group work.

Another dimension of IRT that turned up in student and teacher narratives involved girls' willingness to "experiment" when they did not immediately know how to solve a problem or approach a task. We found examples ranging from working on geometry problems in front of the class using Velcro strips (which allowed girls to move around different parts of the problem), to experimenting with the different elements of Microsoft Word, to building rocket launchers.

Teachers and students described some of the tasks as "challenging" or "frustrating" but reported that the girls felt a sense of pride once the task was accomplished. Ms. Ramsey, a middle school technology teacher, talked about how she observed her students' willingness to take on the challenge of experimenting with different software programs even when they were not exactly sure of how to proceed:

Stepping Out of Their Comfort Zones to Take Risks

This year I have ventured to new territory with my seventh-grade girls by allowing them to select, research, and present an advanced topic in Microsoft Word. Instead of me teaching them these advanced skills, I allowed them to select their own topic and a method to teach their topic. The girls initially struggled with how to research their topics, even though I had given them links to support their various topics. However, once they started experimenting (which I encouraged them to do) they took off and excelled. The final products have come back and are over and beyond my expectations. While each of them has become an "expert" in their specific topic, they have all gained more knowledge and skills from each other. This type of practice supports girls stepping out of their comfort zone and learning to be risk-takers and experiment with new topics. With STEM becoming such a big part of today's education, girls need to be willing to step out of their comfort zones and experiment and/or try new topics and subjects. They need to learn to be risk-takers while being able to be investigators and open-minded learners.

Ms. Ramsey's example beautifully illustrates how IRT can become a regular part of girls' classroom experience through the specific encouragement of the teacher and in the collaborative environment of the classroom. It highlights the importance of teachers' roles in creating spaces that are conducive to students' risk-taking.

Like other teachers in our sample, Ms. Ramsey is very clear about the importance of creating a context in which girls feel free to take intellectual risks. She explicitly connects this behavior to preparing her charges to become successful beyond middle school and high school. Given this understanding, she creates conditions in her classroom that promote IRT such as giving her students the freedom to choose their own research topics and providing them with opportunities for collaboration and experimentation.

Though the presence of a STEAM framework in STEM classrooms is meaningful for all students, it seems to have the potential to be particularly influential for girls. Adding art and creative elements to STEM lessons provides a bridge for some girls, which allows them to move from areas they are confident in to ones that they find scary. It helps girls connect to new material and allows them to feel a sense of self-efficacy and confidence in subjects that they generally become less interested in as they move through adolescence.

STEAM not only adds the arts component, and with it new ways for girls to learn about scientific concepts, but it also emphasizes the interrelatedness of the STEM disciplines to each other, which encourages deeper learning. Rather than learning about mathematical and scientific concepts as independent ideas, identifying and exploring the connections among them make the material more relevant and interesting to girls.

Finally, the introduction of STEAM, and related design-make-play elements, opens the door for increasing girls' opportunities to engage in IRT. The arts and the interdisciplinary elements of STEAM serve as starting points for girls to work outside of their comfort zones by experimenting with different ideas, asking questions about the connections they see between the disciplines, and working collaboratively to develop innovative solutions to assigned tasks.

In turn, teachers who appreciate the value of IRT find ways to promote it within a safe yet challenging classroom environment. This creates a cycle in which girls try new and engaging ways to do the ordinary work of learning math and science subjects, while being challenged to stretch intellectually and emotionally. In the process, they come to see themselves as successful in areas that they have too often avoided in the past. At best, they begin to see themselves as future mathematicians, scientists, and engineers.

KEY IDEAS

What Teachers Can Do to Support Girls in STEM Classes:

- Establish the attitude of a malleable mindset in your classroom around STEM activities by encouraging girls to try things out, and to embrace failure as a learning opportunity rather than as a sign of not having the ability to do something.
- Pay attention to classroom dynamics in terms of student participation: Who gets called on more? Who might be overlooked? What types of feedback are girls being given in your class? What are other students saying to them? What are you saying?
- Work to establish a culture of support in your classroom, in which finding out how to solve problems is emphasized, learning from mistakes valued, and both right and wrong answers are used as information rather than as evidence of success or failure.

- Bring in classroom materials, ranging from articles, to movies and video clips, to books that show women and girls engaged in STEM-related activities.
- Invite women into your classroom who have STEM careers or who have careers where a knowledge of STEM is integral to their work. Have the women talk about their jobs, lead small projects with your students, or invite students to "shadow" them for a day.
- Incorporate design-make-play and art elements into STEM classes, lessons, and projects.
- Encourage girls to take risks in the classroom by having them work collaboratively to solve a task and then present their work to the rest of the class.

What Parents Can Do to Support Their Daughters in STEM Fields:

- Establish the attitude of a malleable mind-set at home focused on STEM subjects by encouraging your daughters to try things out and to embrace failure as a learning opportunity rather than as a sign of not having the ability to do something.
- Encourage your daughters to engage in STEM-related activities by taking them to museums and having them join organizations or attend events that promote girls and STEM.
- Provide opportunities for your daughters to tinker, create, and build by using tools.
- Find science projects that appeal to young girls. Some arrive each month by mail and have great directions for parents and for girls. Many girls find them thoroughly enjoyable and look forward to their arriving each month.
- Encourage your daughters to ask questions, be creative, and to try new things. Where appropriate, do those things with them or alongside of them.

NOTES

1. Diekman, Amanda B., Erica S. Weisgram, and Aimee L. Belanger. "New routes to recruiting and retaining women in STEM: Policy implications of a communal goal congruity perspective." *Social Issues and Policy Review* 9, no. 1 (2015): 52–88.

2. DiPrete, Thomas A., and Claudia Buchmann. *The rise of women: The growing gender gap in education and what it means for American schools*. New York, NY: Russell Sage Foundation, 2013.

3. Spencer, Steven J., Claude M. Steele, and Diane M. Quinn. "Stereotype threat and women's math performance." *Journal of Experimental Social Psychology* 35, no. 1 (1999): 4–28.

4. DiPrete, Thomas A., and Claudia Buchmann. *The rise of women: The growing gender gap in education and what it means for American schools*. New York, NY: Russell Sage Foundation, 2013.

5. Halpern, Diane F., Joshua Aronson, Nona Reimer, Sandra Simpkins, Jon R. Star, and Kathryn Wentzel. *Encouraging girls in math and science: IES Practice Guide.* National Center for Education Research, Institute of Education Sciences, U.S. Department of Education. 2007.

6. Diekman, Amanda B., Erica S. Weisgram, and Aimee L. Belanger. "New routes to recruiting and retaining women in STEM: Policy implications of a communal goal congruity perspective." *Social Issues and Policy Review* 9, no. 1 (2015): 52–88.

7. Diekman, Amanda B., Erica S. Weisgram, and Aimee L. Belanger. "New routes to recruiting and retaining women in STEM: Policy implications of a communal goal congruity perspective." *Social Issues and Policy Review* 9, no. 1 (2015): 52–88.

8. Sanders, Jo. *Gender and technology in education: A research review.* Seattle, WA: Center for Gender Equity, 2005.

9. Sanders, *Gender and technology in education.*

10. Lavy, Victor, and Edith Sand. *On the origins of gender human capital gaps: Short and long term consequences of teachers' stereotypical biases.* No. w20909. National Bureau of Economic Research, 2015.

11. Diekman, Amanda B., Erica S. Weisgram, and Aimee L. Belanger. "New routes to recruiting and retaining women in STEM: Policy implications of a communal goal congruity perspective." *Social Issues and Policy Review* 9, no. 1 (2015): 52–88.

12. Halpern, Diane F., Joshua Aronson, Nona Reimer, Sandra Simpkins, Jon R. Star, and Kathryn Wentzel. *Encouraging girls in math and science: IES Practice Guide.* National Center for Education Research, Institute of Education Sciences, U.S. Department of Education. 2007.

13. DiPrete, Thomas A., and Claudia Buchmann. *The rise of women: The growing gender gap in education and what it means for American schools.* New York, NY: Russell Sage Foundation, 2013.

14. Beede, David N., Tiffany A. Julian, David Langdon, George McKittrick, Beethika Khan, and Mark E. Doms. "Women in STEM: A gender gap to innovation." Executive Summary. U.S. Department of Commerce Economics and Statistics Administration, 2011.

15. U.S. Department of Education Office for Civil Rights. Civil Rights Data Collection, Issue Brief No. 3, Data Snapshot: College and Career Readiness (2014). Available at http://ocrdata.ed.gov/downloads/crdc-college-and-career-readiness-snapshot.pdf.

16. Ibid.

17. Halpern, Diane F., Joshua Aronson, Nona Reimer, Sandra Simpkins, Jon R. Star, and Kathryn Wentzel. *Encouraging girls in math and science: IES Practice Guide.* National Center for Education Research, Institute of Education Sciences, U.S. Department of Education. 2007.

18. Dweck, Carol S. *Mindset: The new psychology of success.* New York, NY: Random House Digital, Inc., 2008.

19. Mueller, Claudia M., and Carol S. Dweck. "Praise for intelligence can undermine children's motivation and performance." *Journal of Personality and Social Psychology* 75, no. 1 (1998): 33.

20. Herbert, Jennifer, and Deborah Stipek. "The emergence of gender differences in children's perceptions of their academic competence." *Journal of Applied Developmental Psychology* 26, no. 3 (2005): 276–295; Simpkins, Sandra D., Pamela E. Davis-Kean, and Jacquelynne S. Eccles. "Parents' socializing behavior and children's participation in math, science, and computer out-of-school activities." *Applied Developmental Science* 9, no. 1 (2005): 14–30.

21. Sadker, David, and Karen R. Zittleman. *Still failing at fairness: How gender bias cheats girls and boys in school and what we can do about it.* New York, NY: Simon and Schuster, 2009; Sadker, Myra, and David Sadker. *Failing at fairness: How America's schools cheat girls.* New York, NY: Simon and Schuster, 2010.

22. Black Girls Code is an organization dedicated to increasing the number of women of color in the digital space through exposing and teaching girls of color ages seven to seventeen to the fields of computer science and technology. http://www.blackgirlscode.com/.

23. IGNITE is an organization that focuses on introducing girls grades 6–12 to technology careers. http://www.igniteworldwide.org/.

24. Gierl, Mark J., Jeffrey Bisanz, Gay L. Bisanz, and Keith A. Boughton. "Identifying content and cognitive skills that produce gender differences in mathematics: A demonstration of the multidimensionality-based DIF analysis paradigm." *Journal of Educational Measurement* 40, no. 4 (2003): 281–306.

25. Eliot, Lise. *Pink brain, blue brain: How small differences grow into troublesome gaps—and what we can do about it.* New York, NY: First Mariner Books, 2010.

26. Yakman, Georgette. "What is the point of STEAM?—A brief overview." *Steam: A Framework for Teaching across the Disciplines. STEAM Education* 7 (2010).

27. Honey, Margaret, and David E. Kanter, eds. *Design, make, play: Growing the next generation of STEM innovators.* Abington, United Kingdom: Routledge, 2013.

28. The Maker Movement is a grassroots movement led by hobbyists, educators, and students that focuses on manufacturing, engineering, industrial design, hardware technology, and education. http://makerfaire.com/maker-movement/.

29. Gilligan, Carol. *In a different voice.* Cambridge, MA: Harvard University Press, 1982.

30. Beghetto, Ronald A. "Correlates of intellectual risk taking in elementary school science." *Journal of Research in Science Teaching* 46, no. 2 (2009): 210–223.

31. Streitmatter, Janice. "An exploratory study of risk-taking and attitudes in a girls-only middle school math class." *The Elementary School Journal* 98, no. 1 (1997): 15–26.

32. Vygotsky, Lev. *Interaction between learning and development. Mind and society.* Cambridge, MA: Harvard University Press, 1978: 79–91.

33. Streitmatter, Janice. "An exploratory study of risk-taking and attitudes in a girls-only middle school math class." *The Elementary School Journal* 98, no. 1 (1997): 15–26.

34. In the interest of others, who like us, had no idea what these were: Protists are "any member of a group of diverse eukaryotic, predominantly unicellular microscopic organisms." https://www.britannica.com/science/protist.

Chapter 9

A School That Works for Girls

It is a place devoted to professional development that is characterized by meaningful self-reflection and continuous self-assessment and improvement among the teaching staff. Teachers support, observe, and teach one another. They also have complete autonomy regarding what they teach, but the school's curricular strands—history, English, science, math, languages, and arts—are integrated, having a clear scope and sequence. The administration uses data to assess how the school is meeting its mission of helping girls develop into strong, competent women, with the courage to voice their views, and the skills to do it in a persuasive fashion that enables them to assume positive leadership roles as they become women. (Observation notes from our visit to The Athena School)

Designing and implementing highly motivating and engaging lessons require a dedicated and talented teacher. In some cases it necessitates particular supplies or technology. However, the success of even the most carefully constructed lesson taught by the most capable and committed teacher also depends on the larger school environment in which it takes place.

While the relationship between what occurs in the classroom and the larger school culture is certainly reciprocal, a school in which teachers are not supported and valued, students are not respected, and virtues of kindness, perseverance, and creativity are not nurtured can rarely be the setting for classroom learning that inspires.

In this chapter, we move from the level of classroom and lesson to the school as a whole. What are the qualities and characteristics of a school community that promotes and reinforces the types of learning we have been describing? And how can schools actively construct that culture?

To better understand the contexts that cultivate the teaching and learning, which girls and their teachers described, we spent time observing in two of the schools that participated in our study. We chose these schools because both their students and teachers wrote particularly rich narratives about lessons that extended across their curricula. In this sense, collectively, the schools reflected best-case examples of what students and teachers told us about the schools in the study.

While our two visits reinforced what we had learned from our analysis of the surveys, they also strengthened our appreciation for how important a school's culture is to promoting memorable teaching and learning for girls. In both schools we saw abundant evidence of relationships between teachers and students being prized as well as of rich and varied curricula that were challenging to girls and that emphasized girls' empowerment.

We call one The Athena School (TAS) and the other The Diana School (TDS). In exchange for extraordinary access, we promised to not share their actual identities. To that end, we have been very careful to avoid describing anything that might make the schools particularly recognizable. While they were exemplary in many ways, each had components of memorable practices that did not emerge in the other. Instead, they complement each other and together show a fuller picture of what works for girls in schools.

The schools had somewhat different cultures and traditions that reveal a range of possible ways to organize schooling. Together, they suggest important lessons for teachers and leaders as well as for school designers. Parents, too, should find the examples helpful in knowing what to look for when searching for a great school for their children.

At the outset, we want to be clear that we recognize that TAS and TDS are highly resourced, independent schools. They are not constrained by most federal and state requirements. They are not bound by the restrictive dimensions of *No Child Left Behind* and its replacement, *Every Student Succeeds*. And, they tend to have class sizes much smaller than many public schools.

We know that many teachers and parents reading this book may wonder how possible it is for their schools to embrace the types of lessons our participants described. Limited resources, large class sizes, ever-increasing demands on teachers and instructional time, academically diverse classes, and the specter of standardized testing may seem to present insurmountable obstacles to attempting ambitious lessons and bringing gender consciousness into the curriculum.

Though special resources, small class sizes, and this kind of freedom from many government regulations are necessary conditions for some of what we found, we also observed many practices that can be accomplished in under-resourced, highly regulated schools. Above all, we want to emphasize that all schools have the potential to foster the kinds of positive relations among the various members of the school community that are essential to girls' success.

We have identified eight qualities of positive school culture that promote excellent teaching and learning. We observed them in action during our visits to TAS and TDS and they are reflected in our broader data, where we see evidence of these qualities in the ways students and teachers described the context in which learning occurs. They also are supported by various fields of research on education, character-building, and living a successful life.

1. Develop and Be Guided by an Action-Oriented Mission Statement

The first essential quality of a supportive environment for girls is an explicit, distinctive mission that celebrates them while making its expectations for them clear. The mission statement is of paramount importance because it should, ideally, call for and help create all the other characteristics of positive school culture that promote student learning and growth.

This means that schools need to craft a mission statement that goes beyond a commitment to "providing a rigorous college preparation program that fosters critical thinking in diverse communities," as can be found in hundreds of school mission statements. At both TAS and TDS we found mission statements that focus on what they imagine for girls, and, crucially, also that address how the schools will help them achieve their goals.

Athena's mission directs the school to cultivate girls' passions and help them reach their highest potential by encouraging their curiosity and critical thinking. The mission values and promotes honesty, ethical behavior, and both intellectual and emotional risk-taking. It asks girls to take up serious intellectual and moral challenges. It encourages girls to develop strong individual voices and advocates that they take responsibility for their own physical and emotional well-being while learning ways to becomes leaders who contribute to broader community needs.

Athena's mission commits to achieving these goals by facilitating collaborative teaching and learning that continually explores how girls learn best. It explicitly values the development of strong, caring interpersonal relationships among all members of its community.

The mission of TDS, like TAS, is clearly focused on girls and their development while also addressing more directly both its value commitments and the role it sees for teachers. The mission statement includes explicit values and a vision for the faculty. It stresses helping girls reach their intellectual potential in the key subject areas beginning with science, then the humanities, and the arts. It also emphasizes the importance of fostering creativity and makes it a central purpose of the faculty to foster girls' capacity to learn and to encourage their sense of wonder.

TDS's mission makes it clear that the school seeks to educate girls to become responsible citizens of their communities and of the world. Service learning is emphasized as is the development of a global perspective. And, it puts front and center the importance of educating girls to develop a strong voice, confidence, and leadership skills.

The mission asks teachers to promote students' appreciation for service to others and the value of managing the natural environment. Overall, it seeks to inspire both teachers and students to use knowledge reflectively in the service of the public good. It emphasizes the importance of accepting differences, acting kindly, being forgiving, and striving to do one's best. Finally, it stresses the values of personal integrity, respect for others, and the development of communal trust and well-being.

In our visits, we observed many ways in which these missions clearly sustain the schools' educational approaches. The all-girl focus was evident and visible throughout the schools. For example, a bulletin board in one hallway proclaimed in bold lettering, "Everyone's voice matters, but only if they use it." Below this announcement, a string of bright letters spelled out, "Our girls speak out for . . ." The rest of the bulletin board was covered with photos of students with comment bubbles and typed paragraphs about what was important to each.

It is clear from our visits, as well as from our experience working in numerous independent and public schools, that great schools have a clear and elevating mission. While many schools have mission statements, not all do. When they do, it is important for its leaders and teachers to assess them to see how well they support girls' learning, growth, and development. When they are absent or unhelpful, it is important to develop one that can help guide the school. In the rare cases where new schools are being created, it is crucial that founders work first to develop a mission statement that expresses their aspirations for their students and their guiding values for the institution.

For girls, the mission needs to focus explicitly on helping them become competent, confident learners. It must be dedicated to exposing them to the rich and complicated roles women have played in history as well as the implications of gender across our society in the twenty-first century.

This means creating spaces where girls may grapple with the special issues and conditions they face as young women. The mission statement should reflect a dedication to helping girls find their voice and the courage to use it both well and wisely. In coed schools, the missions should promote goals appropriate for boys too.

The mission also needs to foster a culture that prizes the importance of strong, positive relationships among girls and between them and the adults in the school. Our data show relational trust is necessary for promoting effective teaching and learning—a finding that is well established in the research on effective schools—for both girls and boys.[1] It is also an important ingredient of the kind of spirit of public happiness we found in our visits.

2. Commit to High-Quality and Ongoing Teacher Professional Development

To achieve their goals for girls, the administrations of both schools we visited put an enormous amount of focus and resources on fostering a learning community for teachers. These communities are designed explicitly to create an atmosphere to directly affect students in positive ways. Thus, while teachers have autonomy to teach as they see fit during their classes, both schools have explicit ways to help them improve instruction.

Teachers and their administrators at TAS and TDS described how school leaders focus on continuous self-assessment and improvement for all faculty members. Indeed, on a school-wide level, we saw leaders across the school, including the heads of school, division administrators, and department chairs, guiding the faculty to use data, research, and educational theory to inform their practice.

Teachers are actively encouraged to continually hone their craft through some combination of advanced courses, observations in other schools, teaching demonstration lessons to their colleagues, attending such demonstrations, and otherwise working together in continuous efforts for self and communal improvement.

In one school, all courses across subjects and grades are aligned by an explicit design for their scope and sequence. Further, that school employs a framework for constructively evaluating teaching using a model developed by the consulting firm Research for Better Teaching.[2] It focuses on improving instruction, strengthening school culture, and using data to improve student learning. More immediately, the framework keeps teachers informed, so they refine and improve their teaching effectiveness, both in their own work and as part of collaborative teaching teams working across the curriculum.

Substantively, solid professional development involves making sure that teachers know much and continue to learn more about their students' psycho-social development. In turn, that means learning just what this study addressed. The more than thirteen hundred students who responded to our survey were very clear about that, and the hundreds of teachers who replied corroborated their views.

To close the circle, effective ongoing professional development must reflect the same educational qualities that work for girls. School leaders must empower and trust their teachers, just as they want their teachers to empower and trust their students. They also need to respect their professionalism.

Chapter 9

Teachers must have control over what they learn and to explore what is relevant and pressing to them. They need the opportunity to collaborate in teams to do this work in an ongoing way. This kind of approach was very much reflected in the ways TDS and especially TAS organized their teaching learning community.

3. Facilitate Interdisciplinary Learning

Closely connected to a learning community for teachers, a commitment to interdisciplinary learning has great benefits for students. Teachers who work together and design—at least on occasion—units of learning that stretch across two, three, or more different subject areas will typically see a huge payoff in student learning.

Such learning helps children make connections and to see relationships among fields they have previously viewed as discreet. Such teaching helps teachers get outside their narrow curricular boxes. It also helps break down the loneliness that can occur when they sit in their own classrooms, day after day, year after year. Overall, interdisciplinary work can help to foster a stronger, more interesting, and more vibrant learning community within the school.

4. Recognize and Address Student Anxiety, Workload, and Stress

Not surprisingly, given their explicit missions to promote girls' welfare, TAS and TDS also collect student feedback regarding homework and stress. One school relies on informal feedback from students gathered by teachers and administrators while the other does it systematically, using surveys. They both employ these data to design better policies to address structural issues. For example, when one school found that at certain times of the year students have too many papers and tests due at the same time, it revised the schedule. More broadly, teachers in both schools are encouraged to take actions to help girls learn to manage their stress as a routine part of their teaching.

Teachers and administrators in both schools seemed particularly attuned to helping students manage their anxiety about receiving feedback on their performance on class work and on more formal evaluations—a problem that is brought to our attention by students in every school in which we work. At one school both the administration and teachers work on this issue regularly. Recent policy changes in its upper school help teachers and students focus on using grades as feedback for learning rather than judgments, while otherwise encouraging efforts to reduce competition and promote collaboration.

At both schools we observed several teachers' attempts to help students manage their anxiety in the days before an upcoming test or quiz. For example, in a tenth-grade English class, the teacher pointed out to his students that their ability to compare *Twelfth Night* to present-day movies—as we observed them doing spontaneously in a student-led, small-group discussion—involved a high-level skill. He also noted it was evidence of their deep understanding of the play and, therefore, their preparedness for their test on it. He then asked the students to share their feelings about the upcoming test and engaged them in a discussion about how best to both prepare for it and manage their anxiety around it.

Beyond the schools' important, day-by-day efforts to help girls become able, self-assured students across the curriculum, and their work to foster students' well-being and enhance their self-esteem, both schools are driven to help girls develop into powerful and confident leaders. For example, in one school, public speaking is emphasized across the curriculum and is viewed as being central to preparing the girls to become pacesetters.

In grades eight and twelve, the students are expected to give speeches in front of their peers and teachers at community assemblies. They work closely with faculty members in their division who serve as "speech mentors," supporting them throughout the process. This focus on public speaking was underscored when one of the school's administrators asked us, when we returned from a tour of the school, if the high school student who had been our guide had been saying "um" too frequently.

Perhaps as important as any of the actual activities and practices we observed, we were struck by how intentional teachers were in supporting the confidence of their students in learning the materials for the day. As part of her review of the steps for balancing a chemical equation, the chemistry teacher paused to give the class a pep talk: "Let's talk about chemistry panic. We get into the middle of the test, and we can't remember what an ion is." She then advised students to "commit to the fact that you don't know it. Own it," and then went on to explain to the class how "it will all work out . . . if you will own what you don't know, you won't miss the whole thing—the things you do know."

In such environments, mistakes are not viewed as failures but as data for making corrections and as feedback that fosters learning. The schools promote—sometimes by name and other times just in spirit—Carol Dweck's notion of a growth or malleable versus a fixed mind-set in their students.[3] When one has a growth mind-set, failures and challenges simply represent what one doesn't know or can't do *yet*. If students have a fixed mind-set, defeatism results. It is especially important that teachers in STEM fields work intentionally and continuously to remind girls they are every bit as capable as boys in these areas, despite the messages that society and even their classmates may explicitly or implicitly give them to the contrary.

Girls also are supported emotionally by teachers and staff who know when they are anxious about an upcoming athletic event, or acting for the first time in a big play, as well as when they have a new sibling or when someone in the family is sick. And then, of course, this kind of positive, developmentally oriented culture will explicitly value and foster the kinds of educational approaches that our respondents prize.

5. Nurture Strong Peer-to-Peer and Teacher-Student Relationships

Supporting girls' emotional needs and helping them manage anxiety about school require, of course, close relationships with them. Teachers must know their girls, and the girls must trust them for any meaningful support to be given or received. We saw evidence of the structures that support the building of these types of relationships at both TDS and TAS.

On our school visits we saw students, teachers, and administrators display genuine courtesy, politeness, and interest in others. This was evident, for example, in the greetings we received in each classroom when we entered, and in our informal conversations with students outside of classes. One of our extraordinarily poised middle school tour guides did an impromptu check-in with us when she saw us during lunch on the second day of our visit: "How is your visit going? Can I help in any other way? Do you have any questions I might answer?"

Peer-to-peer relationships are just as important as those of students with teachers. As we described in our section about the power of collaborative learning, girls working with other girls can make for some of the most effective and memorable learning moments in their school careers. Of course, peer relationships can also be difficult to manage and painful at times. We observed teachers managing and sometimes directly instructing students on working together in mutually beneficial ways.

One pre-calculus teacher encouraged dialogue between his students when there was a concept they did not understand. Thus, the whole class worked together to clarify and solve a problem. Along the same lines, when conferring with us, he praised the flipped classroom method because he felt that it gave students the opportunity "to teach each other," a phenomenon we observed during our visit.

In addition to being very clearly pro-girl and pro-woman, these schools have a palpable spirit of public happiness. We observed firsthand and close-up the results of the missions' emphasis on the importance of relationships. Interactions between members of the school communities appeared to be easy and relaxed.

These interpersonal connections are often particularly strengthened by trips, field days, and other out-of-classroom experiences. While they do not need to happen frequently, schools should commit to having students and teachers have opportunities to challenge themselves, engage in out-of-the-ordinary activities, and, especially, have some fun.

A culture that enshrines relational trust-building and fosters welcoming girls and adults to the school, prizes enjoyment, and builds connectedness and fun into the everyday lives of all its members, will be a place to which students wish to return, day in and day out. Girls will be supported verbally, told they are able, and praised for their achievements.

6. Invest in Technology

Both schools provided a wide variety of technological aids to promote girls' learning. We observed the use of iPads and smartphones for filmmaking and recording interviews. We saw students prepare "radio broadcasts" and make PowerPoints and "Prezis" to support their presentations. We observed teachers making creative use of SMART Boards, laptops, iPads, and an assortment of teaching apps.

The use of such technology requires investment in computer hardware and other technologies, of course, but then can enable an important shift in pedagogy. The teachers employing these technologies were not simply using them as aids to conventional lectures but often were completely upending traditional methods of teaching by flipping classrooms, having girls do online collaborations, and sometimes connecting with students in far-off places relevant to their studies.

7. Practice Gender Consciousness

Though the term was not specifically used, we saw evidence of gender consciousness throughout our time at both TAS and TDS. As noted, their mission statements specifically reference the promotion of girls and a commitment to the realization of their full potential. We saw discussions of girls' issues in history classes, posters with pictures of women scientists in libraries and classrooms, and discussions about gender roles in many classes. On one bulletin board, there was a question asking which women students admire. On small squares of paper, students had pinned up their responses, which included Michelle Obama, CEOs like Sheryl Sandberg, their own mothers, and many others.

Of course, these are girls' schools. In coed schools, it is much less common to see direct references to gender or the specific challenges women face in our society. Schools need to attend to the actions described in chapters 6 and

7 to help ensure that they are breaking down barriers rather than reinforcing stereotypes.

One important component of active gender consciousness is focusing on students' performance and choices in terms of curriculum. At TDS and TAS we were struck particularly by their strong, mission-based investment in promoting their students' interest in and knowledge of subjects involving science, technology, engineering, and math. In the science and math classes we observed, students were engaged in much hands-on, experimental work. The classes where characterized by an aura of high energy, excitement, and involvement.

The TAS seventh-grade life science class exemplified the kinds of active, creative, project-driven work that our study found captures many girls' imaginations. The classroom was decorated from the floor to the ceiling with elaborate models of plant and animal cells, human organs, and biological processes. Colorful drawings and three-dimensional models lined the walls and hung from the ceiling. Brightly painted foam mitochondria hung next to a Q-tip-and-cotton-ball model of a cell membrane, which competed for wall space with a color-coded clay depiction of the phases of mitosis. Students' ongoing science projects crowded every lab table in the room. As we walked around the class, students working alone or in pairs excitedly told us about their projects.

Overall, teachers at TAS and TDS are broadly committed to girls' learning. Many of those we talked with emphasized that they want to prepare the girls to be successful and confident. Supporting girls in STEM subjects and encouraging them to discuss the role of women in history were a few of the examples of ways teachers actively support these goals. Additionally, we observed teachers emphasizing to their students again and again that they were "smart," or "brilliant," and were fully capable of completing whatever assigned task was at hand.

Girls need to develop a critical eye toward the ways in which gender infuses everything they study and do in school: how textbooks frame the knowledge they embody through gender, who is represented in discussions of subjects ranging from history and English to STEM, how athletics are organized, and resources are distributed. Girls benefit from safe spaces to talk about women's issues that are sensitive and vitally important to them. Boys, too, can gain from such reflection in safe spaces in which to discuss sensitive matters without girls.

8. Provide Excellent Leadership

A school, like any organization, needs strong, capable, and committed leadership to thrive. Creating a positive guiding mission for girls is primarily the job of the trustees or board of directors in independent and parochial schools and of elected school board members or principals in public schools. Charter schools are required to formulate a mission statement, and it is typically created by the board organizing its application for a charter.

Missions are usually embedded in school traditions and only revisited when school directors are developing strategic plans. But, of course, it also is always appropriate to reexamine them when school leaders periodically assess how their students are doing.

In public schools and independent coeducational schools, missions must be designed to foster great learning for girls (and boys). Given the extensive research on boys, and the growing understanding of girls, including knowledge based on our findings, it is possible to create mission statements that address both their common and unique interests.

Trustees who develop missions that promote these kinds of girl (and boy) friendly guidelines will set the stage for schools that offer compelling, motivating educations to them. They must then employ strong, school-based leadership to turn their vision into reality for students.

To achieve this, boards need to understand the relationship between the values embedded in the missions and the kinds of heads, principals, and superintendents they hire. Only leaders who are committed to those values and enact them in their daily practice will be able to maintain the culture they reflect.

Once they hire the school leader, boards need to develop an entry plan to facilitate her or his success. At minimum, the board should ensure that the new person has the regular, active, ongoing support of the board chair. Sometimes providing an outside coach for the transition period can also be very helpful. It is easy for new leaders to feel isolated. Having ongoing systems of support in place can ease the transition and ensure the leader's success.

Once the leader has found his or her footing, the board should use his or her success in implementing the mission, and sustaining the values it embodies, as the primary criterion for evaluating performance. A key dimension of the support the head of the board can provide is to have ongoing discussions about how the school leader is doing, so formal assessments do not involve surprises and may address broader questions of strategic importance for the school.

And, finally, the board needs to establish a succession plan that reflects the mission and makes sure it is in place before a leader must leave. Too often when leaders change, their commitments and progress in sustaining a supportive culture are lost as a new leader comes in and makes the school her or his "own."

Successful succession plans provide for finding a new leader attuned to the school's mission. They also nurture and sustain the ongoing internal development of leaders at all levels of the school, from support staff, students, and teachers, to department chairs and administrators.

Effective heads of school will be committed to the school's mission. They will set high standards for teachers and students and then provide them with the kinds of resources and support they need to meet those standards. They also will understand the recursive nature of fostering an ongoing culture. If they want teachers to work with girls in ways that promote the kind of learning our research suggests is so effective, they need to work with teachers in the same way.

This means that if leaders want their teachers to create respectful, collaborative classrooms, they need to create respectful, collaborative schools. They will listen to all their teachers and students and incorporate their ideas for fulfilling and strengthening the school's mission. They will encourage risk-taking and ownership among the adults in the school. Indeed, if they are wise, they will distribute leadership to department heads, teachers, and students, ensuring they and their students develop strong voices within a framework enabling respectful discourse.[4]

Of course, excellent schools must begin with excellent teachers. A school that meets its students' developmental needs and encourages their positive growth, will hire high-quality teachers and gets rid of those who are not up to the challenge: in the words of Jim Collins, a school that "gets the right people on the bus and the wrong people off of it." This is one of the biggest challenges for any school leader, public, parochial, or independent.

It is difficult and often painful to let even an underperforming teacher go. While public and parochial schools with unions sometimes face even more of a challenge, that it is possible is amply demonstrated by effective school leaders[5] and illustrated in a telling example offered by Collins.[6] He describes a young physics teacher who joined a science department and quickly realized that it could be much, much better. When he became department chair, he found the leverage to make the program excellent.

Like many public schools, new teachers in the new department chair's school had a three-year probationary period. The standard for receiving tenure had been that if the teacher's performance were reasonable, and she or he hadn't done anything egregious, they were promoted. The new department chair reframed the standard by telling new hires they were unlikely to receive tenure unless they were outstanding.

When the first person who came up for tenure was simply good, the department chair had the courage to insist on turning him down. Happily, he then was able to hire a terrific young woman as a replacement. Collins explains that once this disciplined approach became part of the department's culture, some of the less strong teachers moved elsewhere and the department became better and better.

But getting caring, respectful, passionate, knowledgeable teachers on the bus and teachers who don't measure up off is only a necessary condition for making sure they have the capacities to matter. Sufficiency requires that leaders provide ongoing professional development that helps teachers relate what they know about their subjects to what we know about girls' needs.

Girls respond very differently to different teachers, different materials, different presentation formats and structures, and to different kinds of instruction. Given this incredible range, for schools to reach all girls, they need to provide a variety of caring teachers with different styles and approaches as well as a large variety of activities both in and out of the classroom.

CAN THESE DIMENSIONS OF GREAT SCHOOLS BE REPLICATED?

All of the qualities of excellent schools for girls are easily transferrable to boys' schools and coed schools. As we have shown, much of what goes into compelling lessons for girls is consistent with what goes into those for boys. Boys and girls are engaged by active learning, project-based lessons, hands-on experimentation, intellectual risk-taking, and the like. They both prosper and grow in schools that promote a strong fabric of interpersonal relationships among students and faculty. Relational trust matters to everyone in a school community.

Of course, finding spaces for gender-conscious discussions in coed schools will require teachers and administrators to think carefully about when to divide their classes and when to bring them together. This is already done effectively is some classes on sex education and other gender-sensitive topics. It can also be done creatively when the curricula in history or English or other key subjects cover topics in which gender-specific discussions may prove fruitful before bringing the full class back together.

A bigger challenge to replication occurs when a school that has built and accomplished much under strong leadership faces a leadership transition or other major disruption. Strong cultures are the antidote to these kinds of events. This is because they provide members of the community—teachers, students, parents, grandparents, and other adults—enduring signposts for what makes the school special and routinize ways of maintaining it. They provide continuity, connection, and meaning in the face of change.

In part, strong cultures are embedded in positive, well-established rituals that involve the entire school community. These can bind people together, help them feel they belong, and sustain them through the inevitable rough spots that are a part of every school's life. Our data as well as our ongoing work in schools offer several examples of such rituals.

Inducting every girl into a "house," "club," or "team" when she joins the school can enhance her sense of belonging. Hogwarts is the central example in popular culture, but several of our schools have been using these methods since they were founded. Regularized, controlled competitions among such groups can foster a sense of fun, team spirit, and enthusiasm. So can going on class outings or doing a ropes course or other challenging team activity on campus.

Requiring every senior to give a substantial speech to her grade or class, having an "old" girl be responsible for mentoring a "new" girl, having a ring or pin ceremony for first-year students to mark the entry into the sister-hood of the school, all can foster a sense of pride, belonging, and continuity. Continuity and pride can also be fostered by having a teachers' and students' dress-up day for an annual Halloween party where the school greets parents and grandparents and puts on a set of performances for them. An environment that is designed to ritualize activities like this helps sustain relational bonds and relational trust in times of trouble.

Strong cultures are also embodied in the ways in which teachers and students are treated. Here again, we are arguing that the lessons we have derived about girls apply to teachers as well. Great schools for girls will have a tradition that deeply respects teachers and safeguards their autonomy within a well-understood set of expectations and behavioral boundaries.

Teachers will have the freedom to teach in ways that work for their students if what girls are learning aligns with departmental expectations for coverage and the appropriate sequencing of materials across grade levels. There will also be built-in, regular opportunities for professional development. A strong culture will reflect the belief that teachers, working together, can discover what they need and often can meet those needs by teaching each other.

Indeed, a culture which manifests constructivist,[7] progressive,[8] maker understandings of learning[9] will best foster both girls' and their teachers' excitement and engagement. Such frameworks emphasize that students and adults are active meaning-makers who must construct their own understand-ings to both learn deeply and feel ownership over what they are learning.

A culture that reflects these notions of epistemology—these understand-ings of what it means for students and teachers to know and how they come to develop knowledge—will invite girls to do projects, hands-on experimen-tation, and team-based work in which students studying together have oppor-tunities to co-construct knowledge.

Teachers in such a culture will employ multiple modalities to tap different ways girls learn. They will cut across the curriculum and be interdisciplin-ary. Beyond conventional lectures and homework, they will invite girls to do activities that involve writing, making videos, using computer programs, expressing research findings through creating art, doing skits, and writing music. Such lessons will challenge girls, stretch them, and require them to get out of their comfort zones to take intellectual and emotional risks.

Leaders in such cultures will do the same. They will help teachers employ different ways of developing their craft. They will foster their exploration, collaboration, and risk-taking. In the end, a school where leadership is distributed, where all adults and students together are engaged in creating the kinds of meaning they need to advance, will form a learning community in which everyone is excited to participate. Much like the two schools we have described, it will become a place of public happiness where people support each other to learn, develop, and grow.

GREAT SCHOOLS MUST BE RESOURCEFUL, NOT HIGHLY RESOURCED

The vast majority of students in the United States go to coeducational public schools. The amount of money per student, per year spent by states varies greatly (from $6,500 in Utah to $20,610 in New York in 2014).[10] Per pupil expenditures by district can vary even more. Few match the per pupil expenditures in the independent schools in our sample, though many exceed those of our two public schools. Given such differences, together with the bureaucratic regulations public schools face, can they hope to promote the kinds of lessons, within the kinds of supportive cultures, exemplified in our two case studies?

While answering this question definitively would require new research in a carefully selected, national sample of public schools, our findings suggest much could be replicated with the right leadership. In concluding our book, and understanding that a full explanation would require another book, we will use examples of lessons and leadership practices to suggest how it is possible.

Lessons that Can Work in Almost All Schools

Happily, having read the narratives in this book, or just by examining the catalog of lessons on our website, you will find that both the girls' and the teachers' examples show that schools do not have to be wealthy or to have wealthy parent bodies to provide many of these diverse and excellent opportunities. They do require resourceful teachers and leaders.

On the website (www.TeachingGirlsWell.com), we provide a list of some of the most memorable lessons from our study. These are the examples, many of them included in this book, that best capture the themes that we found across the student and teacher data. While many of our examples reflect the privileged nature of the independent girls' schools within our sample, most others throughout the book, and in the catalog of excellent lessons, reflect the leveraging of free or easily accessible resources, even those contained within the classroom, school, and neighborhood. We have described lessons employing the air vectors in a hallway, the slopes and terrain of the school playground, the ecology of a local stream or pond, the bounty of a free museum, and even the offerings in a teacher's home. Demanding, challenging, and relevant lessons can occur in almost any venue.

We have organized the lessons by the components of effective practices we found and by subject matter. They provide dozens of examples for teachers searching for proven interventions that girls have found both exciting and motivating. While every example comes from a girls' school, they are absolutely applicable in almost every case to the teaching of boys as well. As we have noted, most of our findings overlap with the qualities Reichert and Hawley found effective for boys.[11]

We also reject categorically the idea that the wonderful lessons described by the students and teachers in our study are at odds with either the requirements of standardized testing or meeting state's academic standards (or whatever requirements your local district or school has in place). While a learning target may be set outside of the classroom, the journey to mastering it will be within the direction of the classroom teacher with assistance from the administration. Finding routes other than boring, usually ineffective test preparation sessions, and "teacher proof" curricula require nothing more than courageous teachers and principals.

Getting students personally invested in learning, structuring effective pair and group work, integrating technology when available, and incorporating the other powerful pedagogical techniques we have described is almost always possible. For example, even many of the resources only available through computers are now within the reach of over 90 percent of middle and high school students.[12] And, while this availability varies by race, class, and the resources of schools, almost all high school students currently have smartphones, which inventive teachers can have them use in lieu of laptops.[13]

Instead of trying to overcome the distractions of students' texting and using of social media in class, teachers can have them use their phones in a variety of educational ways. Students can search the Internet for answers to class questions. They can download and read class materials on them. They can also download sophisticated math calculators, avoiding the need to buy an expensive one. Students can organize their notes on them. They can make films and record interviews on them. And, they can do projects together with them, linking small in-class groups, and even connecting with others from around the globe.

It is our hope that our findings about engaging lessons and the ways they are successfully framed provide many examples for those wanting to hone their craft. We believe that the wonderful descriptions written by girls and their teachers that we have included in this book should indicate useful ways to think about providing rich and varied curricula for all girls. And, since, as we have argued, most are equally relevant for boys, they should be applicable in coeducation classrooms.

Further, while how to make such lessons relevant for boys and girls may vary, the different strategies may be used together. For example, whatever the students' genders, they may focus on substantive questions most applicable to them: What can Caucasian boys learn about how a son during the Civil War supported his family's commitments? What lessons can Black girls learn from the contributions of Black women engineers who worked for NASA? What are the implications for understanding the assumed roles of men and women in the ways in which a novel represents them?

We hope teachers will use the lessons we have described as models to discover ways to incorporate more multimodal activities, employing a variety of different methods to challenge girls. We hope they will encourage those who already use hands-on lessons that they are on a useful track and to help others figure out how to do them. We hope they reinforce the value of ensuring that girls have ownership of their projects. We hope teachers are prompted to create collaborative classroom environments and to foster safe spaces for gender-conscious class discussions.

If teachers work to make their lessons relevant to girls' personal lives, to ensure that there are places to study topics affecting women in history, literature, the arts, and especially in STEM subjects, they will foster more engagement, deepen learning, elicit more enthusiasm, and reach more girls. And if schools come to think of both their whole proximate and broader environments as classrooms, they can not only extend learning but also promote stronger relationships among girls, their teachers, and their broader communities.

Indeed, if anything stands out in this study beyond the central importance of teachers, it is that relationships matter to girls. Many of the stories reveal the importance that girls place on connecting to fellow students and to their teachers. Opportunities to bond and deepen relationships can develop in drama classes; in athletics; in clubs; in field days; on trips, and, of course, in classrooms.

Strong positive relationships encourage girls to take educational and personal risks, to stretch, and to grow. Being able to help others, to support them, as well as to be supported and be helped by others, appears to occupy a central place in girls' imaginations and to reflect a pivotal spot in their hierarchy of needs.

This work—fostering positive relationships among all members of their communities—is *free*, if not easy, for schools to accomplish, no matter how they are situated. Based on our study, we would argue it is among their central responsibilities to ensure.

In closing, we want to return to the idea of strong leadership. We know that in many ways everything we have talked about in this book is connected to—if not completely dependent upon—having a school leader who promotes the type of school culture that encourages these types of activities and fosters strong relationships. We want to share two stories that illustrate what this kind of effective authority can look like.

Effective Leadership in Under-Resourced Catholic Schools

Sister Anne Roderiguez, Ed.D., IHM[14] did a study of Catholic elementary schools in Philadelphia that demonstrated in vivid terms how much strong, clear leadership matters to teachers, to students, and to their achievement. Her findings, described in *Outrageous Leadership: Three Exemplary Principals and the Climate They Create*, support ours about the importance of recursive leadership. She discovered that the most effective school leaders treated the teachers and children as they wanted the teachers and students to treat each other.

After examining the test scores from over thirty schools serving very poor children, Roderiguez picked five with the highest scores. She administered a climate survey in those schools and picked the three with the best school climates. She then surveyed the students and teachers of those schools to discover the kind of emotional tone that characterized them. Finally, she shadowed the principals to see how they created it.

Roderiguez found that the successful principals had strong positive regard for others, were deeply caring, and believed wholeheartedly in the capacity of the students to learn well and the teachers to teach well. They were warm and empathic and fiercely committed to upholding high standards. "Throughout these school communities, [their] empathic validation of individuals and a genuine interest in the presence and wellbeing of others scaffolded interactions and supported the relationship building going on [every single] day."[15]

The emotional stance of the principals was reflected in the cultures of their schools. "Across roles and responsibilities, [positive, empathic] encounters salted the daily routines. A consistency of positive attitudes, encouraging remarks and respectful treatment characterized the calm, cordial and productive atmosphere of these schools."[16]

Dr. Roderiguez was describing precisely what Boyatzis and McKee call *Resonant Leadership*.[17] Resonant leaders have high emotional intelligence, know themselves well, can control their feelings and actions, understand and empathize with others and—because of this understanding—can manage their relationships well. Resonant leaders use their emotional skills to generate goodwill and positive feelings among others.

But having high emotional intelligence is not enough. To create an open, supportive culture, especially in hard-pressed public schools, leaders must also know how to manage openly and effectively, often within distressing financial circumstances. This capacity is illustrated well in a description by James Lytle[18] of his entry into large, urban high school as the new principal.

Effective Leadership in a Time of Budget Cuts, Anxiety, and Change

Within two weeks of assuming the job, Lytle was required to cut 10 percent out of the school's approximately $11,000,000 budget because of severe and ongoing financial shortfalls in the district. He found a demoralized, uncertain staff, faced with possible layoffs, certain loss of resources, and a new, unknown leader.

Lytle brilliantly reframed this situation for himself and the staff by using the required cuts as an opportunity to help the school community clarify its priorities and generate "investment capital." He reasoned that if the school cut fifteen percent rather than ten percent it could create $500,000 for new investments: what he termed the school's "venture capital fund."

Lytle did not try to accomplish these cuts in his office. Instead, he used the necessity to engage the whole faculty. He invented a process that was completely open, writing out the detailed school budget on a blackboard in the staff room. He included salaries for all school positions, costs for books, equipment, maintenance, and the like.

Lytle then invited the community to participate as they tried together to find a way to cut fifteen percent. He and his rostering administrator figured out the cost of each period—based on the school's average teacher salary. The group could then examine the "lost" money for every course reduction teachers had—reductions that rewarded being a department chair, a disciplinarian, or other support positions.

As the community explored the budget, it became clear that the school was devoting ten percent of it to disciplinary issues alone—safety, policing, and school disciplinarians. The staff became clear it was "running a prison, not a school."[19] If they could figure out a way to reallocate this money, they could enhance instruction dramatically.

Of course, such cuts meant two things. Some people would lose their jobs. But much like the department head Jim Collins describes in *Good to Great and the Social Sectors*, getting the wrong people off the bus was as important as getting the right people on it. Lytle used the cuts to accomplish that.

Second, the school had to find another way to think about school discipline educationally, rather than in policing terms.

After going through the entire process, the collaborative effort managed to save half a million dollars beyond the million required by the district. Lytle and the teachers used the money to figure out and then pay for a reorganization plan. It divided the school into six small learning communities, or schools-within-a-school, in which students would take all but their physical education classes.

This plan reframed the school's organizing principle from being policing and departmentally based, to being caring and relationally based within its new, small communities. It also changed the school from being "resource poor to resource rich . . . in the sense that we had money to spend on new programs, good ideas, and professional learning."[20]

The school used the money from its venture capital fund to create a for-profit computer repair business staffed by a skilled teacher and paid students. It invested heavily in new technology. It also worked out internships for students in various organizations within the surrounding community. For example, students were placed in a large university and a major research hospital.[21]

Enough students were situated in the hospital that they not only worked there but also had their academic classes in one of the medical meeting rooms. These were all special education students who had been written off as early as elementary school. Yet now, with a new focus and tutoring from medical staff and students from a nearby university, they completed school and held their graduation ceremony at the hospital. Many ended up working there after they graduated.

Ultimately, what Lytle and his teachers accomplished, through the open and challenging process he initiated, was to reorganize a dysfunctional, disciplinary-driven city high school into a caring community, offering the very kinds of lessons and activities described in this book. Through reorganizing the budget, the school created the kind of wealth it needed to make big changes. Through such programs as the computer business and the work-study internships, students experienced more relevance. Through the small learning communities, stronger, safer relationships among teachers and students and between students became possible.

So, our answer to our question as to whether the great lessons the girls and their teachers in this study described are dependent on highly resourced schools, is emphatically: *No.* The findings of Roderiguez and the case study by Lytle illustrate what can be accomplished, even in the poorest schools, with "outrageous" leadership.

Within contexts led by individuals who have strong emotional intelligence, who are open, and who distribute leaderships broadly, teachers are freer to draw on their own resources, to collaborate, and to take advantage of the kinds of lessons illustrated in our study in ways they would find much more difficult were they trying to do their jobs on their own, in schools that lack community, clear missions, and strong leadership.

KEY IDEAS

- School leaders should focus on eight areas to create and sustain a school culture that promotes learning for all students:
  - Develop and be guided by an action-oriented mission statement
  - Commit to high-quality and ongoing teacher professional development
  - Facilitate interdisciplinary learning
  - Recognize and address student anxiety, workload, and stress
  - Nurture strong peer-to-peer and teacher-student relationships
  - Invest in technology
  - Practice gender consciousness
  - Provide excellent leadership

- Most of the findings from our study do not depend on schools being highly resourced. Developing a strong school culture, promoting quality student-teacher and peer-to-peer relationships, and integrating the qualities and activities of engaging lessons are all possible even in schools with limited budgets. It does require, however, the support of a strong and effective leader and the commitment of dedicated teachers.

NOTES

1. Bryk, Anthony S., and Barbara Schneider. "Trust in schools: A core resource for school reform." *Educational leadership* 60, no. 6 (2003): 40–45.
2. www.rbteach.com. Research for Better Teaching is an organization dedicated to improving teaching and school leadership. It works with schools to help them develop and sustain professional learning communities. It also provides evaluation instruments to track student and teacher progress and consultation directly to schools.
3. Dweck, Carol S. *Mindset: The new psychology of success.* New York, NY: Random House Digital, Inc., 2008.
4. Spillane, James P. *Distributed leadership.* Vol. 4. San Francisco, CA: John Wiley & Sons, 2012.
5. Lytle, James, H. EdD. Personal communication. See also Lytle, James H., *Working for kids: Educational leadership as inquiry and invention.* R&L Education, 2010.
6. See particularly pages 13–17 in, Collins, Jim, *Good to great and the social sectors: Why business thinking is not the answer.* Boulder, CO, 2005.
7. Vygotsky, Lev Semenovich. "Imagination and creativity in childhood." *Journal of Russian & East European Psychology* 42, no. 1 (2004): 7–97.

8. Dewey, John. *Experience and Education.* New York, NY: Macmillan (1938).

9. Halverson, Erica Rosenfeld, and Kimberly Sheridan. "The maker movement in education." *Harvard Educational Review* 84, no. 4 (2014): 495–504.

10. "Education Spending per Student by State." http://www.governing.com/gov-data/education-data/state-education-spending-per-pupil-data.html. Dollars adjusted to inflation for 2014.

11. Reichert, Michael, and Richard Hawley. *I can learn from you: Boys as relational learners.* Cambridge, MA: Harvard Educational Press, 2014.

12. https://nces.ed.gov/programs/digest/d14/tables/dt14_702.10.asp?current=yes.

13. Graham, Edward. "Using Smartphones in the Classroom: Tired of telling students to put away their phones? A veteran teacher shares tips for using mobile devices as learning tools." National Education Association. http://www.nea.org/tools/56274.htm; Kowalski, Kathiann. "When smartphones go to school: Work and grades tend to suffer when there is off-task use in the classroom." *Science News for Students* (2016). https://www.sciencenewsforstudents.org/article/when-smartphones-go-school.

14. Roderiguez, Anne. *Outrageous leadership: Three exemplary principals and the climate they create.* (Dissertation, University of Pennsylvania, 2007). Order No. 3255861, University of Pennsylvania.

15. Roderiguez,Anne. *Outrageous leadership: Three exemplary principals and the climate they create.* (Dissertation, University of Pennsylvania, 2007). Order No. 3255861, University of Pennsylvania, 106.

16. Roderiguez, Anne. *Outrageous leadership: Three exemplary principals and the climate they create.* (Dissertation, University of Pennsylvania, 2007). Order No. 3255861, University of Pennsylvania, 106.

17. Boyatzis, Richard, and Annie McKee. *Resonant leadership: Renewing yourself and connecting with others through mindfulness, hope and compassion.* New York, NY: Harvard Business Press, 2013.

18. Lytle, James H. *Working for kids: Educational leadership as inquiry and invention.* Lanham, MD: R&L Education, 2010. See particularly pages 47–49.

19. Lytle, James H. *Working for kids: Educational leadership as inquiry and invention.* Lanham, MD: R&L Education, 2010, 47.

20. Lytle, James H. *Working for kids: Educational leadership as inquiry and invention.* Lanham, MD: R&L Education, 2010, 48.

21. See Youngblood II, Joseph, and Margaret Beale Spencer. "Integrating normative identity processes and academic support requirements for special needs adolescents: The application of an identity-focused cultural ecological (ICE) perspective." *Applied Developmental Science* 6, no. 2 (2002): 95–108.

Afterword

We hope you have found this book useful. When we began our research in the girls' schools, we were not sure what we would find. Much had been written about boys and their academic struggles. In the past couple of decades, studies also began to show that girls were surpassing their male peers—in grades and achievement, in obtaining leadership positions in high schools, and in college matriculation.

Often, however, these writings lacked nuance and clarity. Relying on average differences, they failed to ask, "Which kinds of boys were failing?" and, "Which kinds of girls were doing so well?" They didn't recognize that children of color and children from under-resourced families and schools were struggling more than those from higher socioeconomic classes, who could avail themselves of schools with abundant resources.

More broadly, these works ignored the fact that even while girls on average were doing better than boys by some measures, they continue to be underrepresented in the hard sciences, math, and engineering. And, they seldom noted that women systematically receive lower pay than men holding equal positions, and only infrequently reach the highest levels of pay or leadership in any fields.

Meanwhile, relatively few studies looked at actual educational practices and how they affected adolescent girls. Worse, almost none bothered to ask students and their teachers what worked for them—not at least until Michael Reichert and Richard Hawley did their groundbreaking research, described in their book, *Reaching Boys, Teaching Boys: Strategies That Work and Why*.

Since no one had asked girls or their teachers about lessons they experienced as effective and memorable, we decided a follow-up study could be very important. We knew that despite their relative academic success, some girls began to lose academic self-confidence during adolescence. Many of them turned away from studying math and science because they came to believe they "weren't good" at those subjects or because, not surprisingly, they responded badly to stereotypes adults had about their lacking "potential" in these areas.

If we could find out about the kinds of teaching that engaged and excited girls, perhaps we could discover ways in which they could be taught more effectively. Might we find ways they could be supported to overcome societal barriers, encouraged to become more self-reliant and self-confident, helped to be more successful? And indeed, our findings do point the way.

We discovered girls prize relevance. They dig in and work hard when they are studying about issues that matter to them, when they can see connections to their lives and circumstances. We found they are motivated to work harder when they experience ownership over what they are learning. They are excited and energized when they are encouraged to take intellectual risks, do hands-on work, and actively experiment with materials, ideas, and questions.

These didactic approaches, which help students construct meaning, are facilitated when girls can work with other girls and find ways to make meaning together. Teachers who foster the development of strong peer relationships lay a foundation for active, collaborative meaning making. Collaboration, fun, and the other qualities and activities of engaging lessons that we have described foster girls' positive development.

Strong student-teacher relationships are equally important. Teachers who connect with their students intellectually, who challenge them while providing them with the support they need to achieve, make a big difference to them. So do teachers who go the extra mile for them; who go out of their way to know them personally and to support them in times of stress and difficulty while celebrating them for their successes and triumphs.

What is striking about these findings is that they are both gendered and they are not. They are deeply gendered because they are about what works for girls. But, the kinds of lessons that are effective for girls are very like the lessons Reichert and Hawley found to be effective for boys.

At one level, our book affirms that teaching rooted in constructivist understandings of how students learn—that they make meaning by experimenting, by getting their hands dirty, by discussing topics in open and lively ways—works equally well for girls and boys. At another level, however, our findings suggest that learning for girls is enhanced when it is personalized within gender-conscious classrooms and schools.

Girls and boys have very different lived experiences. Education that appreciates that and leverages it will work better than teaching that tries to be gender blind. In the end, we hope educators who are committed to improving education will be inspired to adapt our findings about great lessons while also helping to foster a spirit of gender consciousness that underpins everything that goes on in their schools. We hope too that parents can find ways to use these findings as they prepare their daughters to be successful, competent twenty-first-century adults.

Looking forward, we hope that our daughters and granddaughters will continue to make big strides in all areas of their lives: in sports, academics, business, politics, and the arts. We want to see schools that work for all girls by making sure they master the material but, perhaps even more importantly, that they develop the skills, self-awareness, and confidence to reach their goals in school and throughout their lives.

Bibliography

Banaji, Mahzarin R., and Antony, G. Greenwald. *Blindspot: Hidden Biases of Good People*. New York, NY: Bantam, 2016.

Bartolome, Lilia. "Beyond the Methods Fetish: Toward a Humanizing Pedagogy." *Harvard Educational Review* 64, no. 2 (1994): 173–195.

Beede, David N., Tiffany A. Julian, David Langdon, George McKittrick, Beethika Khan, and Mark E. Doms. "Women in STEM: A Gender Gap to Innovation." 2011.

Beghetto, Ronald A. "Correlates of Intellectual Risk Taking in Elementary School Science." *Journal of Research in Science Teaching* 46, no. 2 (2009): 210–223.

Best Beginnings, Alaska's Early Childhood Investment. "Five Areas of Child Development." Accessed July 11, 2016. https://www.bestbeginningsalaska.org/activities-resources/child-development-areas.

Black Girls Code. Accessed January 8, 2016. http://www.blackgirlscode.com/

Boyatzis, Richard, and Annie McKee. *Resonant Leadership: Renewing Yourself and Connecting with Others through Mindfulness, Hope and Compassion*. New York, NY: Harvard Business Press, 2013.

Brown, Lyn Mikel, and Carol Gilligan. *Meeting at the Crossroads: Women's Psychology and Girls' Development*. Cambridge, MA: Harvard University Press, 1992.

Bryk, Anthony S., and Barbara Schneider. "Trust in Schools: A Core Resource for School Reform." *Educational Leadership* 60, no. 6 (2003): 40–45.

Center for American Women and Politics. "Women in the U.S. Congress 2017." Accessed March 1, 2017. http://www.cawp.rutgers.edu/women-us-congress-2017

Christophel, Diane M. "The Relationships among Teacher Immediacy Behaviors, Student Motivation, and Learning." *Communication Education* 39, no. 4 (1990): 323–340.

Collins, Jim *Good to great and the social sectors: Why business thinking is not the answer*. New York: Harper Collins, 2005.

Comer, James P. "Schools that Develop Children." *The American Prospect* 12, no. 7 (2001): 30–35.

Cooper, Joel, and Kimberlee D. Weaver. *Gender and Computers: Understanding the Digital Divide*. Mahwah, NJ: Lawrence Erlbaum Associates, Publishers, 2003.

del Carmen Salazar, María. "A Humanizing Pedagogy: Reinventing the Principles and Practice of Education as a Journey toward Liberation." *Review of Research in Education* 37, no. 1 (2013): 121–148.

Dewey, John. *Democracy and Education.* New York, NY: Free Press, 1966.

Diekman, Amanda B., Erica S. Weisgram, and Aimee L. Belanger. "New Routes to Recruiting and Retaining Women in STEM: Policy Implications of a Communal Goal Congruity Perspective." *Social Issues and Policy Review* 9, no. 1 (2015): 52–88.

DiPrete, Thomas A., and Claudia Buchmann. *The Rise of Women: The Growing Gender Gap in Education and What It Means for American Schools.* New York, NY: Russell Sage Foundation, 2013.

Dweck, Carol S. *Mindset: The New Psychology of Success.* New York, NY: Random House Digital, Inc., 2008.

"Education Spending per Student by State." Governing.com. Accessed August 11, 2016. http://www.governing.com/gov-data/education-data/state-education-spending-per-pupil-data.html

Eliot, Lise. *Pink Brain, Blue Brain: How Small Differences Grow into Troublesome Gaps—and What We Can Do about It.* Boston, New York: Houghton Mifflin Harcourt, 2009.

Emdin, Christopher. "Reality Pedagogy." TEDx Talk at Teachers College, Columbia University (2012). Accessed July 8, 2016. https://www.youtube.com/watch?v=2Y9tVf_8fqo.

Fenaughty, John, and Niki Harré. "Factors Associated with Distressing Electronic Harassment and Cyberbullying." *Computers in Human Behavior* 29, no. 3 (2013): 803–811.

Field-Marvin, Kimberly. *The Making of "Me": Exploring How an Engaging, Student-Directed Learning Environment Influences the Creation of Agency in Early Adolescent Girls.* Unpublished dissertation. University of Pennsylvania. 2016.

Fischer, Kurt W. "How Cognitive & Neuro Science Can Inform Educational Practice." Address to the Annual Round Table of the Center for the Study of Boys' and Girls' Lives. Available at: www.csbgl.org, 2008.

Fischer, Kurt W., and Arlyne Lazerson. *Human Development: From Conception through Adolescence.* New York, NY: Freeman, 1984.

Fish, Amy. "Making Afro-Urban Magic: Zetta Elliott Discusses the Barriers to Black Children's Authors and Writing the Realities of Black Kids." *Transition* 121, no. 1 (2016): 70–80.

"The Five Dimensions of Readiness: From the *National Education Goals Panel.*" *Aspire Institute.* Accessed September 10, 2016. http://teachingcommons.cdl.edu/tk/modules_teachers/documents/5dimensionsdoc.pdf

Gierl, Mark J., Jeffrey Bisanz, Gay L. Bisanz, and Keith A. Boughton. "Identifying Content and Cognitive Skills that Produce Gender Differences in Mathematics: A Demonstration of the Multidimensionality-Based DIF Analysis Paradigm." *Journal of Educational Measurement* 40, no. 4 (2003): 281–306.

Gilligan, Carol. *In a Different voice: Psychological Theory and Women's Development.* Cambridge, MA: Harvard University Press, 1982.

Gilligan, Carol. *Joining the Resistance.* Malden, MA: Polity Press, 2011.

Graham, Edward. "Using Smartphones in the Classroom: Tired of Telling Students to Put Away Their Phones? A Veteran Teacher Shares Tips for Using Mobile Devices as Learning Tools." *National Education Association.* Accessed September 10, 2016. http://www.nea.org/tools/56274.htm.

Grunspan, Daniel Z., Sarah L. Eddy, Sara E. Brownell, Benjamin L. Wiggins, Alison J. Crowe, and Steven M. Goodreau. "Males Under-Estimate Academic Performance of Their Female Peers in Undergraduate Biology Classrooms." *PloS One* 11, no. 2 (2016): e0148405.

Gunderson, Elizabeth A., Gerardo Ramirez, Susan C. Levine, and Sian L. Beilock. "The Role of Parents and Teachers in the Development of Gender-Related Math Attitudes." *Sex Roles* 66, no. 3–4 (2012): 153–166.

Gurian, Michael., and Kathy Stevens. *Boys and Girls Learn Differently: A Guide to Teachers and Parents.* San Francisco, CA: Jossey-Bass, 2010.

Halpern, Diane F., Joshua Aronson, Nona Reimer, Sandra Simpkins, Jon R. Star, and Kathryn Wentzel. *Encouraging Girls in Math and Science: IES Practice Guide.* National Center for Education Research, Institute of Education Sciences, U.S. Department of Education. 2007.

Halverson, Erica Rosenfeld, and Kimberly Sheridan. "The Maker Movement in Education." *Harvard Educational Review* 84, no. 4 (2014): 495–504.

Hart, Lawrence, Juneau Mahan Gary, Christie Creney Duhamel, and Kimberly Homefield. "Building Leadership Skills in Middle School Girls through Interscholastic Athletics." Greensboro, NC: ERIC Counseling and Student Services Clearinghouse, 2003. ERIC ED 479832.

Havighurst, R. J. "Research on the Developmental-Task Concept," *The School Review* 64, no. 5 (May 1956): 215–223.

Heilman, Madeline E., Aaron S. Wallen, Daniella Fuchs, and Melinda M. Tamkins. "Penalties for Success: Reactions to Women Who Succeed at Male Gender-Typed Tasks." *Journal of Applied Psychology* 89, no. 3 (2004): 416.

Henry, Nicola, and Anastasia Powell. "Beyond the 'Sext': Technology-Facilitated Sexual Violence and Harassment against Adult Women." *Australian & New Zealand Journal of Criminology* 48, no. 1 (2015): 104–118.

Herbert, Jennifer, and Deborah Stipek. "The Emergence of Gender Differences in Children's Perceptions of Their Academic Competence." *Journal of Applied Developmental Psychology* 26, no. 3 (2005): 276–295.

Hill, Catherine. "The Simple Truth about the Gender Pay Gap." *American Association of University Women, 2015.* Accessed February 2, 2016. http://www. aauw. org/files/2015/09/TheSimpleTruthFall2015.pdf

Honey, Margaret, and David E. Kanter, eds. *Design, Make, Play: Growing the Next Generation of STEM Innovators.* Routledge, 2013.

Hyde, Janet Shibley. "The Gender Similarities Hypothesis." *American psychologist* 60, no. 6 (2005): 581.

IGNITE. http://www.igniteworldwide.org/ IGNITE.

Johnson, Stefanie K., Susan Elaine Murphy, Selamawit Zewdie, and Rebecca J. Reichard. "The Strong, Sensitive Type: Effects of Gender Stereotypes and Leadership Prototypes on the Evaluation of Male and Female Leaders." *Organizational Behavior and Human Decision Processes* 106, no. 1 (2008): 39–60.

Kafai, Yasmin B. "Learning Design by Making Games." *Constructionism in Practice: Designing, Thinking and Learning in a Digital World*, 1996. 71–96.

Kowalski, Kathiann. When Smartphones Go to School: Work and Grades Tend to Suffer When There Is Off-Task Use in the Classroom. *Science News for Students* (2016). Accessed August 8, 2016. https://www.sciencenewsforstudents.org/article/when-smartphones-go-school

Kunter, Mareike, Yi-Miau Tsai, Uta Klusmann, Martin Brunner, Stefan Krauss, and Jürgen Baumert. "Students' and Mathematics Teachers' Perceptions of Teacher Enthusiasm and Instruction." *Learning and Instruction* 18, no. 5 (2008): 468–482.

Kuzmic, Jeffrey J. "Textbooks, Knowledge, and Masculinity: Examining Patriarchy from Within." *SAGE Series on Men and Masculinities: Masculinities at School.* 11(2000):105–126, Thousand Oaks, CA: SAGE.

Lavy, Victor, and Edith Sand. *On the Origins of Gender Human Capital Gaps: Short and Long Term Consequences of Teachers' Stereotypical Biases.* No. w20909. National Bureau of Economic Research, 2015.

Liberman, Mark. "Sax Q & A." *Language Log Blog.* May 17, 2008. Accessed June 30, 2015. http://languagelog.ldc.upenn.edu/nll/?p=166

Lytle, James H. *Working for Kids: Educational Leadership as Inquiry and Invention.* Lanham, MD: R&L Education, 2010.

Maker Faire. Accessed July 11, 2016, http://makerfaire.com/maker-movement/

McGrath, Daniel. J., and Peter J. Kuriloff. "Unnatural Selection on the Unstructured Playground." *School Community Journal* 9, no. 2 (1999): 41–65.

Miller, Janet L. "Constructions of Curriculum and Gender." *Teachers College Record* 94, no. 5 (1993): 43–63.

Mondschein, Emily R., Karen E. Adolph, and Catherine S. Tamis-LeMonda. "Gender Bias in Mothers' Expectations about Infant Crawling." *Journal of Experimental Child Psychology* 77, no. 4 (2000): 304–316.

Moss-Racusin, Corinne A., John F. Dovidio, Victoria L. Brescoll, Mark J. Graham, and Jo Handelsman. "Science Faculty's Subtle Gender Biases Favor Male Students." *Proceedings of the National Academy of Sciences* 109, no. 41 (2012): 16,474–16,479.

Mueller, Claudia M., and Carol S. Dweck. "Praise for Intelligence Can Undermine Children's Motivation and Performance." *Journal of Personality and Social Psychology* 75, no. 1 (1998): 33.

National Center for Education Statistics. "Number and Percentage of Persons Age 3 and Over Using the Internet and Percentage Distribution by Means of Internet Access from Home and Main Reason for not Having High-Speed Access, by Selected Age Groups and Other Characteristics of all Users and of Students: 2013." Digest of Education Statistics, National Center for Education Statistics. Accessed July 11, 2016. https://nces.ed.gov/programs/digest/d14/tables/dt14_702.10.asp?current=yes

National Center on Safe and Supportive Learning Environments. "School Climate Survey Compendia." Accessed August 10, 2016. https://safesupportivelearning.ed.gov/topic-research/school-climate-measurement/school-climate-survey-compendium

Neilson, Benjamin. "The Shipley School 9th Grade Transition Study: An Exploration of Gender in Independent School Practice." January 1, 2005. Dissertations available from ProQuest. Paper AAI3175650.

Noddings, Nel. *Caring: A Relational Approach to Ethics and Moral Education.* Berkeley, CA: University of California Press, 2013.

Palincsar, Annemarie Sullivan, and Ann L. Brown. "Interactive Teaching to Promote Independent Learning from Text." *The Reading Teacher* 39, no. 8 (1986): 771–777.

Patrick, Brian C., Jennifer Hisley, and Toni Kempler. "'What's Everybody So Excited About?': The Effects of Teacher Enthusiasm on Student Intrinsic Motivation and Vitality." *The Journal of Experimental Education* 68, no. 3 (2000): 217–236.

Pedersen, Sara, and Edward Seidman. "Team Sports Achievement and Self-Esteem Development among Urban Adolescent Girls." *Psychology of Women Quarterly* 28, no. 4 (2004): 412–422.

Phillips Exeter Academy. "The Amazing Harkness Philosophy." Accessed July 3, 2016. http://www.exeter.edu/admissions/109_1220.aspx.

Piaget, Jean. *The Child's Conception of the World.* Lanham, MD: Littlefield Adams, 1951.

Piehler, Christopher. "Survey Reveals Students' Mobile Device Preferences." *The Journal; Transforming Education through Technology.* 2015. Accessed July 12, 2016, https://thejournal.com/articles/2015/09/21/survey-reveals-students-mobile-device-preferences.aspx.

Raider-Roth, Miriam. *Trusting What You Know: The High Stakes of Classroom Relationships.* Indianapolis, IN: Jossey-Bass, 2005.

Reichert, Michael, and Richard Hawley. *I Can Learn from You: Boys as Relational Learners.* Cambridge, MA: Harvard Educational Press, 2014.

Reichert, Michael, and Richard Hawley. *Reaching Boys, Teaching Boys: Strategies that Work—and Why.* Hoboken, NJ: John Wiley and Sons, 2010.

Research for Better Teaching. www.rbteach.com

Rhone, Nedra. "Target's Gender-Neutral Signage a Plus for Consumers." *Atlanta Journal Constitution*, August 17, 2015. Accessed July 3, 2016. http://www.ajc.com/news/lifestyles/shopping/targets-gender-neutral-signage-a-plus-for-consumer/nnKWy/

Roderiguez, Anne. "Outrageous Leadership: Three Exemplary Principals and the Climate They Create." (Dissertation, University of Pennsylvania, 2007). Order No. 3255861, University of Pennsylvania. https://proxy.library.upenn.edu/login?url=http://proxy.library.upenn.edu:2299/docview/304835421?accountid=14707.

Roorda, Debora L., Helma M. Y. Koomen, Jantine L. Spilt, and Frans J. Oort. "The Influence of Affective Teacher—Student Relationships on Students' School Engagement and Achievement: A Meta-Analytic Approach." *Review of Educational Research* 81, no. 4 (2011): 493–529.

Rosenshine, Barak, and Carla Meister. "Reciprocal Teaching: A Review of the Research." *Review of Educational Research* 64, no. 4 (1994): 479–530.

Sadker, David, and Zittleman, Karen, R. *Still Failing at Fairness: How Gender Bias Cheats Girls and Boys in School and What We Can Do about It.* New York, NY: Simon and Schuster, 2009.

Sadker, Myra, and David Sadker. *Failing at Fairness: How America's Schools Cheat Girls.* New York, NY: Simon and Schuster, 2010.

Sanders, Jo. "Gender and Technology in Education: A Research Review." Seattle, WA: Center for Gender Equity, 2005. Accessed June 2, 2015. http://www.josanders.com/pdf/gendertech0705.pdf.

Sax, Leonard. *Why Gender Matters: What Parents and Teachers Need to Know about the Emerging Science of Sex Differences.* Broadway Book, NY, NY, 2005.

Shulman, Lee S. "Those Who Understand: Knowledge Growth in Teaching." *Educational Researcher* 15, no. 2 (1986): 4–14.

Simmons, Rachel. *The Curse of the Good Girl: Raising Authentic Girls with Courage and Confidence.* New York, NY: Penguin, 2009.

Simpkins, Sandra D., Pamela E. Davis-Kean, and Jacquelynne S. Eccles. "Parents' Socializing Behavior and Children's Participation in Math, Science, and Computer Out-of-school Activities." *Applied Developmental Science* 9, no. 1 (2005): 14–30.

Snyder, Kieran. "The Abrasiveness Trap: High-Achieving Men and Women Are Described Differently in Reviews." *Fortune Magazine,* 2014.

Spencer, Steven J., Claude M. Steele, and Diane M. Quinn. "Stereotype Threat and Women's Math Performance." *Journal of Experimental Social Psychology* 35, no. 1 (1999): 4–28.

Spillane, James P. *Distributed Leadership.* Vol. 4. Hoboken, NJ: John Wiley & Sons, 2012.

Streitmatter, Janice. "An Exploratory Study of Risk-Taking and Attitudes in a Girls-Only Middle School Math Class." *The Elementary School Journal* 98, no. 1 (1997): 15–26.

Sweet, Elizabeth. "Toys Are More Divided by Gender Now than They Were 50 Years Ago." Atlantic.com (December 2014). Available: https://www.theatlantic.com/business/archive/2014/12/toys-are-more-divided-by-gender-now-than-they-were-50-years-ago/383556/.

T. Rowe Price. "Fourth Annual Parents, Kids & Money Survey, Detailed Results, March 2012." Accessed June 14, 2014. https://corporate.troweprice.com/Money-Confident-Kids/files/2012-parents-kids-money-survey-detailed-results.pdf.

"Ten Tasks of Adolescent Development." *MIT Raising Teens.* Accessed November 1, 2016. http://hrweb.mit.edu/worklife/raising-teens/ten-tasks.html.

Thompson, Michael, and Teresa Baker. *The Pressured Child.* New York, NY: Ballantine Books, 2005.

Thorne, Barry. *Gender Play: Girls and Boys in School.* Newark, NJ: Rutgers University Press, 1999.

United States Department of Labor. "Women in the Labor Force." Accessed August 8, 2016. https://www.dol.gov/wb/stats/stats_data.htm

U.S. Department of Education Office for Civil Rights. "Civil Rights Data Collection, Issue Brief No. 3, Data Snapshot: College and Career Readiness 1,8 2014." Accessed October 8, 2015. https://www2.ed.gov/about/offices/list/ocr/docs/crdc-college-and-career-readiness-snapshot.pdf.

Vygotsky, Lev. "Interaction between Learning and Development." *Readings on the Development of Children* 23, no. 3 (1978): 34–41.

Vygotsky, Lev Semenovich. "Imagination and Creativity in Childhood." *Journal of Russian & East European Psychology* 42, no. 1 (2004): 7–97.

Yakman, Georgette. "What Is the Point of STEAM?—A Brief Overview." *Steam: A Framework for Teaching across the Disciplines. STEAM Education* 7 (2010), http://www.handshake20.com/wp-content/uploads/whatissteam.pdf.

Youngblood II, Joseph, and Margaret Beale Spencer. "Integrating Normative Identity Processes and Academic Support Requirements for Special Needs Adolescents: The Application of an Identity-Focused Cultural Ecological (ICE) Perspective." *Applied Developmental Science* 6, no. 2 (2002): 95–108.

Zarya, Valentina. "The Percentage of Female CEOs in the Fortune 500 Drops to 4%." *Fortune*, June 6, 2016. Accessed October 4, 2016. http://fortune.com/2016/06/06/women-ceos-fortune-500-2016/.

Index